THE SABAN CENTER
for MIDDLE EAST POLICY
at THE BROOKINGS INSTITUTION

ANALYSIS PAPER

Number 7, February 2006

A SWITCH IN TIME

A NEW STRATEGY FOR AMERICA IN IRAQ

KENNETH M. POLLACK
AND THE IRAQ POLICY WORKING GROUP OF
THE SABAN CENTER FOR MIDDLE EAST POLICY
AT THE BROOKINGS INSTITUTION

FEBRUARY 2006

Copyright © 2006
THE BROOKINGS INSTITUTION
1775 Massachusetts Avenue, N.W., Washington, D.C. 20036
www.brookings.edu

A Switch in Time: A New Strategy for America in Iraq may be ordered from:
Brookings Institution Press
c/o HFS
P.O. Box 50370
Baltimore, MD 21211-4370
800/537-5487; 410/516-6956
Fax: 410/516-6998
www.brookings.edu

Library of Congress Cataloging-in-Publication data are available
ISBN-13: 978-0-8157-7151-7
ISBN-10: 0-8157-7151-7

The paper used in this publication meets minimum requirements of the American National Standard for Information Sciences—Permanence of Paper for Printed Library Materials: ANSI Z39.48-1992.

9 8 7 6 5 4 3 2

TABLE OF CONTENTS

The Author

Kenneth M. Pollack is the Director of Research at the Saban Center for Middle East Policy and a Brookings Senior Fellow. He has served as Director for Persian Gulf Affairs and Director for Near East and South Asian Affairs at the National Security Council, Senior Research Professor at the National Defense University, and Iran-Iraq military analyst for the Central Intelligence Agency. Pollack's most recent book, *The Persian Puzzle: The Conflict between Iran and America* was published in 2004. He is also the author of *The Threatening Storm: The Case for Invading Iraq* and *Arabs at War: Military Effectiveness, 1948–1991* (both published in 2002). Pollack received a B.A. from Yale University and a Ph.D. from the Massachusetts Institute of Technology.

PREFACE

This report is the first in a series from the Iraq Strategy Project of the Saban Center for Middle East Policy at the Brookings Institution. Although it was drafted by Kenneth M. Pollack, the Director of Research of the Saban Center, it resulted from the discussions of the Saban Center's Iraq Policy Working Group. The members of the group, which met during November and December 2005, included:

Raad Alkadiri, PFC Energy Consulting

Frederick Barton, Center for Strategic and International Studies

Daniel Byman, Saban Center for Middle East Policy at the Brookings Institution and Georgetown University

Noah Feldman, New York University

Paul Hughes, United States Army (ret.), United States Institute of Peace

Brian Katulis, Center for American Progress

Andrew Krepinevich, Jr., United States Army (ret.), Center for Strategic and Budgetary Assessments

Andrew Parasiliti, Barbour, Griffith & Rogers

Kenneth Pollack, Saban Center for Middle East Policy at the Brookings Institution

Irena Sargsyan, Saban Center for Middle East Policy at the Brookings Institution

Joseph Siegle, Development Alternatives, Inc.

Nearly all of the ideas contained in this report came from the discussions of the Iraq Working Group. This report is a distillation of the thinking of the members of the group as interpreted by the principal drafter, Kenneth Pollack. However, *none of the ideas within this report should be attributed to any individual member of the group, except where explicitly stated.* The members of the group provided substantial comments on various drafts of the report, but were not asked to agree to the final version. As a result, *the opinions expressed in this report should not necessarily be construed as the views of any member of the Iraq Working Group.* In some cases, members of the group may agree entirely with its recommendations; in other cases only partially, or not at all.

We would also like to thank by name some of those who assisted us, such as by providing input for the report, or by reviewing draft versions. They include, at the Saban Center at Brookings, Ambassador Martin Indyk, Avi Dicter and Andrew Apostolou; in Foreign Policy Studies at Brookings, Michael O'Hanlon and Nina Kamp. Outside of Brookings, we drew on Amatzia Baram; Eliot Cohen; Bathsheba Crocker; Janine Davidson; James Dobbins; Colonel Thomas X. Hammes, United States Army (ret.); Major General James "Spider" Marks, United States Army (ret.); Phebe Marr; Steven Metz; Lieutenant Colonel John Nagl; Ambassador Mark Parris; Lieutenant General David Petraeus; Fareed Yaseen; General Anthony Zinni, United States Marine Corps (ret.); members of the headquarters staff of U.S. Central Command; and other serving U.S. military officers and government officials who must remain anonymous.

Above all, we wish to thank Nemir Kirdar, whose generosity and devotion to the future of Iraq made this report possible.

GROUND RULES OF THE REPORT

"A Switch in Time" is intended to provide an alternative, comprehensive approach for American strategy in Iraq. It begins with the assumption (not necessarily shared by all members of the Iraq Working Group) that although the current U.S. approach is encountering considerable difficulties and appears unlikely to produce a stable Iraq within the next two to five years the alternative proposed by some Bush Administration critics—a rapid withdrawal—would also not serve U.S. interests. While many thoughtful experts and policymakers have attempted to offer a realistic third course of action, none have so far succeeded in doing so. This report proposes such a strategy.

The one aspect of Iraq policy that this report deliberately does not address is domestic American politics. Determining what is politically possible for U.S. policy in Iraq is an inherently difficult proposition. Moreover, U.S. domestic politics lie beyond the writ of the Saban Center and the expertise of the Iraq Working Group. The guiding principle behind this report was to ask non-partisan specialists with relevant expertise to devise an optimal strategy for producing a stable, pluralistic Iraq within the foreseeable future. Whether that strategy is domestically politically viable and what is required for its adoption by the U.S. government and the Congress is a question for others. We believe, however, that a vital element of the U.S. domestic debate over Iraq is a realistic assessment of what "staying, but doing it right" requires.

Finally, another rule we have tried to adhere to is not to place blame on specific individuals for events or decisions. This report discusses the many mistakes and failings that currently hinder reconstruction, both political and economic, in Iraq for the sole purpose of identifying what must change and how. The intent of this report, and of the Iraq Working Group, is to identify the steps that the United States must take to put the reconstruction of Iraq on a path to success. The task of deciding the responsibility for mistakes is best left to future historians.

EXECUTIVE SUMMARY

The reconstruction of Iraq is not doomed to fail, but the Bush Administration does not yet have a strategy that is likely to succeed. The progress made so far is an insufficient basis for a durable solution to Iraq's problems. Many of the positive developments are fragile or superficial, and conceal deeper underlying problems that could easily re-emerge. U.S. policy often focuses on the wrong problems and employs the wrong solutions. The most basic flaw stems from April 2003 when the fall of Saddam Hussein created a security vacuum in Iraq that the United States has never properly filled. This security vacuum has given rise to two separate but related problems:

- An insurgency, based principally in the Sunni tribal community of western Iraq; and,

- A failed state, in which the governmental architecture has essentially collapsed and has not yet been effectively replaced by new, capable military and political institutions.

The United States has devoted considerable energy and resources to fighting the insurgency, but it has consistently employed the wrong strategy. However, more damaging has been the consistent failure to rebuild Iraq's failed state. *Until the United States succeeds in helping the Iraqis build strong, new political and military institutions, a massive commitment of external military forces and economic assistance will continue to be necessary to forestall a civil war.*

Time is already working against the United States. The many disappointments of reconstruction are increasingly eroding Iraqi popular support, prompting a growing number of Iraqis to cast their lot with insurgent or militia groups who offer them immediate relief, even if most Iraqis understand that this is an extremely dangerous path. Until now, the promise of a new government just around the corner has kept Iraqis from defecting in large numbers. But the installation in 2006 of Iraq's new "permanent" government—the fifth since Saddam's fall—means that it will be four years before Iraqis can shift their hopes to a new horizon. It is therefore essential that this government not disappoint Iraqis as its predecessors have.

The United States must therefore approach 2006 as a make-or-break year in Iraq. Either the new Iraqi government with U.S. backing starts to fix Iraq's problems or continued failure will propel Iraqis into the arms of the militias, likely generating a full-blown civil war. However, the situation is not yet hopeless because so many Iraqis still fear that turning away from reconstruction will mean civil war. If the U.S. and Iraqi governments can begin to produce positive results, they can still win the hearts and minds of most Iraqis.

SECURITY AND MILITARY OPERATIONS

Security is the most important prerequisite for the reconstruction of Iraq. Although there is no guarantee that reconstruction will succeed with adequate security, it is guaranteed to fail without it. *The key flaw in U.S. military strategy in Iraq has been its inability to provide basic safety for Iraqis. Providing that safety, not chasing insurgents, must be the new priority of U.S. policy.*

Adopt a traditional counterinsurgency strategy. To improve the chances of providing adequate levels of security for reconstruction in Iraq, the United States should adopt a traditional counterinsurgency (COIN) strategy which will, by its very nature, address the dual needs of defeating the insurgency and building a viable state. *The key requirement of COIN is to achieve a ratio of about 20 security personnel per thousand of the population.* For the 22 million Iraqis living outside of Kurdistan, that would require about 450,000 security personnel—well beyond current U.S. and Iraqi capabilities. However, traditional counterinsurgency strategy initially focuses on creating such a favorable ratio only in those parts of the country that are both the most important and the most supportive of reconstruction. These locations become secured enclaves and, with economic resources pouring in, emerge as successful models of reconstruction. They then provide the base from which reconstruction can slowly expand across the country as more security forces become available. These areas are like an "oil stain" or "ink spot" that gradually spreads throughout the country, pacifying and rebuilding those areas that it touches.

Such a strategy in Iraq would begin by reducing the resources devoted to stamping out the insurgency in western Iraq. These would be shifted to securing the critical enclaves of Kurdistan, Baghdad, much of southeastern Iraq, and a number of other major urban centers, along with the oilfields and some other vital economic facilities. The concentrated security focus and development effort should ensure meaningful local economic and political progress. In turn, public opinion within the secured enclaves would likely solidify in favor of reconstruction, while Iraqis outside the secured enclaves would see that the government can offer a better alternative than the militias and insurgents. The United States would train additional Iraqi forces within the permissive environment of the enclaves to allow them to build unit cohesion, trust, and command relationships.

For this counterinsurgency strategy to work, the United States will need to:

- *Make protecting the Iraqi people and civilian infrastructure its highest priority, training Iraqi security forces a close second, and hunting insurgents a distant third.* The single most important mission of counterinsurgency forces is to provide basic safety for the population so that it no longer lives in fear.

- *Shift the strategic emphasis from offensive to defensive military operations, but go on the offensive in the political and economic realms.* Military offensives should only be mounted as immediate counterattacks for insurgent actions or when intelligence has clearly identified a high-value target.

- *Focus on reducing the influence of militias and organized crime in central and southern Iraq, which cripples economic development and threatens civil war.* The militias established themselves there because the United States never properly filled the post-Saddam security vacuum. The only way to reverse this trend is to fill the security vacuum by deploying significant Iraqi and Coalition forces into these regions.

- *Create a unified command structure fully integrating civilian and military operations.* Only a fully-integrated approach is likely to produce success. The United States and the Iraqi government must create a hierarchy of joint committees to integrate military, political, and economic decision-making both horizontally and vertically. These committees should consist of all key players in reconstruction and governance. The Bush Administration's nascent plan to deploy Provincial Reconstruction Teams (PRTs) in Iraq falls far short of what is needed because it will not erect a national integrated hierarchy.

The United States' newly-proclaimed "clear, hold and build" strategy also fails to meet these criteria. In particular, it is being implemented in the wrong part of the country—western Iraq—thereby drawing off forces from central and southern Iraq where popular support for reconstruction is highest but is souring because of insecurity. Consequently, these critical parts of the country are falling under the control of vicious sectarian militias which could fragment the country and drive it into civil war.

Adopt more appropriate tactics. The change in U.S. strategy must be accompanied by changes at tactical level. Two examples of the many changes to tactical conduct that this report advocates are:

- *De-emphasize detainee counts.* The military has replaced the Vietnam metric of the body count with a new and equally counterproductive metric in Iraq, the detainee count.

- *To facilitate population control, conduct a nationwide census and create a biometric identification card system.* A nationwide census would help identify insurgents and their supporters, and a biometric ID card would make it extremely difficult for insurgents to hide their identities, obviating their ability to mingle freely with the population.

Organizational and personnel changes. This report recommends a great many changes to the personnel, organizational and structural policies that the U.S. military has pursued in Iraq. One example is that all U.S. Army and Marine battalions should be "paired up," with one of the pair always in Iraq in the same area of responsibility (AOR) and the other at home, resting and training for the next rotation. The two would continue to swap for as long as the U.S. deployment lasts. Officers would be able regularly to exchange information and provide each other with lessons learned. The intelligence sections of the paired battalions would function as "rear" and "forward" elements. "Pairing up" is the best way to deal with the problems of turnover, loss of institutional memory, and the need for frequent rotations to deal with "burnout."

A better integrated reconstruction effort. Another important failing of the U.S. effort in Iraq has been the dearth of civilian personnel from key agencies: USAID, CIA, the Departments of State, Energy, Agriculture, and others. Very few of Iraq's 18 provinces have more than a half-dozen American civilian government personnel working in them. State and USAID must commit far greater numbers of personnel—particularly those with Arabic and knowledge of the Arab world—to the reconstruction of Iraq, even if this means reducing the manning of posts elsewhere. Far more personnel need to be assigned to missions outside the Green Zone in Baghdad.

Training the Iraqi armed forces. The training of Iraqi security forces is progressing better than ever before, but there is still a long way to go before they will be able to shoulder the burden of providing security in Iraq alone. Political pressure to quickly produce more trained Iraqi units to replace U.S. soldiers is the overarching problem that has plagued U.S. efforts. The only way to generate Iraqi troops sufficiently capable of shouldering the burden of securing their country is to give them the time in both formal and informal training to develop.

At this point, roughly 40,000–60,000 Iraqi security force personnel appear capable of contributing in some meaningful way to COIN and stability operations in Iraq. Although far short of the number necessary to secure the country without U.S. military forces, this represents a considerable increase over the past year, and suggests that Iraqi forces should be able to pick up more of the security burden in coming years. However, before this can happen, the United States must address three key problems:

- U.S. military personnel will need to place greater emphasis on the selection and training of Iraqi military officers, especially at tactical levels.

- The U.S. and Iraqi high commands need to make a greater effort to create integrated Iraqi security formations.

- The U.S. will have to make rebuilding Iraq's military support infrastructure a higher priority if the Iraqi armed forces are to take over full responsibility for securing the country.

BUILDING A NEW IRAQI POLITICAL SYSTEM

The United States will need to help develop a new political system that will secure the trust of Iraqis by persuading them that there are effective, non-violent means to address their problems; that others will not use violence against them; that they will have equal opportunities; and that the state has institutions capable of addressing their needs.

The new Iraqi government's legitimacy will depend on whether it can improve the lives of its people through providing higher employment, more constant electricity, more readily available clean water and gasoline, and the security that underpins all of these necessities.

There are four major problems afflicting the Iraqi body politic:

- Iraq is now a deeply divided society and those divisions are creating animosity, fueling the violence, and preventing the efficient functioning of the Iraqi government.

- Iraq's central government is now fully-constituted but essentially powerless.

- Iraq's political parties have only tenuous connections to the Iraqi people and mostly limit their interaction with their nominal constituents.

- The United States, as the principal occupying power and the driving force behind reconstruction, lacks the personnel, capabilities, know-how, and even the necessary resources to rebuild the Iraqi nation.

Power sharing and national reconciliation. Like security, some form of national reconciliation compact, coupled with a new power-sharing arrangement, is a precondition for any progress in Iraq. The greatest obstacle to national reconciliation is the fact that many Sunni Arabs feel alienated from the political reconstruction process by the Shi'ah, the Americans, and, to a

lesser extent, the Kurds. Regardless of these grievances, the Sunnis will still have to make some major concessions. In particular they will need to accept that their share of Iraq's resources will be strictly proportionate to their numbers. The Shi'ah and Kurds will need to reciprocate this and other Sunni concessions by:

- Revising the de-Ba'thification program and establishing a formal truth and reconciliation process.

- Reintegrating Sunnis into the armed forces and civil service.

- Providing greater protection for minorities.

- Revising electoral laws to prevent sectarian chauvinists from running.

- Providing Sunni tribal shaykhs with resources if they stop attacking roads, power lines, oil pipelines, and Coalition forces in their territory, and prevent other groups from doing the same.

Another key goal for the United States is to rein in the Shi'ah. Since the fall of Saddam, there has been an alarming tendency by some Shi'i leaders to overreach. Some now talk about splitting off all of southeastern Iraq to form an autonomous region, much like Iraqi Kurdistan, keeping the revenues from the southern oil fields for themselves. They expect the Kurds will do the same in the north, leaving no oil revenues for the Sunnis. This would be a disastrous development for Iraq as it likely would spark civil wars both within the Shi'i community and between the Shi'ah and Sunni Arabs.

Since the fall of Baghdad, Kurdish political leaders have been the most willing to argue for actions that are in the best interests of Iraq, while jealously guarding Kurdistan's prerogatives. As long as they do not push a maximalist agenda of immediate secession, full ownership of all revenues from the northern oilfields, or an arbitrary solution to competing property claims in Kirkuk, the *status quo* on issues related to them should not preclude solutions to Iraq's other political problems.

They will want something in return for concessions to the Sunni Arabs. The United States should offer them a more equitable slice of foreign aid so that they can demonstrate to their constituents that there are real benefits to remaining part of Iraq.

Decentralization. Iraq's ministries are crippled by corruption, undermanned, and remain tied to sclerotic bureaucratic practices inherited from the former regime. Accordingly, the United States and the new Iraqi government should begin moving toward a federal system in which the central government retains control of the armed forces, foreign policy, monetary policy and currency, national standards including regulation of the media, and regulation of the oil sector (but not oil income distribution). Most other powers should devolve to local governments. This report suggests a range of actions that could assist the process of decentralization, the most important of which are:

- Funds from foreign aid and oil revenues should be provided directly to local governments.

- Control of Iraq's police should be transferred from the Ministry of the Interior to local officials.

A new oil-revenue distribution system. The success or failure of political reconstruction in Iraq probably hinges on establishing a fixed and equitable system for the distribution of its oil revenues. Without such a plan, it is impossible to imagine real national reconciliation because all the parties will continue to fight over the spoils, distracting officials and technocrats from the job of running the country, let alone rebuilding it. Moreover, a fixed distribution plan is necessary to ensure that all the revenues do not go into central government coffers as pure discretionary funding because this breeds rampant corruption and concentrates financial power in the hands of the federal government.

However, it is critical that Iraq's oil-revenue distribution system consist of multiple "baskets" into which the oil revenues would be deposited. This report proposes five separate baskets:

- Basket 1: Federal government funding for national security, foreign affairs, monetary policy and other central government functions.

- Basket 2: Infrastructure development.

- Basket 3: Distribution directly to local governments based on the population in their municipalities.

- Basket 4: An additional pool of revenue divided among the provinces on an annual basis by the Council of Representatives (Iraq's parliament), giving the average Iraqi a tangible interest in the performance of his or her national representatives who would have to fight for as much of this basket for their constituents as possible.

- Basket 5: Direct funding to the Iraqi people. Money from oil revenues should be deposited in individual bank accounts for every Iraqi, earmarked for specific purposes—education, retirement, healthcare, etc., to give Iraqis a direct stake in opposing organized crime and the insurgents who steal the oil and destroy oil industry infrastructure.

Building central government capacity by tackling corruption. Corruption is probably the single greatest factor inhibiting the creation of credible Iraqi political institutions. Like the problem of insecurity, with which it is intertwined, corruption undermines nearly every aspect of reconstruction. This report details over 40 different prescriptions that the United States and the government of Iraq should adopt to fight corruption, including:

- Reducing the monetary size of individual aid and reconstruction contracts.

- Creating an independent NGO responsible for issuing annual "report cards" on the Iraqi fiscal and monetary systems.

- Establishing a special court for cases of corruption to be presided over by a panel of judges, including at least one foreign judge to ensure impartiality.

- Changing Iraqi perceptions of corruption by educating the Iraqi media so that they are better able to expose corruption.

Reforming the Iraqi political process. The early U.S. decision to allow a group of exiles and Shi'i chauvinists to determine the shape of Iraq's democratic process has resulted in a political structure that is exacerbating many of the problems plaguing the country and could eventually prove disastrous. Iraq's electoral system is based on proportional representation which hinders the emergence of many key features of democracy because it forces Iraqis to vote for party slates. All party leaders have a vested interest in maintaining this system because it rewards party loyalty and favors weak national parties over strong individual candidates. But the result is that the parties currently in power do not adequately represent the aspirations of the Iraqi people, their electoral victories notwithstanding. And the party leaders have few incentives to make the kinds of compromises necessary either to achieve national reconciliation or to address the needs of the people. Instead, they have every incentive to pocket as much public wealth as they can while they remain in office.

It would be preferable for Iraq to move to a version of direct geographic representation, as used in Great Britain and the United States, because this would encourage parliamentary compromise and national reconciliation, and force legislators to pay close attention to the needs of their constituents. Candidates from districts representing mixed populations would have a strong incentive to find solutions that would secure them support across sectarian lines. Of course, the current parties will be reluctant to give up the current system. *One solution could be to encourage Iraq to adopt a hybrid system like Germany's, with half of the seats in the Council of Representatives being decided by proportional representation and the other half by geographic direct election.*

Even without such a major overhaul of Iraq's current electoral system, there are many changes that could be adopted to reduce sectarianism, make Iraqi political

leaders more conscientious about securing the needs of their constituents, and moderating extremists. One example of the ideas presented in this report would be to make it mandatory by the 2009 or 2013 elections for candidates for the Council of Representatives to have served on either a local or provincial council. If each member of the Council of Representatives has first to serve on local and provincial councils it forces the political parties to pay attention to elections for these lesser assemblies.

Increasing international assistance. Now that the December 2005 elections have ushered in a permanent government, the United States should try to hand over some of the burden of guiding Iraq's reconstruction to an international body. It would be better for the United Nations or some other international actor to take the lead in prodding the Iraqis. *Moreover, the United Nations, through its various agencies, can call upon a vast network of personnel and resources vital to various aspects of nation-building.* But securing greater international assistance from NGOs, the United Nations, and other nations will largely depend on two factors:

- The willingness of the United States to allow the United Nations and foreign countries to play a leadership role—particularly on the political and economic tracks—in the reconstruction of Iraq.

- The willingness of the United States to adopt a true counterinsurgency strategy that would make key sectors of the country safe enough for civilians to perform their missions. Only by creating safe zones in Iraq can the United States hope to entice large numbers of foreigners back.

ASSISTING IRAQ'S ECONOMIC DEVELOPMENT

Meaningful progress in improving Iraq's economy depends on commensurate improvements in Iraq's security and political fortunes. While the Iraqi economy is not doing well, it is not listless either. Foreign aid continues to flow into Iraq. Although far too much of

Iraq's oil money is siphoned out of the country in the form of graft, much still remains—even if that too is tainted by corruption. The influx of money and the U.S. decision to lift all import duties after the fall of Baghdad, has brought in a flood of foreign consumer goods. So much foreign aid was earmarked for infrastructure repair that Iraq's construction industry boomed. This has taken some of the edge off unemployment while putting money into the hands of Iraq's working classes. Nevertheless, all of these advances tend to be fragile: the influx of foreign aid and cheap imports will not last forever. Iraq's manufacturing, agricultural, and service economies are moribund, crippled by a lack of investment, excessive corruption and inefficient management.

The United States and the new government of Iraq have two economic challenges ahead of them:

- The pressing need to provide more tangible benefits to the Iraqi people within the next 6–12 months, as Iraqis assess whether this new government will be any different from its predecessors.

- The need to help Iraq deal with its various structural problems so that the Iraqi economy can eventually operate under its own steam and provide for the Iraqi people without prodigious external assistance.

There is tension between these short-term and long-term requirements. It is therefore critical that the United States and the new government of Iraq set clear priorities for economic policy for the next year. Immediate growth is needed in the sectors that are most important to the short-term well-being of average Iraqis. In all other areas of the Iraqi economy, the emphasis should be on long-term structural reform.

Short-term efforts. Those issues in the Iraqi economy targeted for short-term improvement should be those that Iraqis have identified as of greatest concern to them—employment, electricity, oil production and export, corruption, agriculture, decentralization, banking and investment, and foreign aid projects.

Lack of jobs is one of the greatest complaints of Iraqis. However, this is one area where short and long-term needs run at cross purposes. Nearly three years into the reconstruction effort, Iraq should be moving away from aid programs that fund what are often nothing more than make-work projects concentrated in construction and infrastructure repair. Iraq needs to be shifting its emphasis to more economically viable and productive methods of employing its work force. However, because progress in Iraq's economy has largely been limited to just a few sectors, jobs do not yet exist in the economy to absorb large numbers of Iraqis if these make-work programs are ended. *Thus, despite their inefficiencies, the United States must maintain adequate levels of funding for current Iraqi construction projects and other programs that generate large numbers of jobs.*

The revival of Iraq's agricultural sector, critical to the economic reconstruction of Iraq, has been badly neglected. Iraq has some of the most fertile land in the Middle East and was at times a net exporter of agricultural products. Enhanced agricultural production could help diversify Iraq's economy away from its current dependence on oil. Moreover, agriculture is far more labor-intensive than oil, making it an excellent way of curbing unemployment. This report advocates a number of steps for the revitalization of Iraq's agricultural sector such as ensuring that the Iraqi government stops importing food for its ration basket and devolves to local governments control over contracting and administration of agricultural programs.

Electricity blackouts are a constant complaint of Iraqis. Immediately after Saddam's fall, Iraqis ran out to buy every type of household appliance imaginable. As a result, demand for electricity to run these items quickly outpaced every Coalition effort to repair and expand the capacity of Iraq's electricity generation and distribution sector. Thus, while the United States and other foreign donors must continue to increase generating capacity (and the grid's ability to import electricity from neighboring countries), it is equally important that the Iraqi government move to curb demand by installing meters in every Iraqi home and business while ending electricity subsidies.

The longer term. The United States will also have to ensure that Iraqi economic growth is sustainable over the long-term. Iraq's economy remains hobbled by costly subsidies dating to Saddam's era and before. The principal subsidies on food, gasoline and electricity constitute 21 percent of the Iraqi government's budget. Imports of gasoline and other refined petroleum products—which are then sold at subsidized prices—cost the government another 10 percent of the budget. These subsidies negate and distort market forces. Because these are all "sacred cows," quickly eliminating them is probably impossible. Instead, these subsidies should be phased out over the next several years. In particular, most poor and middle class Iraqis remain dependent on rations provided by the government since the imposition of UN sanctions against Iraq in 1990. It will be impossible to do away with the food basket overnight and there are concerns about its monetization because of problems with corruption and violent crime. *Consequently, it might benefit Iraq to employ a system of food stamps for underprivileged Iraqis in the meantime.*

There is nothing more important to Iraq's long-term economic prosperity than improving the state of its educational system. The United States and the international community have already provided considerable assistance, largely in terms of building schools, raising the pay of teachers, providing revised textbooks, furnishing school supplies, and eliminating Saddam's worst flunkies from university positions. There is still a great deal more to be done. Iraq suffers from the same problems in education as other Arab states: there is little emphasis on interactive learning, rote memorization is employed in every subject (including the sciences); creativity tends to be stifled; there is an overemphasis on the humanities (including religion) at the expense of science and math; teachers are provided with few incentives to stimulate or engage with their pupils; and the entire process is rigidly prescribed by the central government. The result is that, like elsewhere in the Arab world, students graduate from the educational systems with few of the kinds of job skills needed to compete in the globalized economy. This report offers a number of suggestions regarding the revival of education in Iraq, including the funding of new programs to teach English, scholarships for Iraqi students to study in the United States, and the commissioning of a high-level and comprehensive study of Iraqi education by leading American educators.

THE IMPORTANCE OF AN INTEGRATED APPROACH

One of the principal themes of this report is the essential need to integrate military, political and economic programs to foster reconstruction across the board. There are always bound to be successes and failures in an effort as grand as the reconstruction of Iraq. Proper integration, however, increases the prospects for success in one field which can help generate symbiotic achievements in others, creating a self-reinforcing process. Unfortunately, the opposite is also true.

A Switch in Time
A New Strategy for America in Iraq

Introduction

Iraq hangs in the balance. The elections of December 2005 again demonstrated the desire of Iraqis for prosperity, pluralism, and peace. There should be little doubt that the vast majority of Iraqis want reconstruction to succeed. This is the most powerful of a range of positive factors in Iraq that could be the foundation of a new Iraqi state capable of overcoming sectarian differences and serving as a force for stability in the Middle East. Yet the Iraqi and American peoples are becoming increasingly frustrated at the persistent failings of reconstruction. Both continue to believe in the importance of reconstruction there, but understandably worry that both the U.S. and Iraqi governments do not have a strategy that can succeed.

For this reason, 2006 could prove to be decisive for the future of Iraq. Reconstruction must finally begin to make progress and show tangible results in building strong Iraqi political and military institutions capable of holding the country together on their own, or else people on both sides of the Atlantic will begin to lose faith that they ever can. Reconstruction must start to climb upwards in a clear, unambiguous fashion, or else

it is likely to begin to spiral downward, toward possible chaos and civil war.

The reconstruction of Iraq is not doomed to fail, but Washington does not yet have a strategy that can produce a stable, pluralistic and independent Iraq. The Bush Administration can point to areas of progress and promise, but these are an insufficient basis for a durable solution to Iraq's problems. Despite the sometimes positive evolution of U.S. policy, it often focuses upon the wrong problems and employs the wrong solutions.

Consequently, the reconstruction of Iraq is hobbled by a wide array of deep-seated problems. In some cases, these problems are masked by a superficial aspect of success. For instance, there is somewhat greater security in many parts of Iraq. Yet the improvement in security is largely superficial and contains within it the seeds of its own destruction because it is being delivered by sectarian militias while looters and petty criminals have been consolidated into organized crime rings.[1] Parts of Iraq may seem "safer" because the militias and criminals are in charge, but over the

---

1 Throughout this report "militia" refers to the irregular military forces of Shi'i and Sunni Arab groups, and to a lesser extent the Kurdish *peshmerga*. The Mahdi Army and the Badr Organization are both militias. Most of the Sunni "insurgent" groups are essentially just Sunni militias, functionally equivalent to the Shi'i militias. The principal difference is that the Shi'i feel empowered by reconstruction and so are not attacking Americans or Iraqi government officials, whereas the Sunnis, feeling threatened by it, are launching such attacks. The *peshmerga* fall into a slightly different category. The *peshmerga* are militias and are guilty of some of the same reprehensible behavior as the Arab militias, especially in ethnically mixed cities such Mosul, Kirkuk and Khanaqin. Nonetheless, the *peshmerga* are very different from the Shi'i and Sunni groups because they are long-standing security forces of a functional society ruled by a largely autonomous and mostly functional, if imperfect, administration. Consequently, the *peshmerga* do not pose the same threat to Iraq's stability as the Shi'i and Sunni militias and insurgents, although they are not entirely benign and do not promote *unity* in Iraq.

long-term their influence will prevent the emergence of a viable state and economic development. Taken together these persistent, underlying problems raise the prospect that in the next 6–24 months the process of reconstruction may begin to break down, and in so doing raise the specter of civil war.

The most damaging of all of these deep-seated problems is the U.S. failure to fill the security vacuum that we created in April 2003. *The security vacuum led to two intimately related phenomena: a full-blown insurgency, largely based in the Sunni tribal community of Western Iraq, and a failed state, in which the governmental architecture has essentially collapsed and has not yet been effectively replaced by new, capable military and political institutions.* As a result, Iraq has a daunting combination of insurgency-related problems similar to those of the wars in Vietnam, Northern Ireland, and Algeria, compounded by failed-state challenges similar to those of Lebanon in the 1970s and 1980s, the former Yugoslavia in the 1990s and the Congo today.

To tackle these challenges, the United States requires a strategy that will both defeat the insurgency and rebuild the state and end its chronic dysfunctions. At present, however, the United States has no such strategy and Iraq is held together almost entirely by the U.S. military presence.

Unfortunately, the Bush Administration has focused principally on the insurgency, and not the failed-state. This has allowed a host of new threats to emerge. To defeat the insurgency requires strong Iraqi political and military institutions with popular support. Iraq, however, is trapped in a vicious cycle in which its inadequate institutions cannot deliver basic necessities like security, jobs, electricity, and clean water to Iraqis, which in turn undermines popular support for reconstruction and for each newly-elected government.

While the United States has energetically attacked the

insurgency, it has not launched a similar effort to address the population's most pressing needs. Even when the United States has tried to remedy these problems, its efforts have generally been disjointed, uncoordinated, under-resourced, or misdirected.[2]

Instead, persistent problems are eroding Iraq's institutional capacity and popular support for U.S.-led reconstruction. Corruption is rampant in Baghdad and has rotted-out nearly every Iraqi ministry. Two-and-a-half years after the fall of Saddam's regime, the Iraqi central government has little ability to effect real change anywhere outside Baghdad's heavily protected Green Zone.[3] Rather than build ties to their people and improve the lives of their constituents, many Iraqi politicians are becoming disconnected from society at large and more pre-occupied with dividing up the country's wealth among themselves. Although the training of the Iraqi Army is progressing better than ever before, it is still incomplete. By focusing the limited U.S. and Iraqi military assets that are available on chasing insurgents in the "Sunni Triangle", the United States has denuded the most populous regions of Iraq of adequate security forces. This has left the majority of Iraqis vulnerable to crime and inter-ethnic attacks. This security failure is part of the vicious cycle as it drives Iraqis into the arms of ethnic and sectarian militias that can provide a semblance of security. Meanwhile, Iraqis increasingly resent the U.S. military presence, sometimes out of sheer nationalism, but more often because the U.S. occupation has added burdens to their lives without providing the basic necessities of security, jobs, electricity, gasoline, clean water, and sanitation.

None of this suggests that Iraq is stable, or that it is likely to stabilize in the near future. Instead, it indicates that current U.S. policies at best will solidify the unpalatable *status quo*. At worst, Iraq could slip into a Lebanon-style civil war. Given the gradually-building momentum behind these underlying problems, the

---

2 The same failures occurred in Vietnam until the imposition of the CORDS and Phoenix programs, both of which largely succeeded but did so only when it was too late.
3 Formally renamed the "International Zone," as if relabeling makes any difference.

worst-case scenario seems distressingly more likely than the best case.

THE RISKS OF A PRECIPITOUS WITHDRAWAL

Nevertheless, the rapid withdrawal of U.S. forces suggested by Bush Administration critics is also not the correct answer to the challenges that the United States faces in Iraq. *Iraq's political and military institutions are not yet strong enough to allow the country to survive without comprehensive U.S. support, and are unlikely to be able to do so for several years.* A precipitate withdrawal of U.S. forces before Iraq has developed capable institutions would almost certainly plunge the country into civil war. Existing armed groups would immediately seize as much wealth and territory as they could and some would mount pre-emptive attacks on other groups whose intentions they suspected. Meanwhile, the zealots in each major community, the Sunnis, Shi'ah, and Kurds alike, would indulge in the full-scale ethnic cleansing they have been pressing for since the fall of Baghdad.

A civil war in Iraq would likely destabilize Iraq's neighbors. Civil wars often have spillover effects on neighboring states—such as refugee flight and armed groups moving in to seek sanctuary there. Neighboring states often intervene to prevent such spillover or to grab territory, which would be especially tempting in oil-rich Iraq. For instance, the Lebanese civil war of the 1970s and 1980s imposed damaging spillover effects on both Syria and Israel, while civil strife in Afghanistan in the 1990s exacerbated the problems of Central Asia, Iran and Pakistan. The collapse of the Democratic Republic of Congo from the late-1990s onwards has embroiled six neighboring countries in southern and eastern Africa and caused millions of deaths. A civil war in Iraq might well spread instability into already fragile states such as the major oil producers of Saudi Arabia, Kuwait, and Iran; our NATO-ally Turkey; our friend, Jordan; and even

our sometimes foe, Syria—an enormous risk to vital U.S. national interests. Experts already fret over the long-term stability of each of these countries. Allowing Iraq to fall into civil war and further threaten the well-being of these other states would be running an enormous risk to vital U.S. national interests. *For the United States, to leave Iraq in a state of civil war would be as reckless as having invaded Iraq without being adequately prepared to prevent civil war.*

Moreover, President George W. Bush is no doubt correct that if Iraq were to fall into chaos and civil war, it would probably become a haven and breeding ground for terrorist groups to an even greater extent than it already is. Lebanon in the 1970s and Afghanistan in the 1990s are examples of this phenomenon. Iraq was not the central front of the war on terrorism before the U.S.-led invasion. By invading and failing to stabilize the country, however, it has become the central front. Today, many Salafi Jihadist[4] recruits are traveling to Iraq to learn the trade of terrorism and to test their mettle in direct combat with the Americans. If the United States leaves Iraq in chaos, terrorists will establish training camps and bases from which to attack the United States and its allies throughout the world, just as al-Qa'ida used Afghanistan to mount the East Africa bombings, the attack on the USS Cole, and September 11. Moreover, if we left Iraq prematurely, this would be seen across the Muslim world as a great victory for the Salafi Jihadist cause—greater even than their part in defeating the Soviets in Afghanistan. This would be a major spur to terrorist recruitment.

Finally, just as successfully establishing a stable, pluralist government in Iraq should eventually and subtly advance the cause of liberal reform across the Middle East, its failure could doom such change. The *status quo* in the Middle East is unstable. The region's regimes are rotten and their only credible political opposition is comprised of Islamists who do not offer a better alternative. It is a vital long-term interest of the United States, the Arab world, and the global

---

4   The radical Sunni Muslim fundamentalists exemplified by al-Qa'ida.

community that Arab regimes begin a gradual process of comprehensive reform. Unfortunately, Arabs are watching closely the grand experiment in democracy and free market economics occurring in Iraq and they are not impressed. The opponents of reform, within the autocratic regimes and among their Islamist enemies, want to see reconstruction fail in Iraq, because that will allow them to claim that democratic reform cannot work in the Arab Middle East. They will argue that the United States failed to democratize Iraq despite sending 150,000 troops and spending hundreds of billions of dollars, which they will argue means that reform cannot succeed anywhere in the Muslim Middle East—and many Arabs (and many Americans) will agree.

We should not fool ourselves into believing that we can walk away from Iraq without serious repercussions. In that sense, Iraq is not Vietnam. America's retreat from Vietnam cost it little in material terms because Vietnam was a poor, peripheral country. Iraq is an asset rich country in the heart of an economically-vital and fragile region. Indeed, failure in Iraq could dramatically undermine America's principal goals in the Middle East: diminishing the threat of terrorism and improving the stability of the region. Failure in Iraq would almost certainly spur the opposite, making the threat to the United States from terrorism worse, and creating grave risks to the stability of the Middle East—and with it, the global economy. As Andrew Krepinevich has remarked, the war in Iraq began as a war of choice, but it has become a war of necessity.

BUYING TIME

Yet all is not yet lost for the United States in Iraq. It is possible to imagine a different strategy that would have a better chance of success. This report describes such an approach, both in its broad themes and many of its key details.

The Bush Administration is correct to observe that there are still many positives in Iraq. The most impor-

tant is the determination of the vast majority of Iraqis to see the political and economic reconstruction of their country succeed. They want a better future and are terrified that failure will mean civil war. Consequently, they have endured the injustices and disappointments of reconstruction thus far, and most remain hopeful and committed to improving the process of reconstruction. As long as the majority of Iraqis continue to take that view, reconstruction can be turned around to produce a stable, pluralistic Iraq.

Nonetheless, we must recognize that time is working against us. Setting aside the impatience of the American public, which is beyond the scope of this report, the underlying problems are gradually eroding Iraqi public support for reconstruction. Put differently, Iraqis have waited a long time for the meaningful improvements that they hoped for and were promised after the fall of Saddam. The longer that these hopes are frustrated and they are deprived of basic necessities—security, jobs, constant electricity, gasoline, clean water, sanitation—the more despondent they will become. Over time, that frustration has made many Iraqis conclude that the United States and the Baghdad government cannot or will not provide them with these necessities. Many Iraqis are therefore forced to look "elsewhere" for security and their basic needs—and in Iraq, elsewhere means the militias and insurgents, particularly rejectionists like Muqtada as-Sadr. Taking a page from Hizballah in Lebanon and Hamas in the Palestinian territories, the militias are providing average Iraqis with a semblance of security, social services, health clinics, jobs, and whatever else is required to gain their loyalty.

Many of the militias and insurgents have slowly begun to battle for control over parts of Iraq and to violently expel those who are not members of their ethnic or religious group. Although this scramble for turf and ethnic cleansing is not yet widespread, the fear that it will become generalized is starting to convince those Iraqis who might otherwise support reconstruction that they must cast their lot with the militias or insurgents. Many Iraqis understandably believe that because the government has failed them, only "their" ethnic or religious militia can provide protection from rival ethnic or religious militias.

There is a real risk inherent in the political process as well. Since April 2003, Iraqis have seen four governments come and go: Jay Garner's Office of Reconstruction and Humanitarian Assistance; L. Paul Bremer's Coalition Provisional Authority (CPA) and its partner, the Iraqi Governing Council (IGC); the interim government of Ayad Allawi; and the transitional government of Ibrahim Ja'fari. On each occasion, Iraqis were elated and relieved when the new government took power, believing that they would now have an authority that would deliver security, jobs, electricity, clean water, gasoline and other basic necessities. On each occasion, these governments failed to do so. This alone turned some against reconstruction, but in every case a (diminishing) majority set its sights on the next new government, which was already scheduled to take power in a matter of months, only to be just as disappointed when that new government took power and failed them in the same fashion as its predecessors.

Such a trend clearly cannot continue indefinitely. In December 2005, Iraq elected a new parliament, the Council of Representatives that will sit for four years and will select a "permanent" government with a similar four year mandate. Iraqis are even more emphatic that this government must finally address their needs. They also are well aware that they may be shackled with this parliament and the government for four years, so there is no other new government on the horizon that they can shift their hopes to should this one fail them as the others have. The failures to date have to an extent been alleviated by the safety valve of seeing governments change frequently and the opportunity to go to the polls. Now, however, if demonstrable progress on reconstruction is not forthcoming, then the temptation of supporting militias or insurgents that can deliver, as opposed to yet another government that cannot, could prove too great to resist.

For these reasons, the United States must approach 2006 as a watershed year in Iraq. The new Iraqi government and the United States must begin to fix Iraq's problems, or our continued failure will propel Iraqis into the arms of the militias and a full-blown civil war. *Therefore, the Bush Administration's approach of gradual, evolutionary policy changes in Iraq will no longer suffice.* Within the next six to twelve months, Washington and Baghdad must pursue sweeping policy changes to prove that they understand Iraq's deep-seated problems and that they have the correct schemes to address these problems.

Our critical need right now is to buy ourselves and the Iraqis more time. Only very time-consuming programs of training, construction, education and reform can solve many of Iraq's underlying problems. Therefore, we must convince Iraqis (and Americans) to give us that time. Iraqis will understandably demand to see material improvements this year and Washington must respond accordingly. *By the same token, because so many Iraqis fear that turning away from reconstruction will mean civil war, there is every reason to believe that if the U.S. and Iraqi governments can demonstrate that they are making major changes, that the changes are the right ones, and that these changes are beginning to produce positive results for the average Iraqi, most will continue to support reconstruction at least for as long as it keeps moving in the right direction.*

GOALS AND ENDSTATES: SUSTAINABLE STABILITY

Since a "strategy" is a course of action intended to produce a specific goal, it is important to know what the goal is.

Our goal in Iraq should now be "sustainable stability." This means that the United States must leave an Iraq that will not cause us the regional and global problems that we would suffer in the event of a full-scale civil war. To prevent civil war, we need successful political and economic reconstruction. We cannot allow Iraq to remain the haven for terrorists that it is now, let alone allow it to become an Afghan-style terrorist state. We cannot allow Iraq to devolve into chaos and civil strife and so threaten the stability of the wider region. We cannot allow Iraq's reconstruction to be seen as a failure, thereby jeopardizing the prospects for liberal reform in the Middle East and delivering a galvanizing victory to the Salafi Jihadist terrorists. Only when we have achieved sustainable stability will U.S. forces be able to withdraw fully from Iraq.

Aiming for sustainable stability might seem to set the bar for U.S. strategy in Iraq quite low. Yet, given the complexities of Iraq and the negative effect of past policy errors, the opposite is the case. Sustainable stability is more demanding than it seems:

• *Sustainable stability will require some degree of pluralism coupled with meaningful power sharing.* We cannot expect a full-fledged democracy in Iraq anytime soon. Nonetheless a certain amount of democratization and the checks and balances that this entails will be vital for sustainable stability. There is no other form of government that has any chance of producing this endstate. Iraq's various ethnic and religious groups are now so polarized, and so heavily-armed, that they will all demand their "fair" share of power. None will be willing to accede to the dictatorship of one of the others, and they will fight to prevent it. Even an inter-ethnic and inter-religious oligarchy would fail because it would inevitably devolve into an unpopular kleptocracy challenged by militias and sliding towards civil war—not unlike what Iraqis have seen in the Baghdad Green Zone for the past two and a half years.

While some Americans hope to find a new military dictator to rule the country, there is no such person. No Iraqi political or military leader has demonstrated the necessary charisma, generalship, or resources to keep Iraq intact by force. Indeed, it is worth noting that Saddam was the first Iraqi dictator to achieve "stability"—which he did by employing near-genocidal levels of violence.

Therefore, only a government in Baghdad that is genuinely pluralist will be able to hold the country together and prevent a civil war. All Iraqis must feel represented by the new government and believe that there are political processes to resolve their disputes. Iraq's minorities must believe that they have sufficient safeguards against the majority so that they participate fully in the new political process.[5] There will have to be sufficient transparency and accountability for Iraqis to believe that no one group is taking advantage of its positions within the government to oppress or steal from the others. Thus, a form of pluralism is the only political system imaginable for Iraq that has any hope of achieving sustainable stability.[6]

• *Sustainable stability will require considerably improved public safety.* Sustainable stability requires a certain minimal level of public safety because its absence is undermining reconstruction. The rule of law will have to prevail to the extent that Iraqis are not obliged to seek protection from militias and insurgents. This does not mean stamping out every last terrorist and extremist. Rather, Iraq will need a level of public safety roughly equivalent to that of Israel, where acts of political violence are infrequent enough that they do not prevent the functioning of society.

• *Sustainable stability in Iraq will require improved economic performance.* Iraq's institutions will have to be able to deliver the basic necessities of life to Iraqis, thereby obviating a key appeal of the militias and insurgents.

---

5 In Iraq minorities are both national (Sunnis and Kurds) and regional (Shi'a in Sunni areas and vice versa).

6 It is important to note that while the United States must continue to press for a certain degree of democracy because this builds stability, it is not the case that democracy is all that is necessary to provide stability, as some within the Bush Administration consistently suggest. Iraq needs pluralism, but we should not make the pursuit of democratization our only priority in the mistaken belief that democratization alone will solve all of Iraq's other problems.

The objective of sustainable stability in Iraq is a lower threshold than the lofty goals the Bush Administration proclaimed when it invaded in 2003. Sustainable stability, should not, however, be confused with merely finding a "decent interval" before retreating or an autocracy slightly better than Saddam's tyranny. Sustainable stability is the minimum acceptable but is still considerably more demanding than abandoning the Iraqis to their fates.

I. SECURITY AND MILITARY OPERATIONS

Security is the most important prerequisite for the reconstruction of Iraq. *Although there is no guarantee that reconstruction will succeed with adequate security, it is guaranteed to fail without it.* The United States invaded Iraq lacking both the troops and the plans to provide immediate security for the population. As a result, we were unable to prevent looting; we could not reassure the bulk of the population, which favored Saddam's overthrow but was uncertain about our motives; nor could we overawe those elements of Iraqi society considering armed resistance. This failure created a security vacuum that has never been properly filled and that is the single greatest underlying problem in Iraq today.

Although the struggle for Iraq cannot be won without determined and competently implemented political and economic programs, without some degree of security nothing else is possible. Thus, everything begins with security and the military operations designed to create it. As Lt. Gen. James Mattis, commander of the 1st Marine Division during the conquest of Iraq said, "The military has one duty in a situation like this, and that is to provide security for the indigenous people. It's the windbreak behind which everything else can happen."[1]

Lt. Gen. Mattis' remark cuts to the heart of the problem. The key flaw in U.S. military strategy in Iraq has been its inability to provide basic safety for Iraqis. As noted earlier, Iraq suffers both from an insurgency and from being a failed state, and it is the first rule of both counterinsurgency operations and stabilization operations (which are the military operations designed to address the problems of failed states) that the highest priority of military and police forces is to provide security for the populace. In particular, as every successful counterinsurgency campaign has demonstrated, this starts with (but is not limited to) tactical *defensive* operations to ensure public safety. In this, the United States has failed badly. Too much of the U.S. military (and now of newly-trained Iraqi formations) have consistently been devoted to fruitless, and often counterproductive, tactical *offensive* operations to try to kill or capture Iraqi insurgents.

President Bush remarked on June 28, 2005 that, "The principal task of our military is to find and defeat the terrorists, and that is why we are on the offense."[2] While this is an accurate description of the American military approach, it is, unfortunately, wrong in terms of what is needed. The right formulation would be that, "The principal task of our military is to protect the Iraqi

---

1 James Fallows, "Why Iraq has no Army," *The Atlantic Monthly*, December 2005, p. 64.
2 "National Strategy for Victory in Iraq," The National Security Council, November 2005, p. 29, available at
<http://www.whitehouse.gov/infocus/iraq/iraq_national_strategy_20051130.pdf>.

people, and that is why we are mainly on the defensive." Better still would be to make clear that our military strategy is principally defensive to make it possible for the United States and the government of Iraq to go on the offensive in the economic and political spheres.

Instead, we are committing the cardinal military sin of reinforcing failure by concentrating too many of our forces in Iraq's western provinces (the "Sunni Triangle") where the insurgents are thickest and where support for reconstruction is thinnest. This approach has repeatedly resulted in counterinsurgency failures throughout history. Our efforts to "take the fight to the enemy" and mount offensive sweep operations designed to kill insurgents and eliminate their strongholds have failed to eradicate the insurgency so far, and likely will continue to do so, as was the case in Vietnam and other lost guerrilla wars. Moreover, by emphasizing offensive operations we have also committed the cardinal sin of stability operations—ceding control over much of the population to militias and other forces of anarchy.

In his seminal study of the failure of U.S. counterinsurgency strategy during the Vietnam War, Andrew Krepinevich warned of the false promise of hunting guerrillas:

> Should government forces attempt to defeat the insurgency through the destruction of guerrilla forces in quasi-conventional battles, they will play into the hands of the insurgent forces. Insurgent casualties suffered under these circumstances will rarely be debilitating for the insurgents. First, the insurgents have no need to engage the government forces—they are not fighting to hold territory. Second, as long as the government forces are out seeking battle with the guerrilla units, the insurgents are not forced to maintain access to the people. Therefore, *the initiative remains with the guerrillas*— they can "set" their own level of casualties (probably just enough to keep the government forces out

seeking the elusive big battles), thus rendering ineffective all efforts by the counterinsurgent to win a traditional military victory.

As a result of these circumstances, the conventional forces of the government's army must be reoriented away from destroying enemy forces toward asserting government control over the population and winning its support.... Winning the hearts and minds of the people is as desirable for the government as it is for the insurgent. This objective can only be realized, however, after control of the population is effected and their security provided for.... Nevertheless, even though the attempts to co-opt the insurgents may prove successful in winning the hearts of the people, they will be for naught unless the government provides the security necessary to free the people from the fear of insurgent retribution should they openly support the government.[3]

Large scale offensive operations are unlikely to succeed against a major insurgency and can be counterproductive. The guerrilla does not need to stand and fight when counterinsurgency (COIN) forces sweep his area. He can run or melt back into the population and thereby avoid crippling counterinsurgency losses. If the counterinsurgency forces do not remain and pacify the area over the long term, the guerrilla will return within months, or maybe just weeks. Meanwhile, concentrating forces in sweep operations means diverting resources away from securing the population. In Iraq, sweep operations in the "Sunni Triangle" have netted relatively few true insurgents, while the bulk of the insurgents generally return to the swept areas soon thereafter because the U.S. presence cannot be maintained properly—with so few troops, the only way to maintain the offensive is to send U.S. forces elsewhere to attack new insurgent bases.

Moreover, by concentrating U.S. and Iraqi forces in western Iraq, we have denuded central and southern Iraq of the forces desperately needed to maintain order, to enable

---

3   Andrew F. Krepinevich, Jr., *The Army and Vietnam* (Baltimore, MD: Johns Hopkins University Press, 1986), pp. 11–12. [Emphasis in original].

economic revival and to prevent militias from taking control. While there needs to be an offensive element in any strategy, in COIN campaigns the offensive component should primarily consist of limited attacks upon unequivocally clear and important insurgent strongholds, or immediate counterattacks against insurgents.

The United States' newly-proclaimed "clear, hold and build" strategy is not much of an improvement. The "clear, hold and build" strategy is being implemented in the wrong part of Iraq—western Iraq—thereby drawing off forces from central and southern Iraq where popular support for reconstruction is souring because of insecurity. Yet, even in western Iraq, the United States is not employing sufficient troops to actually "hold" areas or the resources needed to "build" there. For instance, as part of Operation Iron Hammer, the U.S. 3rd Armored Cavalry Regiment with nearly 5,000 troops cleared Tal Afar, but was replaced a few weeks later by a battalion roughly one-tenth that size—too few troops to "hold" Tal Afar. Similarly, after the Marine reduction of Fallujah in November 2004, the United States left behind only a brigade-sized formation, large enough to prevent Fallujah from reverting to insurgent control, too small to preserve security and stability to facilitate reconstruction. In Fallujah, and elsewhere in western Iraq, the U.S. and Iraqi governments have generally failed to make good on their promises of economic assistance and reparations for damage to innocent victims. Thus far, "clear, hold and build" has proven to be little different from the misguided offensive military operations that that have been the norm throughout the American occupation.

The consequences of this mistaken emphasis on offensive military operations have been devastating and have been reinforced by the interrelationship of the insurgency and Iraq's failed state. Many of the country's main population centers in central and southern Iraq are under militia control because of the insufficient U.S. and Iraqi military presence. Many Iraqis have been driven to seek protection from "friendly" militias, lending these groups a degree of legitimacy because Coalition forces cannot provide the populace with protection from crime, insurgents, and rival militias.[4] The absence of Coalition forces has also allowed both insurgent groups and the militias to begin low-level ethnic cleansing, assassinations, and other forms of internecine warfare that could prove to be the first skirmishes of a civil war. National Public Radio's Anne Garrels filed a chilling story from a formerly mixed Sunni-Shi'i village near Samarra. In October 2005 a Sunni militia began killing Shi'i villagers, prompting 200 Shi'i families to flee:

GARRELS: Samir says the Shiite community appealed for help from Ayatollah Ali al-Sistani, the most influential Shiite religious figure in Iraq.

Mr. MOHAMMED: (Through Translator) He [Sistani] said that we ought to be silent until this is over.

GARRELS: But when, they ask, will it be over? They're running out of money and patience. One of their local religious leaders, Sheikh Hadi Abdul Rahim al-Garawi (ph), fled after he escaped a kidnap attempt and threats. He's a student of Sistani's. And his father was Sistani's representative in Samarra until he also left. They're obliged to follow Sistani's orders without question, but Sheikh Hadi Abdul Rahim too is running out of patience.

Sheikh HADI ABDUL RAHIM AL-GARAWI: (Through Translator) We keep meeting and meeting, getting nothing. These meetings are useless. No one does anything. The people need help.

GARRELS: In his desperation, he's threatening to

---

4 Again, a considerable number of the Sunni "insurgent" groups are more properly understood as Sunni militias fighting against the Shi'ah and the Kurds (and their American rivals) because they believe that their opponents mean to oppress them just as Saddam's Sunni-based regime oppressed the Shi'ah and Kurds.

turn to radical cleric Muqtada al-Sadr and his armed militia.

Sheikh AL-GARAWI: (Through Translator) I was never a member of the Sadr line, but I really respect them because they are decisive. The people who have had to leave Samarra feel more and more that patience is the same as cowardice. I never wanted to reach this stage but I cannot tolerate the situation much longer. Why shouldn't I fight? Let it be civil war.[5]

This is a textbook example of how civil wars can begin. They often start not because two groups decide to have a civil war, but because the collapse of the central government creates a security vacuum that allows extremists to use violence to seize territory, settle old scores, and simply eradicate those that they don't like. Fear of these extremists causes the majority—that often lives harmoniously in integrated communities and dreads civil war—to seek protection from "their" extremists (Shi'ah turning to Muqtada as-Sadr, Sunnis to the insurgents). The inherent aggressiveness of the extremists guarantees ever increasing violence, given their determination to control more territory, given the need to "cleanse" intermingled population centers, and the desire to strike the first blow against the other side and so gain the advantage. The result is a vicious cycle that plunges the country into civil war.[6]

THE IMPACT OF INSECURITY

In Iraq, the security vacuum has had additional deleterious effects beyond allowing the spread of the insurgency and the rise of the militias. For instance, crime has blossomed throughout the country. Initially of the random, unorganized variety as a great many Iraqis sought to take advantage of the lawless situation and grab as much as they could, crime in Iraq has become increasingly organized, and therefore

increasingly more debilitating. Kidnap rings continue to flourish. Anything not guarded is quickly vandalized or stolen and goods (and people) are frequently lost on the roads to bandits. Murder for profit is as common as murder for political causes.

The insurgency, the growth of the militias, and the spread of organized crime have crippled Iraq's economy. Again, there have been superficial improvements. Iraq's consumer spending has rebounded to a considerable extent, largely because of the default deregulation of the economy and the lifting of most import fees. In the long-run, however, consumption and trade in consumer goods alone will not create a viable economy. In contrast, Iraq's manufacturing sector is crippled by a dearth of foreign investment. The agricultural sector is hamstrung because goods cannot move around the country. The service sector is floundering for lack of adequate investment capital. There is no functional banking system. Unemployment remains at excessively high levels and underemployment and low-productivity are chronic. (All of these problems are also exacerbated by the pervasive corruption of the Iraqi central government, although this is only indirectly related to the security vacuum.)

Insecurity also distorts Iraq's political process. Iraqis often support the candidates who promise immediate security regardless of their broader political platforms, which is part of the reason why the political wings of Iraq's militias and insurgent groups have fared so well in recent elections. In other cases, militias or insurgents have been able to take over areas and intimidate the local population into voting for them because of the absence of Coalition forces. Similarly, economic difficulties force many Iraqis to turn to the militias for jobs, food, medicine, shelter and other basic necessities. The price these groups extract is political support. This trend explains the growing popularity of both the

---

5 Anne Garrels, "Violence plagues Iraq, despite constitution breakthrough," National Public Radio, *Morning Edition*, October 14, 2005. *The New York Times* reports that events similar to this were occurring in at least 20 towns in central Iraq by November 2005. See Sabrina Tavernise, "Sectarian Hatred Pulls Apart Iraq's Mixed Towns," *The New York Times*, November 20, 2005.

6 This pattern was first recognized and described in Barry Posen, "The Security Dilemma and Ethnic Conflict," *Survival*, vol.35, no.1 (Spring 1993), pp.27–47.

Supreme Council for the Islamic Revolution in Iraq (SCIRI) and Muqtada as-Sadr, rather than any popular enthusiasm for their political platforms. Indeed, opinion polls consistently demonstrate that Iraqis staunchly oppose the Iranian-style theocracy at the heart of SCIRI's ideology. Yet SCIRI is the most "popular" party in Iraq in terms of its performance in national and regional elections.[7]

The problem is not merely a mistaken strategic approach but also clumsy U.S. military tactics that alienate Iraqis, particularly among the Sunni tribal community. Many U.S. units see the targets of their raids as their enemies and treat them as such—invariably turning them and their neighbors into enemies even if they were neutral or favorable to the United States beforehand. Often, the priority that American units place on force protection comes at the expense of the larger mission—the safety, psychological disposition, and dignity of Iraqis. There is a price to be paid for busting down doors, ordering families to lie down on the floor, holding them down with the sole of a boot, searching women in the presence of men, waiving around weapons, ransacking rooms or whole houses, destroying furniture, and confiscating weapons which all Iraqis believe they need to protect themselves and their families. Iraqis become less cooperative, more withdrawn and less willing to provide useful information. Indeed, it is not uncommon for the wrong house to be raided because too much of the intelligence that is received is of poor quality. All too often, U.S. forces are directed to raid a house, or arrest a person by an informant acting on a grudge who uses the Americans to settle a score.

The consistent priority that U.S. military personnel place on force protection at the expense of Iraqi public

safety has played a key role in turning average Iraqis against the U.S. military presence. Too often, skittish troops will fire at any Iraqi car that seeks to overtake them on the road. In other instances, American military vehicles drive along major highways displaying signs warning "Do not approach within 100 meters or you will be fired upon," and they are usually true to their words. Likewise, U.S. forces devise elaborate barriers and security procedures for entry into their facilities that force the Iraqis to congregate outside in long lines that make tempting terrorist targets. All of this behavior convinces Iraqis that the United States places no value on their lives, the precise opposite of the message that U.S. forces should be sending. U.S. commanders must protect their troops, but this cannot come at the expense of the mission which is to protect the Iraqi people.

Finally, while the training of Iraq's security forces is better than it ever has been before, these forces are still incapable of shouldering Iraq's security burden alone. Although the senior U.S. military leadership has made training Iraqi military forces its highest priority, in practice many lower down the chain of command treat it as a lesser priority than hunting insurgents. The training programs instituted by Gens. Eaton and Petraeus appear to be bearing fruit, as is the embedding of U.S. special forces with Iraqi units. However, many Iraqi formations are being trained by conventional U.S. units that lack the know-how, the inclination, or the time to properly teach counterinsurgency and stability operations. Moreover, Iraqi combat formations are still not always receiving the right kinds of training, and are often being pressed into service too soon after their formal periods of training (typically twelve to sixteen weeks). After training, too few Iraqi units are allowed to operate in permissive environments

---

7 For instance, two polls conducted in late 2003 when the militias were still comparatively weak, and therefore Iraqi political perspectives were still largely uncontaminated, showed very little support for an Iranian style theocracy. In a Zogby poll conducted with *American Enterprise* magazine in August 2003, respondents were asked which foreign country they should model their new government on. The United States got the most (24 percent), while Iran got the least (3 percent). Zogby International Survey of Iraq, August 2003, p. 2. Available at <http://www.taemag.com/docLib/ 20030905_IraqpollFrequencies.pdf>. Likewise, a Gallup Survey in Baghdad found that Iraqis believed that a multiparty parliamentary democracy was both the preferred form of government (39 percent) and the form that was most acceptable to the respondents (53 percent said that such a system would be acceptable to them). By comparison, an Islamic theocracy such as Iran's was preferred by only 10 percent, and was acceptable to only 23 percent. The Gallup Poll findings are in Appendix Table 2 of Dina Smeltz and Jodi Nachtwey, "Iraqi Public Opinion Analysis," U.S. Department of State, October 21, 2003, p. 13. Available at <http://www.cpa-iraq.org/government/political_poll.pdf>.

for enough time to develop critical relationships, such as unit cohesion, command relationships, and familiarity with procedures.[8] The risk is that Iraq's fragile security forces could collapse en masse in the face of a major challenge from insurgents or militias, as occurred in southern Iraq in April 2004 and around Mosul in November 2004.

Iraq's security forces are beset by three further problems. First, virtually all of Iraq's most capable formations are single-sect units that are almost entirely composed of either Sunni Arabs, or Shi'i Arabs, or Kurds. Some of these units contain a few officers from one of the other major ethnic groups—some excellent largely Kurdish units have a sprinkling of Sunni Arab officers—but this hardly qualifies them as ethnically mixed units. Indeed, many of these units were previously militia formations that have been inducted whole into the security forces. Some of these have been implicated in inter-ethnic atrocities; many are not welcomed in the towns of other ethnic or religious groups. And of course, their loyalty to the new Iraqi states is questionable.

Second, while the U.S. has done an admirable job of training Iraqi combat battalions, it has so far failed to build either combat support or combat service support structures to sustain the Iraqi armed forces in counterinsurgency and stability operations. As a result, the Iraqi armed forces lack a functional logistics system, command and control, communications, training, and other vital support elements. Instead, they are wholly reliant on the U.S. military to provide such functions. Were the United States to withdraw its forces from Iraq under present circumstances, the newly-trained Iraqi combat battalions would quickly become incapacitated for want of support.

Third, Iraq's police remain largely a disaster. In counterinsurgency and stability operations, a capable police force is a vital ally for the armed forces. Yet the Iraqi police force is riddled with graft; thoroughly penetrated by the insurgents, militias, and organized crime; under-armed and under-trained; and victim to attacks from all sides.

STRATEGIC CHANGES—A TRADITIONAL COUNTERINSURGENCY CAMPAIGN

The most important changes that the United States needs to make to improve its chances of succeeding in Iraq lie in the realm of military strategy.[9] There needs to be a clear shift towards a true counterinsurgency campaign. Since the fall of Baghdad, the United States has employed a "post-conflict stabilization" model of security operations. The key element of this strategy is trying to provide simultaneous security for the entire country by concentrating Coalition forces in those areas of greatest insurgent activity to quell the violence quickly and prevent its spread. Had the United States brought sufficient ground forces to blanket Iraq immediately after Saddam's fall and had other mistakes not been made, such as failing to provide troops with orders to maintain law and order, this strategy might have succeeded. That is now a topic for historians. What matters today is that this strategic approach has failed.

In recent months, the Bush Administration has finally begun to acknowledge this and is modifying its military approach. In particular, several senior American generals, along with Ambassador Zalmay Khalilzad and his team in Baghdad, have shown considerable perspicacity in pressing hard for changes in all aspects of U.S. policy, including military operations. Consequently the U.S. military is slowly revising its approach.

---

8 It is worth noting that the U.S. General Accounting Office (GAO) reported that according to a senior U.S. military officer, "Iraqi forces have more quickly progressed from level 3 (of MNF-I's four-stage readiness coding) to level 2 in those areas that have experienced fewer insurgent attacks, such as southern Iraq." Joseph A. Christoff, "Rebuilding Iraq: Enhancing Security, Measuring Program Results, and Maintaining Infrastructure are Necessary to Make Significant and Sustainable Progress," Testimony before the Committee on Government Reform, Sub-Committee on National Security, House of Representatives, October 18, 2005, p. 14.

9 Military experts may quibble that the discussion that follows actually relates to the operational level of warfare, not the strategic. This is largely correct. However, this report is intended to be accessible to a general readership for whom the divide between strategy and tactics is clear, whereas introducing an unfamiliar term like "the operational level of warfare" might confuse more than it would clarify.

Unfortunately, the changes underway are almost entirely in the realm of tactics, not strategy. Even if the tactics are improving, and in some cases they are, such changes will have little impact unless the United States also fundamentally alters its strategic approach. The fact that U.S. forces continue to mount operations like "Iron Hammer" and "Steel Curtain" against the towns of western Iraq, even with better tactics, is proof that America's civil-military leadership has not recognized the need for a fundamental strategic shift.

What is required is more than just tinkering around the edges of military operations; it is the adoption of a traditional counterinsurgency strategy along with its attendant tactics.[10] For a variety of reasons, COIN strategy also lends itself easily to dealing with the problems of failed states like Iraq. The overlap between counterinsurgency and stability operations means that such a strategic shift could involve easily tailored approaches to fit Iraq's dual needs of defeating the insurgency and building a viable state.

The core concept of a traditional COIN strategy is that insurgents require access to the population to survive. The insurgents need to be able to move about freely among the population, using the people for camouflage, recruitment, procurement of supplies, and as a human shield against government retaliation. If the population is not supportive, then in contrast the insurgent is constantly on the run and vulnerable at any moment to arrest or attack. As Mao famously observed, insurgents are like fish that swim in the "sea" of the people. The goal of a true COIN campaign is to deprive insurgents of that access, leaving them like fish out of water.

The COIN force begins this process by first securing a base of operations in one portion of the country that is denied to the insurgency. This area can be as large or as small as the COIN force can handle. Within this area, the COIN force provides the population with security in all senses of the word. In Iraq, this would mean security from insurgent attack, from militias and from criminals, whether organized or not. Ideally, the COIN force would then pour resources into this secured area to make it economically dynamic and thereby cement popular support for the COIN campaign. By securing this area, the COIN force creates a space in which political and economic life can revive, which is also a key requirement of stabilization operations to address the problems of a failed state. Those living outside the secured area, witnessing its revival, will have an incentive to support the counterinsurgency campaign when it arrives in their region.

The increasing attractiveness of such secure areas also helps solve the intelligence problem that COIN forces inevitably face. Ultimately, a counterinsurgency cannot gather sufficient intelligence on insurgent forces through traditional means to comprehensively defeat them. Instead, the only way to gather adequate information on the insurgents is to convince the local population to volunteer such information, which will only happen if they enthusiastically support the counterinsurgency campaign and feel largely safe from insurgent retaliation. When these conditions are met, the counterinsurgents enjoy a significant intelligence advantage, greatly easing the further eradication of the insurgents. By contrast, in Iraq at present the advantage lies with the insurgents. The population knows that any assistance to U.S. or Iraqi forces will be met by savage insurgent reprisals because, as has been repeatedly demonstrated, the insurgents will

10 The literature on counterinsurgency practices is vast and, remarkably, consistent about how such operations are best conducted. Some of the best works include, Colonel Richard L. Clutterbuck, *The Long, Long War: Counterinsurgency in Malaya and Vietnam* (New York: Praeger, 1966); Thomas X. Hammes, *The Sling and the Stone: On War in the 21st Century* (Wisconsin: Zenith Press, 2004); Frank G. Hoffman, "Principles for the Savage Wars of Peace," CETO, U.S. Marine Corps Warfare Laboratory, available on the web at <http://www.smallwars.quantico.usmc.mil/search/Articles/SavageWarsofPeace.pdf>, downloaded on December 4, 2005; David Galula, *Counterinsurgency Warfare: Theory and Practice* (New York: Praeger, 1964); Krepinevich, *The Army and Vietnam*, op.cit.; Mark Moyar, *Phoenix and the Birds of Prey* (Annapolis, MD: Naval Institute Press, 1997); Thomas Mockaitis, *British Counterinsurgency in the Post-Imperial Era* (Manchester, UK: Manchester University Press, 1995); John Nagl, *Counterinsurgency Lessons from Malaya and Vietnam: Learning to Eat Soup with A Knife* (Westport, CT: Praeger, 2002); Kalev I. Sepp, "Best Practices in Counterinsurgency," *Military Review* (May-June 2005), pp. 8–12; Robert G.K. Thompson, *Defeating Communist Insurgency: The Lessons of Malaya and Vietnam* (New York: Praeger, 1966).

generally return after U.S. forces depart.

In addition, the COIN forces use these "secure zones" to train indigenous forces that can assist them in subsequent security operations. Once this base of operations is truly secure and can be maintained largely by local forces, the COIN forces then spread their control to other parts of the country, performing the same set of steps as they did in the first area.

This approach is typically referred to either as a "spreading ink spot" or a "spreading oil stain" strategy because the COIN forces slowly spread their control over the country, depriving the insurgents of support area by area. In Andrew Krepinevich's words,

> Once the security of the population and its attendant resources is accomplished, the initiative in the war will pass from the insurgent to the government. The insurgent will either have to fight to maintain control of the people or see his capabilities diminish. If the insurgents decide to fight, they will present themselves as targets for the government mobile reaction forces.[11]

The key, as counterinsurgency experts observe, is to start in one area by securing the population and providing them with material incentives, in the form of genuine security and a thriving economy, which will cause them to reject the insurgency and support the COIN campaign. A traditional COIN strategy is best understood as one that reinforces success. The counterinsurgents concentrate their forces where their support is strongest and where they therefore can do the most good, stacking the odds in their favor. The approach that we are employing in Iraq means reinforcing failure because we are concentrating our forces in Iraq's western provinces where the insurgents are thickest and support for reconstruction weakest.

A traditional counterinsurgency strategy in Iraq would focus on securing enclaves (Kurdistan, much of southeastern Iraq, Baghdad, and a number of other major urban centers, along with the oilfields and some other vital economic facilities) and reducing the resources and attention paid to stamping out the insurgency in western Iraq. The Coalition would consolidate within these enclaves, thereby increasing the ratio of security personnel to civilians, and so allowing a major effort to secure these areas. The Coalition would likewise redirect its political efforts and economic resources to emphasize development in the secured enclaves, to ensure that they prosper—and because in the short-run the secured areas would be the only regions worth investing in. The concentrated security focus should allow meaningful progress in terms of local economic and political development. In turn, public opinion within the secured enclaves would likely swing back in favor of reconstruction, while Iraqis outside of the enclaves would realize the dangers of the militias and insurgents and see that the government can offer a better option. Within the enclaves, the United States would train and initially deploy Iraqi soldiers, because these secured areas would be precisely the permissive environments that these troops need to build unit cohesion, trust, and command relationships.

Five other key changes at the strategic level follow from the need for the United States to shift to a true counterinsurgency strategy:[12]

1. Make protecting the Iraqi people and civilian infrastructure our highest priority, training Iraqi security forces a close second, and hunting insurgents a distant third. There is a large, coherent body of literature on counterinsurgency warfare and what is most remarkable about it is that it all draws the same lessons. Moreover, the principal lesson of every one of these works is that the single most important mission of counterinsurgency forces is to provide basic safety

---

11 Krepinevich, op.cit., p. 15.
12 For an excellent parallel endorsement of these various changes by an American general who performed extremely well in Iraq because he grasped the nature of the problem, see Major General Peter W. Chiarelli, USA, and Major Patrick R. Michaelis, USA "Winning the Peace: The Requirement for Full-Spectrum Operations," *Military Review*, July-August 2005, pp. 4–17.

for the population against attack, extortion, threat, and fear. If the population is afraid to leave its homes or is afraid even while in its homes, the insurgents and other forces of chaos have in effect won. The people will not support the government, they will be susceptible to the insurgents, and they will not go about their normal business, thereby undermining the economy and the political system. The Iraqi insurgents are largely accomplishing these goals because Coalition forces are too thinly stretched and have left the cities of central and southern Iraq vulnerable to insurgent and terrorist attacks, to militia takeover, and to general lawlessness. For this reason, Coalition forces must fundamentally reorient their priorities towards "area security"—protecting towns and neighborhoods.

As part of the area security mission, U.S. and Iraqi forces must make a greater effort to protect critical infrastructure, including oil pipelines, roads and the electrical grid. Protecting infrastructure is best accomplished by a combination of regular patrols, checkpoints and other fixed defenses, sensors, passive barriers and quick-reaction forces. Oil pipelines and their pumping stations are the easiest to guard. Passive barriers, usually fences, with embedded sensor technology can be run along either side of a pipeline with quick reaction forces standing by and guarding key nodes like pumping stations. Roads are tougher, but a combination of regular patrols, complemented by airborne assets including high-endurance drones, checkpoints, passive barriers, defensive deployments at vulnerable locations, controls on access to the road, and quick-reaction teams to counterattack or pursue those attacking the road can make most routes quite safe. The best example of this is the recent U.S. operation to secure the road from Baghdad to the airport, which transformed it from one of the deadliest routes in Iraq to one of the safest by employing these measures.[13] The electrical grid is the most difficult to protect, but much of the problem can be solved both by increasing the redundancy of facilities and transmission lines (see Chapter 3) and by guarding large electrical generation

facilities and substations. The insurgents will have become little more than a nuisance if all they can achieve is to cut the power lines of a system that possesses sufficient redundancy to allow power to be rerouted around broken links.

2. Shift the strategic emphasis from offensive military operations to defensive military operations, go on the offensive in the political and economic realms. Another cardinal sin of the United States in Iraq so far has been that we have insisted on remaining on the offensive militarily. While even COIN strategies require some offensive components, they should not be their principal focus. Typically offensives should only be mounted in immediate counterattack to an insurgent action or when intelligence has clearly identified a high-value target. Even then, the degree to which offensive operations are emphasized is relative to troop numbers. Offensive operations can be employed more liberally only when there are more than enough troops for the defensive missions that are the crux of a COIN campaign. In Iraq at present, offensive operations need to be de-emphasized because there are not enough troops for vital defensive missions. Offensive operations, particularly large raids, should *not* be the default mode of security forces as it is for many U.S. and U.S.-trained Iraqi units.

Concentrating on defensive operations in the military realm has been a key element of every successful COIN campaign of the past century. As respected former Director of Central Intelligence William Colby explained when describing the highly-successful (but too little, too late) CORDS program in Vietnam:

Certain areas were delineated as 'national areas of precedence.' Others were listed for priority treatment within certain provinces. Large areas of the country were left unspecified, meaning that we would worry about them later. These priorities followed our knowledge of population density, so that the geographic precedence that was established we

---

13 For instance, see Jackie Spinner, "Easy Sailing Along a Once-Perilous Road to Baghdad Airport," *The Washington Post*, November 4, 2005, p. 15.

directly adapted from Marshal Lyautey's 'ink spot' pacification strategy developed decades before in Morocco: starting with the population centers we were gradually spreading outward, so that the base was first consolidated, then expanded. We were using tactical defense in a strategic offensive.[14]

There appear to be two reasons that the United States has clung so stubbornly to an offensive mindset. First, the U.S. political leadership seems unwilling to admit that there are parts of Iraq that are not really under U.S. military or Iraqi government control. This seems to have placed pressure on U.S. military commanders to secure areas like western Iraq that would have been difficult to pacify even with adequate numbers of troops. Second, the U.S. military broadly, and the U.S. Army in particular, adheres to the notion that only offensive operations can prove decisive, which is valid for *conventional* military operations but in counterinsurgency warfare, the reverse is the case. Unfortunately, COIN doctrine is not popular in the U.S. armed forces, particularly in the U.S. Army. COIN specialists do not typically have highly-rewarding careers and are often passed over for promotion in favor of ambitious officers trained in conventional mechanized combat. As Maj. Gen. James "Spider" Marks has put it, "We are a Phase III Army in a Phase IV world."[15] The determination of a great many U.S. military officers to persevere with conventional military approaches—despite all the evidence that this is a mistake—is a major hindrance to creating genuine security in Iraq.

Consequently, the U.S. and Iraqi security forces must focus first on defensive operations to make the Iraqis feel safe in their homes, their streets, and their places of business. This does not mean simply deploying soldiers in defensive emplacements around Iraqi population centers. It means establishing a constant presence throughout those areas to be secured to reassure the population and to deter and defeat insurgents and militias. This means constant patrols (principally on

foot); checkpoints; security personnel deployed at major gathering points like markets, entertainment, religious and political events, and main intersections and thoroughfares among other measures. Security personnel should routinely search persons entering large facilities, such as businesses or apartment complexes, street markets or shopping arcades, or sports arenas. Fixed defensive positions, checkpoints, or ambushes can be employed against known routes of insurgent infiltration. Above all, offensive operations should become the exception rather than the rule.

A potential objection to such a defensive strategy is the fear that this will allow insurgents and terrorists in areas beyond the "oil stain" the freedom to plan and prepare operations in relative peace, thereby greatly increasing the threat. Moreover, in the age of suicide bombers there is an assumption that "the bomber will always get through," to borrow an equally inaccurate belief from an earlier age of warfare. Underlying this objection is the notion that only offensive operations that harry insurgents and terrorists and leave them with no sanctuary can succeed.

Although this concern appears to be common sense, it is unfounded because it exaggerates the threat and the difficulty of dealing with the threat. If enough suicide bombers try, some will inevitably get through. However, strong, comprehensive security measures can prevent all but the most determined, best prepared, and luckiest of terrorists and insurgents from penetrating defenses. Thus a country can greatly reduce the threat of suicide bombings by dramatically raising the costs of such attacks while diminishing their likelihood of success.

For instance, although Americans often focus on Israel's offensive counterterrorism measures, particularly targeted killings of high-ranking terrorists, these are only a fraction of its total counterterrorism efforts. Most Israeli counterterrorism is defensive, including: a ubiq-

---

14 William Colby with James McCargar, *Lost Victory: A Firsthand Account of America's Sixteen-Year Involvement in Vietnam* (NY: Contemporary Books, 1989), p. 264.

15 In U.S. military parlance for planning major military operations, Phase III is the combat phase, while Phase IV is the post-conflict phase.

uitous security presence, frequent searches, constant patrols and numerous checkpoints manned by police or military personnel, a population trained to watch for suspicious activity, aggressive intelligence gathering to identify attacks and attackers beforehand, massive information-sharing systems to ensure terrorist suspects are caught or denied freedom of movement, and physical barriers (including, but not limited to, the security fence) to hinder infiltration. Of course the Israelis do still suffer from suicide bombings, but they catch or prevent many others and, because their defensive measures are so extensive, they greatly raise the costs and risks to Palestinian terrorist groups, diminishing the number of attacks these groups can mount because they are forced to invest far more in each attack to have some chance of it succeeding. As a result, Israel today suffers far less from suicide bombings than does Iraq.

Obviously, Washington and Baghdad cannot replicate all Israeli measures in Iraq, but we can adopt many of them, thereby diminishing the incidence of suicide attacks in Iraq substantially. If the United States could reduce the damage done by terrorist attacks in Iraq to the levels experienced by Israel over the past 15 years, it will have achieved a miracle.

3. Emphasize population security in the south and center of Iraq to reduce militia and organized crime influence, which cripples economic development and threatens civil war. The militias established themselves in central and southern Iraq because the United States never properly filled the post-Saddam security vacuum. The only way to reverse this trend is to fill the security vacuum by deploying U.S., Iraqi and other Coalition forces there. Very few of the Shi'i militias have ever tried to resist Coalition forces when they moved into an area in strength, because they understood that doing so was essentially suicidal. Once the Coalition has concentrated sufficient forces to move back into a population center in central or southern Iraq, it should be able to do so. Coalition forces must then remain in strength over time, and thereby obviate the need that drove the locals to support the militia. This is critical in Iraq not only to create a basis for

defeating the insurgency, but to prevent the failed-state aspects of Iraq from causing the country to spiral into chaos and civil war.

Once these initial enclaves are secured, and as additional Iraqi security forces are trained, they should be slowly expanded to include additional communities— hence the metaphor of the spreading "oil stain." In every case, the Coalition would focus the same security, political, and economic resources on each new community brought into the pacified zone. If implemented properly, a true counterinsurgency approach can win back the entire country.

However, employing such a strategy means superficially ceding control over parts of the country at first and accepting that it will take time before all of Iraq will become a stable, unified, pluralist state. Objectionable though that might appear at first glance, it is worth remembering that the U.S. military and the Iraqi government do not currently control much of Iraq. Thus, the "oil stain" strategy simply *acknowledges* that we can only control part of Iraq with the forces currently available and that our control over other regions is at best nominal. It means focusing our efforts on controlling the most important areas where roughly half the Sunni Arabs live, and where the bulk of the Shi'ah and Kurds, the strongest supporters of reconstruction, reside. We should concentrate our resources on holding those regions properly, rather than squander them playing "whack-a-mole" with insurgents in areas that we cannot control. Over time, a traditional counterinsurgency strategy will allow us to slowly expand our control over the rest of the country as more resources become available.

4. Force protection must be a constant concern of American military commanders at all levels, but it cannot jeopardize the mission of U.S. forces in Iraq. U.S. forces are generally penned up in formidable cantonments where they are largely cut off from the population. Although some commanders have made a determined effort to get out and patrol more, there is still too much emphasis on the occasional raid to boost detainee counts and too little emphasis on day to day presence patrols. It is a constant and justified complaint of Iraqis that the Americans have no presence and thus have little impact on street crime, militia control, or insurgent attacks. In particular, U.S. troops should employ foot patrols backed by helicopters or vehicles similar to those used by the British Army in Northern Ireland and NATO forces in the Balkans rather than mounted patrols in Humvees and Bradley fighting vehicles. This is the only way that American forces can get out, reassure the Iraqi civilians, find out from them where the troublemakers are, and respond to their problems.

5. Create a unified command structure fully integrating civilian and military operations. Another well-known counterinsurgency and stability operations lesson which the United States continues to ignore is unity of command.

First, there needs to be a single "campaign chief" heading the entire effort. That person should have absolute control over both the civilian and military sides of the U.S. effort, and ideally the Iraqi side as well. In time, the campaign chief should be an Iraqi, but at first it will probably have to be an American. The historical evidence is mixed as to whether the campaign chief should have a military or civilian background. What matters is that the person appointed be determined and decisive; familiar with the principles of counterinsurgency and stability operations; adaptive and willing to experiment, because even the tried and tested principles of COIN always need to be adjusted to local conditions. In particular, the person must be a consummate bureaucratic warrior who can extract results from vast government agencies.[16] The campaign chief requires the authority to take executive decisions on all matters. It would be preferable if America's "proconsul" in Iraq were either the supreme U.S. military commander there or an extraordinary civilian position created solely for this

mission and endowed with all necessary authority. The campaign chief's deputy should be a civilian if the campaign chief is a military officer, or vice versa.

Beneath the campaign chief and his or her deputy must be a fully integrated chain of command. On the military side, every division, brigade and battalion must be part of this chain of command, as should the personnel of every civilian agency in country and their Iraqi counterparts. Additional deputies should be appointed on a functional basis to ensure that all of the civilian agencies are cooperating with one another and with all of the military units. Moreover, there needs to be an emphasis on *integrated* operations that has so far been lacking in Iraq. Civilian authorities must coordinate their efforts to support military operations and military commanders must coordinate their efforts to support political and economic initiatives. This will undoubtedly require far more personnel from the civilian agencies than are currently deployed to Iraq and those personnel will have to deploy out of the "Green Zone" in Baghdad. This is another reason why it is so critical to concentrate Coalition military forces on creating secured zones, so that there are areas in which civilian personnel can operate on a regular basis.

Ideally, the United States would create reconstruction committees at every level of the chain of command (discussed in greater detail in Chapter 2). These committees would regularly bring together the relevant military commander, the relevant State Department officer, a United States Agency for International Development (USAID) official, an intelligence officer (either from the CIA, the Defense Intelligence Agency (DIA), or one of the military services depending on the level of the committee), and personnel from any other departments and agencies pertinent to the level in the chain of command and the specific region.[17] The reconstruction committees should also include the Iraqi counter-

---

16 The inability of Ambassador Lodge to unify American efforts in Vietnam is a warning that the campaign chief probably should not be the U.S. ambassador in country as that post rarely has the necessary status.

17 This is a different but related concept from the Provincial Reconstruction Teams (PRTs) used in Afghanistan and which Washington has finally agreed to try in Iraq as well. The PRTs are self-contained and have a set number of people who then try to coordinate assistance for local Afghans. PRTs on the Afghan model are also transitory. They only move around with massive amounts of force, and when a particular task is complete they move on; there is no sustained security presence that makes a difference for local citizens. Although the PRTs in Iraq are intended to work with Iraqis, they will not include Iraqis in their structure. Instead, the proposed reconstruction committees would replicate the inter-agency coordination embodied in the PRTs at every level of the U.S. hierarchy in Iraq, with varying numbers of personnel and representation of Agencies based on the echelon within the hierarchy and the problems of the region it was operating in. Thus there would be multiple reconstruction committees, each reporting to another higher in the chain of command. Ideally, the PRTs would grow quickly into such a committee system.

parts to the various U.S. officials present. At the very least they should include an appropriate Iraqi military *and* civilian official participating at every level, with the goal of expanding Iraqi involvement over time.

At present, U.S. military personnel are often the only Americans in any town or neighborhood. They have neither the skills, the resources, nor the time to devote to such matters as aid contracts, political negotiations and engineering projects. These are all jobs that should be handled by U.S. civilian agencies, but because their personnel rarely leave the Green Zone these tasks fall to military officers. Many officers have risen admirably to that challenge, but it is one they should not have to bear. Reconstruction can only succeed in the 99.9 percent of Iraq outside of the Green Zone if U.S. civilian personnel are out there, working alongside the military and coordinating their efforts.

Only a fully-integrated political/military/economic approach is likely to produce success. For 40-years we have worked to get U.S. military forces to cooperate in "joint" warfare. In the words of Irena Sargsyan, we now need to take the next step beyond "joint" warfare in Iraq to "comprehensive warfare" in which all of our diplomatic, political, intelligence, economic, financial, and other capabilities are interwoven with military operations at every level.

DEFINING THE INITIAL OIL STAIN

A proper counterinsurgency strategy would divide Iraq into different zones based upon their priority for pacification. This should not be a simple split between those parts inside the "oil stain", where conditions are already favorable for reconstruction, and a "wild west" outside of the "oil stain." Instead, Iraq should be divided into five areas, each with different pacification and reconstruction priorities. To a great extent, central Iraq (including Baghdad), Kurdistan and as much of southeastern Iraq as possible (given initial troop levels), should be the highest initial pacification prior-

ities. Western Iraq (the "Sunni Triangle") should have the lowest priority and host the fewest number of Coalition and Iraqi forces. The rest of the country will fall into a middle ground designed to minimize the Coalition troop commitment there, but without fully ceding the area to the insurgents.

The initial "oil stain" should consist of Baghdad, central Iraq and Kurdistan, and should extend as far southeast as possible. As additional troops and resources become available through rising Iraqi troop numbers and the pacification of these areas, the next round of areas for inclusion in the "oil stain" should be the remaining pockets of the southeast.

Baghdad and central Iraq. Iraq's capital is the heart of the nation. As Andrew Parasiliti and Puneet Talwar have remarked: "Baghdad is the key to the success of our efforts. It remains the nation's political and cultural capital, and the most representative city in terms of Iraq's demographic diversity, with roughly 20% of the country's population. It is home to the most influential professional, business, and opinion leaders. In short, the national political transition will depend upon our success in stabilizing Iraq."[18] It is the largest city by far with roughly 5 million inhabitants and is Iraq's political and economic dynamo. For these reasons, the "oil stain" must start with Baghdad and the mixed Sunni-Shi'ah areas to its north, south and east. It is important that Sunnis in Baghdad and nearby towns be included in the Baghdad "oil stain" so that the COIN strategy does not appear to be an effort to protect the Shi'ah and the Kurds exclusively. The "oil stain" should also extend north through towns such as Baqubah and Khanaqin to eastern Kurdistan, so that central Iraq and Kurdistan can be tied together.

Kurdistan. Safe within their mountains, with their 70,000 *peshmerga*, and their separate language and culture—which provides considerable protection from Sunni insurgents and Shi'i militias—the Kurds are the best off of all Iraqis. Although in theory a "militia,"

---

18 Puneet Talwar and Andrew Parasiliti. *Iraq: Meeting the Challenge, Sharing the Burden, Staying the Course.* A Trip Report to the Members of the Committee on Foreign Relations, United States Senate. (S. Prt. 108–31), July 2003, p. 7

in practice the *peshmerga* are a functioning police and security force that is doing what the United States and the central government of Iraq have thus far failed to do—protect their people. Moreover, the Kurds have been clear that they will not surrender the *peshmerga* under any circumstances, which is understandable given their history and their aspirations to eventual statehood. Thus, there is no reason for Coalition troops to protect Kurdistan. Indeed, a Korean brigade sits outside of Erbil, the largest city of Kurdistan, protected by the *peshmerga* rather than the other way around, and they are probably safer there than they would be if they were deployed along the Korean demilitarized zone.

Although Kurdistan does not require pacification, it is because it is largely secure that it must be part of the initial "oil stain" and should be part of the effort to improve economic and political conditions by focusing reconstruction assistance there. Although the Kurds are doing better than the rest of Iraq, and have made some intelligent decisions about their economic future, they are hardly an economic miracle. Unfortunately, the United States has consistently cut funding for Kurdistan, instead redirecting assistance to other parts of Iraq, such as the "Sunni Triangle" where funds disappear into the black hole of the security vacuum.

Depriving the Kurds of reconstruction aid is shortsighted for two reasons. First, because most Kurds favor immediate independence, Kurdish leaders need to show their people that there is tangible benefit to remaining part of Iraq. Kurdish politics has become a battle, with the leadership arguing that for the time being autonomy within Iraq is preferable to what their constituents want—independence outside of Iraq. These same Kurdish leaders have to deliver material benefits to their people if they are to contain the tide of Kurdish separatism. Second, traditional counterinsurgency dictates that pacified areas need to prosper economically and politically so that the local population maintains its support for the counterinsurgency and so that those outside the pacified area want to become part of it. Since Kurdistan must be part of the initial "oil stain," it therefore must share in its economic prosperity to convince other parts of the country of the benefits of being part of the secured area.

Western Iraq. Western Iraq, and specifically the "Sunni Triangle" that runs from Baghdad west to Ramadi and ar-Rutbah and then northeast to Mosul, should be the lowest priority for pacification. The fewest numbers of Coalition and Iraqi troops should be deployed there. The large numbers of American and Iraqi units currently deployed there to chase insurgents should be withdrawn almost entirely. They should be redeployed to increase troop density in higher priority areas in central and southeastern Iraq.

Coalition forces should not, however, simply abandon western Iraq. The United States and the new Iraqi government have an interest in not allowing western Iraq to become a terrorist haven, but we will have to tolerate a considerable amount of insurgent activity, crime and lawlessness. (These problems already exist, but since April 2003 the United States has refused to tolerate them, resulting in a massive expenditure of military and economic resources for little gain). Instead, we should seek to moderate the chaos in western Iraq through other means. First among them should involve striking deals with the Sunni tribal shaykhs.

Tribal shaykhs still command considerable respect and authority in western Iraq. However, much of their power typically derives from their ability to dole out such patronage as cash, land, valuables, jobs, and contracts to their followers. For the past two to three hundred years, the tribal shaykhs have received patronage from the rulers in Baghdad, whether the Ottomans, the British, the Hashemite monarchy, the republican dictators, and even Saddam. In return, the tribal shaykhs kept order in their areas by protecting the roads and pipelines, and refraining from attacking these potential targets themselves. Starting in late April of 2003, numerous delegations of tribal shaykhs have approached the United States and the new Iraqi government to cut the same deals. Although such deals with the Sunni shaykhs would not eliminate the insurgency entirely, or the potential for western Iraq to become a haven for terrorists and Sunni militias, they could have a very significant effect on maintaining order in western Iraq. Of course, such deals would create new challenges of their own such as ensuring that the shaykhs kept their end of the bargain, but these are risks worth taking.

The United States would also want to maintain a considerable intelligence presence in western Iraq to prevent terrorists and insurgents from turning the region into a sanctuary from which to attack the secured zones with impunity. This would require an integrated network of human sources and technological surveillance platforms to monitor activity there, along with regular, long-range patrols by U.S. or Iraqi reconnaissance personnel. The United States could then mount discrete military operations to eliminate targets such as major concentrations of insurgents, large bomb factories, training bases and arms caches whenever they were detected.[19] In addition, the United States might conduct targeted killings of important terrorists on the Israeli model. The U.S. already employs various means for just such missions, the Hellfire-armed Predator drone being the best known. This program could simply be continued in western Iraq so that if U.S. forces ever were to pinpoint Abu Musab az-Zarqawi or any of his key henchmen, the Coalition would have the capability to eliminate him discretely.

Targeted offensive actions would need to be accompanied by restraint. We should maintain a high threshold for action lest we slip back into the misguided practice of major military sweeps in western Iraq. This is another lesson worth learning from the Israelis, who after withdrawing from Gaza and the West Bank population centers, only mount targeted killings against the highest-value terrorists and only raid Palestinian

facilities if convinced that they pose a very significant threat. Israel refrains from attacking a great many terrorists and terrorist facilities it knows about because they are not a sufficient threat to justify the military resources, the risk of a protracted engagement or the possibility of civilian casualties.

The northwest and the southeast. The remaining two regions, the southeast and the northwest, are difficult to categorize. Intuitively, the largely Shi'ah southeast should be in the "oil stain," while the heavily Sunni northwest should not. The reality, however, is more complicated. Instead, a more nuanced approach is needed for these two regions.

There are four arguments for including all of southeastern Iraq, including Basra, Iraq's second-largest city, in the initial secured area of the "oil stain." First, the southeast consists largely of Shi'ah who strongly support reconstruction, and a key rule of COIN is to start pacifying where the population is the most supportive.[20] Second, southeastern Iraq accounts for roughly two-thirds of Iraq's oil production. Third, the southeast is the most heavily populated region of Iraq after Baghdad and a COIN priority is to make people feel safe, rather than making territory safe. Last, the southeast is the home of a number of the strongest and most dangerous militias. Some of the militias in the south are very large, such as the Badr Organization and Muqtada as-Sadr's Mahdi Army. They exercise real control over swathes of territory where they have created a semblance of order. The sooner these militias can be neutralized, the lower the chance of an Iraqi civil war.

In addition, there appear to be strong arguments against including the northwest in the initial "oil stain" arguments that might push it into the same category as western Iraq. Northwestern Iraq is less populous

---

19 For a fuller discussion of this topic see Andrew F. Krepinevich, Jr., "How to Win in Iraq," *Foreign Affairs,* September/October 2005.

20 It is important to bear in mind the great Shi'i holy cities of Najaf and Karbala in assessing how much of southeastern Iraq the initial "oil stain" should include. The Shi'i have been ambivalent about a U.S. presence there. On the one hand, they generally have demanded the U.S. forces stay out of the cities, or at least of the neighborhoods closest to the holy sites. On the other hand, they have blamed the U.S. troops for their absence following major terrorist attacks in those same areas. To avoid offending the religious Shi'ah it may be necessary to devise special arrangements for the holy sites. For instance, it might be agreed that only Iraqi Army units would be present near the holy sites, although U.S. rapid reaction teams might be deployed nearby.

than the southeast, and has virtually no oil. Unlike other areas, the population is not overwhelmingly favorable to reconstruction. The northwest contains many Sunni Arab tribals who are ambivalent or hostile to reconstruction. The Sunni Arabs, Shi'i Arabs, and Kurds in the northwest who support reconstruction are not dominant.

However, there are also a number of arguments that mitigate against leaving the northwest entirely out of the initial pacified zone, even if extending that area some degree of protection would have to come at the expense of areas of the southeast that appear to be much better candidates for initial inclusion.

The first of these is the paradoxical reason that while the militia dominance of the south east is deeply problematic over the long term, it is tolerable in the short term. Because many of the Shi'i militia leaders are members of the government in Baghdad and/or respect Ayatollah 'Ali Sistani, they are, in their own way, supportive of aspects of reconstruction and unwilling to cross either the Americans or the central government as long as it is seen as having a chance to survive. Moreover, some of the militias in the southeast are very big, like the Badr Organization and the Mahdi Army, and they exercise real control over parts of the country, and in so doing they create a kind of order and protection for the locals—indeed, that is why the popularity of the militias is rising at the expense of the central government. Consequently, Washington and Baghdad can assign a lower initial priority for troops and pacification to some parts of southeastern Iraq. These areas can be expected to continue in their current state for some months to come without significantly endangering the overall prospects for reconstruction. These areas are unlikely to deteriorate dramatically before the securing of the first "oil stain" area and before capable Iraqi security forces are brought in.

In contrast, the militias in the northwest are smaller and weaker and their allegiances run the gamut from Sunni to Kurdish to Chaldean to Turkoman.

Moreover, this is reflective of the far more heavily mixed population of the northwest. Mixed populations are tinder boxes for sparking civil strife, the Balkans being the best known example of this. For all of these reasons the northwest has been unstable and the United States has had to maintain a heavier troop presence in the north than in the south to prevent intercommunal strife. In addition, the northwest contains Iraq's third-largest city of Mosul, a location too important to be put in the same category as Fallujah.

So while the instability of the northwest theoretically makes it a low pacification priority, in practice withdrawing the U.S. presence could be a huge mistake. The result could easily be widespread ethnic cleansing and internecine strife in the northwest that could trigger reactions by all of Iraq's various ethnic and religious communities

It is unlikely that the United States, Iraq and the Coalition will have enough troops to pacify both the northwest and the southeast simultaneously (in addition to central Iraq). Therefore, in the northwest the United States and Iraqi governments should employ what the military calls an "economy of force:" current troop levels should be maintained—although their tactics need to change—but not expanded. The goal should be to keep the northwest in its current state without drawing off any more resources from those areas that can be pacified and so should be the highest priority. By contrast, southeastern Iraq should be within the initial "oil stain" to the extent possible depending upon troop levels. Those militia-infested parts of the south east not in the initial "oil stain" would then be the highest priorities for the second wave of pacification.

TROOP NUMBERS

A key question that any discussion of changing strategy in Iraq automatically generates is whether doing so will require more U.S. troops. Many unfamiliar with traditional COIN strategy assume that its application to Iraq would require a substantial reinforcement of U.S. forces. However, this is not the case. Traditional COIN strategies work by building popular support, thereby denying that same support to the insurgency, as well as generating indigenous forces capable both of fighting the insurgency and protecting ever greater portions of the population. Correctly employed , it is a self-generating and self-sustaining strategy—drying up the sea of popular support in which the insurgents seek to swim.

The number of troops required is, broadly, related to the time that a traditional COIN strategy requires to succeed. *Thus, there is no reason that the United States could not shift to a traditional COIN strategy right now, without increasing troop levels*—doing so would just mean that it would take longer for the strategy to bear fruit. Of course, if the United States hopes to win quickly in Iraq, it will probably need a significant increase in troop strength (and even then "quickly" would still mean several years).

Numbers in warfare are always slippery, but it is impossible to avoid them for planning purposes. For both COIN operations and stability operations, the canonical figure is that there needs to be 20 security personnel per 1,000 of population.[21] These security personnel do not all need to be crack Green Berets. Many can be police or local paramilitaries with little ability to do more than defend their own town or neighborhood. As long as they are willing to fight, possess minimum levels of military training, are deployed as part of a traditional COIN strategy and employ appropriate tactics, then they can play an important security role.

The population of Iraq today is roughly 26 million people, which suggests the need for 520,000 security personnel. However, the roughly 4 million Kurds who live inside Iraqi Kurdistan enjoy considerable safety because they are protected by approximately 70,000 *peshmerga*—they need not be included in these calculations. *To secure the remaining 22 million people therefore requires approximately 440,000 security personnel—the baseline figure for what will be required ultimately to stabilize Iraq.*

Unfortunately, we are far from that number. At present, the United States has between 135,000-160,000 troops in Iraq at any given time. They are joined by roughly 10,000 British and Australian troops, along with a grab bag of other detachments that may withdraw in 2006 and so should not be considered for planning purposes. There are probably some 40-60,000 Iraqi security personnel in the Army, National Guard, Police and other units that can meaningfully participate in security operations—although they are not without their problems (see below).[22] This yields a total of 185-230,000 Coalition security personnel, which should be capable of securing a population of 9 million–11.5 million, or roughly half of Iraq's population outside Kurdistan.

If the United States and the Iraqi government were to begin with only this baseline of troops and were to employ a traditional COIN strategy—withdrawing most of their forces from those areas of Iraq most opposed to reconstruction, and instead concentrating the troops and resources on areas of high importance and high support for reconstruction—its starting oil stain could encompass Baghdad, all of central Iraq,

---

21 Bruce Hoffman, "Insurgency and Counterinsurgency in Iraq," Washington, D.C., RAND Corp., June 2004; Kalev I. Sepp, "Best Practices in Counterinsurgency," Military Review (May–June 2005), p. 9; James T. Quinlivan, "The Burden of Victory: The Painful Arithmetic of Stability Operations," *RAND Review*, Summer 2003. Available at <http://www.rand.org/publications/randreview/issues/summer2003/burden.html>. Also, James T. Quinlivan, "Force Requirements in Stability Operations," *Parameters*, Winter 1995, pp. 56–69. Quinlivan has demonstrated that stabilizing a country requires roughly 20 security personnel (troops and police) per thousand inhabitants just as COIN operations do. In his words, the objective "is not to destroy an enemy but to provide security for residents so that they have enough confidence to manage their daily affairs and to support a government authority of their own."

22 The number of Iraqi troops capable of participating in "meaningful" security operations is based on numerous conversations with U.S. military officers and Iraqi government officials. It also corresponds very well with the figures cited by President Bush in his November-December 2005 speeches on Iraq in which he cited 40 battalions capable of "leading" combat operations with another 40 capable of other, presumably less-demanding, missions. See the President's address in Annapolis, "President Outlines Strategy for Victory in Iraq," November 30, 2005, available online at <http://www.whitehouse.gov/news/releases/2005/11/20051130-2.html>, downloaded December 1, 2005.

and a significant portion of southern Iraq with a smaller "economy of force" presence in northwest Iraq to prevent the situation from deteriorating there. Some strategists might draw the "oil stain" differently, but that is a very large secured area to start with. Although some southeastern cities might have to temporarily remain under the sway of the militias, in time the "oil stain" would expand to include them. As additional Iraqi security forces were trained, vetted, tested, and certified as ready for action, and as areas within the "oil stain" were pacified, security resources would be freed up for deployment to these southeastern cities. Next on the agenda would be the cities of the northwest. Progress in the initial "oil stain" area should bolster the position of those in the northwest who support reconstruction, while those who are ambivalent about reconstruction and pacification would see that it had benefited major swathes of Iraq. Finally, once the rest of the country were secured and, hopefully, thriving, the Coalition would turn its attention to western Iraq, ("the Sunni triangle") and begin incorporating its towns into a secure new Iraq.

It is worth considering that the population of all of central and southern Iraq (including both Baghdad and Basra) is roughly 17 million people. Employing the canonical ratio of 20 security personnel per 1,000 of population yields a requirement for approximately 340,000 security personnel to secure that population for both COIN and stability operations. If that were achieved, over 80 percent of Iraq's population would soon be living in secured areas.[23] That would be a phenomenal achievement by the historical standards of previous COIN campaigns. It likely would take another two years to properly train the additional 110,000-125,000 Iraqi troops required to fill the gap between current Coalition force levels and the 340,000 needed if securing central and southern Iraq were our initial objective. However, if half that gap could be filled with troops provided by the United States and other foreign nations, it might take as little as a year to train the

necessary Iraqi forces. This is why troop strength is more relevant to the speed of a COIN campaign than to its ultimate success.

Thus, a traditional COIN strategy will *not* require any additional foreign troops, but if they were available they could speed the process and so move up the date at which U.S. troop levels could be significantly brought down. Paradoxically, therefore, increasing the troop levels would be the fastest (responsible) way to begin ultimately decreasing them.

As a final point on this subject, the only strategy that would require a massive augmentation of U.S. troop strength is our current strategy of trying to secure the entire country simultaneously. Coalition military commanders simply do not have the troops on hand— American, allied, or capable Iraqis—to handle the number and extent of the tasks at hand. We do not have the forces to provide security in Iraq's populated areas and to suppress the insurgency in western and southern Iraq. Indeed, we do not have sufficient troops for either of these missions independently. Consequently, with our current force structure we can reduce towns in western Iraq, but we cannot secure these urban areas long term. Inevitably, the forces needed to seize an insurgent stronghold are needed to move to attack the next one, which allows the last one recaptured to slip back into insurgent control. The Bush Administration's claim that we have left behind troops to secure places like Tal Afar and Fallujah is actually proof of the contrary—in both of those places the number of troops left behind was far less than what was employed to recapture the city and is too few to properly hold it. As a result, those left behind must fight a constant, losing struggle to maintain security. In the Tal Afar operation, the highly-regarded commander of the 3rd Armored Cavalry Regiment, Col. H.R. McMaster, addressed the question bluntly: "Is there enough force here right now to secure this area permanently? No. Are there opportunities for the enemy in other areas within our region? Yes."[24]

---

23 "Soon" is a relative term in this sentence. Even once the proper density of troops has been established for a location, it can take 6–36 months to create real security.
24 Ellen Knickmeyer, "U.S. Claims Success in Iraq Despite Onslaught," *The Washington Post*, September 19, 2005, p. A1.

In short, moving to a true COIN strategy is not only strategically sound, it is the only strategy that the current U.S. military can possibly sustain and have a reasonable chance of bringing stability to Iraq.

Iraqi public opinion and American troop levels. A question often linked in many minds about U.S. troop levels in Iraq is whether more troops—or even just sustaining the current level of troops—will help or hinder the cause of reconstruction. The answer is complicated, but the bottom line is that *what matters most is not how many U.S. troops are in Iraq but how they are being employed.* At the time of the fall of Baghdad in April 2003, Iraqi opinion on the U.S. presence ran the gamut from joyful welcoming to utter rejection. Some Iraqis truly were delighted to see the U.S. troops, and others were humiliated and appalled. The vast majority of Iraqi Arabs would probably have preferred not to see U.S. troops conquering their country, but for them the U.S. invasion was a necessary evil to liberate them from the horrors of Saddam's regime. They also wanted to rebuild their country along the lines that the Bush Administration was proclaiming, and they understood that a U.S. military presence would be essential to achieving that goal.

What has changed since then is that a great many of those middle-ground Iraqis, who were both grateful and ambivalent, have become increasingly frustrated with the U.S. presence (and the new Iraqi central government that Washington has created). Often, this frustration is expressed, especially in badly-constructed public opinion polls, by the sentiment that the United States "should just leave Iraq." However, a little more digging usually reveals a more subtle and far more common opinion among Iraqis: that they want U.S. forces to stay, but they wish that our troops were doing more to help them. Many Iraqis are souring on the U.S. presence because U.S. military forces sometimes treat Iraqis badly (see below), place U.S. force protec-

tion ahead of Iraqi public safety, make little effort to secure the streets on which Iraqis live and guard the infrastructure that is essential to the Iraqi people's quality of life, and because they see little real progress being made toward the promised goals of reconstruction. *The evidence strongly indicates that Iraqis still see the U.S. military presence as a necessary evil. However, they increasingly seem to see it as a little more "evil" and a little less "necessary" than in the past.* Moreover, their motive in desiring the U.S. to remain has largely become the negative one of avoiding civil war. A wide majority of Iraqis believe, probably correctly, that Iraq would slide quickly into civil war in the absence of sizable U.S. military forces.[25]

It is incorrect to suggest that more U.S. troops will simply stimulate more terrorist attacks either because they will provide more targets or because they will generate more animosity. The insurgents have repeatedly demonstrated that they oppose not just the U.S. presence, but the entire project of reconstruction and, for the Sunnis who comprise the vast bulk of the insurgency, the ascendance of the Shi'i majority. The insurgents have committed far more acts of violence against other Iraqis than they have against U.S. forces. Similarly, many of the leading insurgents have made it clear that they believe they are already waging a civil war against the Shi'ah, whom the Salafi Jihadists regard as apostates and for whom they reserve far greater venom than for "infidel" Americans.

All of the evidence available indicates that were U.S. forces to leave Iraq without first securing it, the insurgents would be even less restrained and would greatly increase their attacks on the new Iraqi government, on the Shi'ah, on the Kurds, and on their other enemies. They would be joined ("opposed" might be more accurate) in this escalation of violence by the various Shi'i militias, and possibly by Kurdish and Turkoman groups as well, who would retaliate for insurgent

---

25 Program on International Policy Attitudes, *What the Iraqi Public Wants: A WorldPublicOpinion.org Poll conducted by the Program on International Policy Attitudes,* January 31, 2006, available at <http://www.worldpublicopinion.org/pipa/pdf/jan06/Iraq_Jan06_rpt.pdf> and Michael O'Hanlon, Nina Kamp, Adriana Lins de Albuquerque, *Iraq Index: Tracking Variables of Reconstruction & Security in Post-Saddam Iraq,* the Brookings Institution November 17, 2003 onwards, available at <http://www.brookings.edu/iraqindex>.

attacks, attempt to seize as much territory as possible, and/or pre-empt feared attacks by other groups. Again, this is exactly how many civil wars have started.

Maintaining (or even increasing) the number of U.S. forces in Iraq and redeploying them to Iraq's populated areas and to guard key infrastructure would probably be resented by some Iraqis. A great many others, however, would likely feel that such measures were long overdue. *Especially if additional American forces were deployed to provide security for the bulk of Iraq's population, were deployed in mixed formations with Iraqi units, were deployed on regular foot patrols and encouraged to get to know the residents of the neighborhoods in which they were stationed, the available evidence suggests that Iraqi responses would range from grudging acceptance to positive relief.* Thus, the key to maintaining or increasing U.S. force levels in Iraq lies in how those forces are employed—what matters is the military mission, not the military mass. If the troops are employed in such a way that the average Iraqi believes that he or she is benefiting, the Iraqis will likely accept this. But for as long as U.S. troops continue to be employed in the same manner as at present and do not alter their conduct, then they will soon wear out their welcome regardless of how many or how few of them there are.

TACTICAL CHANGES

The U.S. military has made considerably more progress making tactical changes consistent with counterinsurgency and stability operations than our nation's political-military leadership has in adopting a true counterinsurgency strategy. U.S. units are now being trained in COIN techniques before deploying to Iraq. Officers who have developed effective solutions to problems that they have encountered are devising ways to disseminate this knowledge to their peers and to their successors. There is a greater emphasis on training indigenous Iraqi forces and employing them in opera-

tions than was the case previously. Counterinsurgency doctrine is finally being introduced into some military education programs. Some military leaders have begun discussing the need for their subordinates to employ COIN tactics and more U.S. units are doing so. Nonetheless, much remains to be done.

In large measure, the problems and the solutions are about personnel. Most of the progressive changes to military tactics have been the product of a relatively small number of military officers who recognized the circumstances and were willing to do what was necessary to adapt to them. Unfortunately, there are still many other officers who steadfastly refuse to adapt to the circumstances of Iraq or to embrace counterinsurgency and stability operations. To some extent, this reluctance is institutional. The U.S. military, and the U.S. Army in particular, is committed to conventional warfare and the vast majority of its training, education, doctrine, and career incentives are all geared toward it. For many officers, principles and tactics of conventional combat is all that they know—and all that they believe they need to know. As a result, many find counterinsurgency operations counterintuitive because COIN principles are, in many respects, the reverse of conventional warfare principles. In the words of one American special forces officer, "most guys in the Army are taught how to kill people and destroy things, but COIN warfare is about how to protect people and build things."[26]

Flexibility. The only immutable law of counterinsurgency warfare is that nothing else is immutable. In particular, *while the principles of COIN operations must be followed to have success, their tactical application must always be tailored to the specifics of the situation.* COIN operations are tremendously complicated, far more so than conventional military operations— because they involve not just using force to achieve political objectives, but using force to enable political and economic activity, to change proverbial "hearts

---

26 This same officer also commented that "COIN is a thinking man's war; it is graduate level warfare." Pollack interview with U.S. military personnel, northern Iraq, November 2005.

and minds." Thus, the culture, history, traditions, topography, economy, political system, and a host of other intangibles all must be factored into COIN operations. The result is that tactics that worked marvelously in one war may not work at all in another because of the different context: a different culture, economics, politics, or other factors.

What this means for Iraq is that commanders must be willing to look to COIN warfare principles as guides to action and inspirations to tactics, but they must also be prepared to experiment, to learn and to adjust quickly when lessons become manifest. Personnel should be encouraged to try out tactics and ideas that are consistent with COIN principles. If they are successful, the chain of command must be ready, willing and able to employ them elsewhere. If they fail, they must quickly learn that lesson too, discontinue the deleterious practice, and be prepared to try something else.

Systemic changes. Some of the most important changes that the U.S. military needs to make to improve its performance in Iraq relate to the functioning of the system as a whole.

- *De-emphasize detainee counts.* One of the most pernicious influences on every aspect of U.S. and Iraqi military operations at the tactical level is the pressure to produce a high "detainee count." The military learned from Vietnam not to talk about body counts, but they do not seem to have understood why that metric was so counterproductive and so have replaced it with the detainee count. This is just as damaging to good COIN operations as the emphasis on the body count was in that earlier conflict. It encourages lower-level commanders to mount raids and other offensive operations, and to

arrest people based on little more than "hunches" that frequently turn out to be wrong. Everything about this emphasis is misguided and harmful to the conduct of operations. It creates precisely the wrong set of incentives for commanders on the ground, suggesting to them that all Iraqis are potential detainees, that any piece of intelligence regardless of source or corroboration should be acted on, and that their first priority is to catch bad guys rather than to protect good guys.

- *Dedicate personnel and create a structure within the military hierarchy in Iraq for learning lessons and disseminating them back to units in the field in the form of doctrine, best practices, and orders.* Although it has been two-and-a-half years since they were first employed to address post-invasion security measures, U.S. forces in Iraq still have no effective system to collect, analyze, and disseminate lessons for all aspects of operations in Iraq.[27] To a great extent, this effort has been left to the Center for Army Lessons Learned, which has done yeoman service collating after-action reports from units returning from Iraq and helping to make changes to the training for units deploying to Iraq. Nonetheless, this is no substitute for an in-theater element performing a similar function for tactical formations on a constant basis and so able to affect ongoing operations.

Units of all kinds in Iraq must regularly file situation and after-action reports, indicating that the information is available for such an effort. However, where these reports go and how they are used is unknown. Of greater importance, there appears to be no dedicated effort in the military command structure in Iraq to absorb these lessons and then

---

27 In 2005, Generals Abizaid and Casey did invite a leading expert on COIN warfare, Kalev Sepp, to Multi-National Force-Iraq (MNF-I) headquarters in Baghdad to lay out for them what a proper COIN campaign might look like. This was an extremely positive development as Sepp is a true master of the art. Many of the tactical changes that U.S. forces in Iraq have been making appear to have resulted from Sepp's critique. However, this is no substitute for a dedicated system in Iraq designed to collect and analyze field reporting and then devise new COIN techniques that can be disseminated to field techniques. In some senses, it speaks to the problem that someone like Sepp needs to be called in to devise a COIN doctrine for MNF-I rather than their having done so for themselves. In addition, COIN warfare is a dynamic contest by its nature, and no matter how brilliant Sepp's analysis and recommendations, they will have to be modified over time based on changing circumstances, including the inevitable reactions of the enemy themselves. Only a dedicated team in Baghdad can do this.

make them available to forces in the field in anything like real time. If such an effort is being made, it is having little impact on the troops in the field.

This is inexplicable and inexcusable. Personnel in every kind of unit from civil-affairs to line infantry to Special Forces desperately want such distillations of best and worst practices because they recognize the utility of learning from their comrades' successes and mistakes. It is certainly true that the principle of flexibility in COIN operations warns that techniques that succeeded in one time and place may not succeed at another, but it would still be extremely helpful for personnel to know what other units have done elsewhere and with what results. They can then take these as examples to be tailored to their circumstances and then try to see if they work.

The proof that there is such a need is that, to their great credit, junior officers have created their own websites and are sharing their own experiences via the internet. While this is much to be admired, it does not exonerate the failure of the military command to provide a formal system to provide this critical function. Many officers see these unofficial websites as the sources of "optional" doctrine and procedures, thus leaving the need for a formal process that would make such changes mandatory for all field commanders in Iraq. Learning and adaptation is one of the keys to victory in COIN operations, and the lack of a formal structure designed to learn and diagnose adaptations within the military network in Iraq goes a long way to explain the persistence of our many failings there.

• **Regularize operations in all military areas of responsibility (AORs) so that all U.S. (and Iraqi) military formations are applying techniques from the same counterinsurgency principles.** A problem closely related to the lack of a system for formulating best practices for waging the war in Iraq is the lack of any uniformity in the approach to military operations across U.S. AORs. To a great extent, every division and brigade commander is being allowed to fight his own war the way that he wants to fight it. Some commanders understand COIN operations and so employ appropriate tactics in their AOR, inevitably demonstrating a rapid improvement in the situation there. Unfortunately, the commander of the neighboring formation—or their successor, as is often the case—may know little and care less about COIN warfare and so will not employ any of the same approaches. In part, this problem is a direct outgrowth of the previous point: because no one in the U.S. military command in Baghdad is analyzing best/worst practices and disseminating them, lower level commanders are free to conduct operations as they see fit. It is important to keep in mind that all of the good work that one unit with a good commander may do in 12 months can be undone in a matter of weeks by a unit not employing the same methods.

• **Counterinsurgency operations must be incorporated into all U.S. Army and Marines training and education programs, with a particular emphasis on how those techniques should be applied in Iraq.** As noted above, some of this is already happening. For instance, the Army War College recently added a rigorous assessment of COIN operations to its program. Likewise, when Lt. Gen. David Petraeus took over the Army's Combined Arms Center, which has authority over the Command and General Staff College (CGSC) at Fort Leavenworth, he insisted on adding 18 hours of COIN warfare education to their curriculum.[28] That Petraeus did so was important, but the fact that it was not already being taught speaks to the overarching problem that still exists in many other guises. For instance, many courses for military officers being promoted to new ranks and responsibilities do not include any training or education on COIN warfare. Even those that do teach COIN warfare teach far too little given the importance of the mission in Iraq and how likely it is that U.S. forces will be prosecuting this war for some time to come.

---

28 Lt. Gen. Petraeus is also presiding over a highly-sophisticated and much-needed revision of the Army's manual on counter-insurgency warfare.

Operational changes. Despite numerous changes in Coalition operating procedures in Iraq, the situation is still far from perfect. In some cases this is because command decisions have not yet made themselves fully felt in the field. In other cases, it is because making the approved changes takes a great deal of time in a bureaucracy as large as the U.S. armed forces. However, there are still a number of areas in which necessary changes have not yet been recognized or ordered, others where a good idea is being implemented improperly, and still others where the "every-division-for-itself" decentralization of the war has allowed lower echelon commanders to effectively ignore their superiors' stated priorities. All of these problems need to be addressed quickly. (Since many of the operational changes that U.S. forces need to make to prosecute the war more effectively have already been addressed in other sections, much of the following list has been abbreviated).

• *Make it a priority to take back territory currently controlled by the various militias in central and southern Iraq.* The militias cannot be allowed to control any "turf" in the key population centers, oilfields, and transportation lines of central and southern Iraq. In other words, once the Coalition forces determine the contours of the initial "oil stain", they must move to eliminate any "competition" from the militias. Coalition forces (and ultimately Iraqi forces) must have a monopoly on violence in secured areas, which is the very definition of "secured." Any militia that resists must be dealt with quickly and forcefully by Iraqi and U.S. units. As the "oil stain" expands, a key element will involve taking back whatever areas are being held by the militias in the territory into which the "oil stain" grows.

• *Concentrate on area security by saturating Iraqi population centers with checkpoints, foot patrols, snipers, screening at major gathering points, and other methods of demonstrating presence and deterring crime and attacks.* The importance of foot patrols, over the mounted patrols that U.S. units still favor cannot be overemphasized. If troops are not out in the streets,

they will see nothing, they will not develop any rapport with the population, they will not reassure the innocent nor will they deter the guilty. Our model should be the kind of pervasive security presence that Israel employs as part of its day-to-day life.

• *To the greatest extent possible, operate in mixed formations of U.S. and Iraqi units.* Ideally, U.S. squads should be attached to Iraqi platoons and U.S. platoons attached to Iraqi companies. The larger number of Iraqis typically allows them to interact more easily with the population and takes the edge off of whatever humiliation the civilians may feel; the U.S. complement then can serve as a quick reaction force, can provide heavy firepower if there is trouble, and also helps reassure other Iraqi civilians (who often fear Iraqi units for being corrupt, or members of an unfriendly sect or ethnic group) that the Iraqi soldiers will not hurt them. Throughout Iraq, such mixed formations have proven highly successful whenever they have been employed.

• *Protect Iraq's critical infrastructure, including roads, oil pipelines, communications and power lines.*

• *U.S. military doctrine and operational procedures must be wholly revamped to emphasize restraint and the discriminant use of force.* This is another archetypal principal of COIN and stability operations. Excessive force results in civilian deaths which, no matter how unintended, typically aid insurgents by increasing their recruitment and creating more supporters. In Northern Ireland, this problem led the British to develop the famous Yellow Cards that every soldier carried. These laid out strict rules of engagement designed to minimize the likelihood of collateral damage. The enemies that Americans face in Iraq are far more willing to use indiscriminate force against Coalition units than the Provos were against the British, indicating that U.S. personnel cannot be bound by quite such high standards as the Yellow Cards. However, there is still a great deal that can be done—such as forbidding Americans from arbitrarily firing on cars on the road that seem suspicious to them, refraining from the use of tank cannon and other heavy weapons in built-up areas, and prohibiting all air strikes in urban areas except in the most extraordinary circumstances (and then requiring approval from the commander of the Multi-National Force-Iraq, MNF-I, to do so).

• *As part of the emphasis on the discriminant use of force, offensive military operations such as raids and sweeps, should only be conducted when they are based on extremely sound intelligence derived from an equally sound intelligence process.* As Thomas Mockaitis has concluded in his seminal study of British post-war COIN operations, "A long-term intelligence picture must be built up before an operation can be mounted and then the operation might best be left to special forces. Soldiers trained to think in terms of seizing the initiative might naturally believe that they are denied the information which would allow them to achieve results. They fail to see that their real contribution is in the violence they prevent by their very presence."[29] Maj. Gen. Spider Marks, the former chief of U.S. military intelligence in Iraq, observes that it is critical—and especially for counterinsurgency and stability operations—to have a sound process of collecting, analyzing and disseminating intelligence to create the proper context for new information before taking any "kinetic" actions. Only in this way will operations be properly targeted to disrupt the enemy's operations while minimizing any harm to the civilian population, whose security is the entire campaign's center of gravity. Another example of such a process is when Israel conducts a targeted killing or raid into the Palestinian territories. Israeli officials go through a tortuous process of identification and vetting to ensure that when they launch the operation, they are as close to certain as possible that the target has been properly identified and there will be minimal collateral damage. As one former, senior Israeli security official warned, "You don't act without pinpoint intelligence, and you don't act unless you are sure about a target." U.S. operations in Iraq are often triggered by the flimsiest information, employ excessive force, and often target huge numbers of people indiscriminately in the expectation that a few bad guys will turn up in every dragnet full of Iraqis. These operations, often called "block parties" because they involve rounding up all of the males between 15 and 60 in an entire city block (which could mean 300–400 people), rarely turn up any real insurgents. However, they frequently anger all of the families on the block, diminishing their willingness to cooperate with the Coalition, and potentially driving some to join an insurgent group or militia.

• *Treat all Iraqis with dignity and respect.* This is a simple point, but it is symptomatic of the larger failures of America's handling of Iraq that it needs to be made. While many (perhaps most) U.S. military personnel go out of their way to treat Iraqis with kindness and dignity, too many others treat Iraqis—both civilians and military—in a manner that the Iraqis find distasteful and disrespectful. It is probably not a majority, but too many Americans appear to regard the Iraqis as obstacles to be overcome or avoided, as enemies to be killed or subdued, or as livestock to be ordered about for their own good. Iraqis are hyper-sensitive to such disrespect and it creates tremendous anger among the Iraqi people, who are the key to reconstruction. Moreover, tolerance for such callousness among U.S. military personnel leads to a whole range of pernicious behavior, from breaking down doors and furniture to treating respected local figures with derision to ordering Iraqi military personnel to conduct demeaning behavior that erodes support for the U.S. military presence and boosts insurgent and militia recruitment. Such behavior would never be condoned if the Iraqis were U.S. citizens, and this divergence is a key failing of the U.S. military presence in Iraq. To some extent, this may be a case of a "few bad apples spoiling the bunch," but the few are far too numerous,

---

29 Thomas Mockaitis, *British Counterinsurgency in the Post-Imperial Era* (Manchester, UK: Manchester University Press, 1995), p. 118.

and if this is the case, they are causing damage out of all proportion to their numbers.

- *All U.S. military personnel must be taught to treat Iraqis with the same degrees of respect, concern and politeness as if they were U.S. citizens.* This is critical to winning the "hearts and minds" of the people, which is the key to counterinsurgency operations. India waged a half-dozen COIN campaigns during the Cold War, and this was one of the most important lessons they learned, even though it was often more honored in the breach than in the observance. U.S. troops would do well to pay heed to an Order of the Day from India's Army Chief of Staff during the COIN campaign against the Nagas in northeast India in the 1950s and '60s: "You must remember that all of the people of the area in which you are operating are fellow Indians. They may have different religions, may pursue a different way of life, but they are Indians and the very fact that they are different and yet part of India is a reflection of India's greatness. Some of these people are misguided and have taken to arms against their own people, and are disrupting the peace of this area. You are to protect the mass of the people from these disruptive elements. You are not there to fight the people in the area, but to protect them."[30] Similarly, India's great prime minister, Jawaharlal Nehru, warned the Indian Army that "the Nagas were fellow-countrymen who had to be won over, not suppressed."[31]

Until all U.S. forces come to respect the Iraqi people and treat them as being worthy of U.S. military protection, it is not realistic to expect U.S. military personnel to take that mission seriously, no matter how vital it is to success in Iraq.

- *Diminish the numbers of U.S. contract security personnel in Iraq as quickly as possible.* Iraq is a dangerous place and many of the private firms operating in Iraq require private security forces to protect their personnel in country. Some of these private security contractors have hired high-quality former U.S., British and other military personnel, but others hire minimally-trained and poorly-equipped novices. Their mission ultimately is different from that of U.S. or Coalition military forces and this often means that they will operate in ways that can be unhelpful to the U.S. mission. They are not counterinsurgent forces and so do not apply COIN techniques in executing their tasks. *Often, they execute their missions even if it means alienating Iraqis.* Indeed, it seems clear that at least part of the anger that Iraqis direct toward "Americans" for disrespectful behavior and indiscriminate uses of force are actually directed at contractors, not U.S. soldiers and U.S. Marines. Unfortunately, the Iraqis have a hard time distinguishing among them. Of course, contract security personnel will be necessary in Iraq for as long as the areas in which civilians operate are not safe. This is still another reason to adopt an "oil stain" approach that would allow the securing of the areas of Iraq where the civilian presence should be highest, thereby diminishing their need for private security guards.

Information warfare changes. The history of counterinsurgency campaigns makes crystal clear that good intelligence work and effective psychological operations (PsyOps) are essential to victory. All warfare is psychological, but counterinsurgency warfare is even more so than conventional conflict because the decisive contest is waged for the "hearts and minds" of the population. Thus the goal is to convince the population to support the COIN effort and turn against the insurgents—and provide information on the insurgents' whereabouts and activities to make it impossible for them to operate and possible for the COIN force eventually to destroy them. Part of that psychological contest is reassuring the people that the COIN force has a good handle on the insurgency, is able to target

---

30 Rajesh Rajagopalan, "'Restoring Normalcy:' The Evolution of the Indian Army's Counterinsurgency Doctrine," *Small Wars and Insurgencies*, Volume 11, No. 1 (Spring 2000), p. 49.
31 Rajagopalan, op.cit, p. 47.

them effectively, and is able to discriminate between insurgents and innocents.

- *Military operations, particularly offensive military operations, must be the product of painstaking intelligence work to ensure that they have the highest likelihood of success and the lowest likelihood of incorrectly or indiscriminately targeting innocents.* One of the worst practices of U.S. military personnel in Iraq is to act on bad and uncorroborated intelligence. In some cases U.S. forces behave this way because of the pressure to produce a high detainee count, pushing them to grasp at straws. In other cases they do so out of the mistaken belief that they need to be aggressive and when a piece of information comes in they need to act on it while it is fresh, before the "bad guys" get away. In still others, they do this because they lack dedicated intelligence specialists or any training in intelligence work, let alone in Iraqi culture, and so do not understand what constitutes reliable information. As a result, U.S. raids and other offensive operations are too often misguided. They target the wrong people based on the wrong information. Instead, U.S. forces in Iraq must exercise restraint and stay on the defensive until intelligence has been carefully assembled and analyzed and targets can be identified with a very high degree of certainty. Only under those circumstances should raids and other offensive operations be undertaken. Our default mode should be to do nothing, rather than to act precipitously on unverified information. This too is highly counterintuitive for U.S. military personnel and so must be ingrained at all levels of command in all possible ways.

- *Military operations should be conducted with an eye toward intelligence gathering.* Intelligence in COIN operations is generally a "bottom-up" system meaning that most of the intelligence must come from the lowest echelons of the chain of command—soldiers manning checkpoints, conducting dismounted patrols, mingling with the population and approaching local leaders to help them with their security needs. These are the best ways to gather the information needed to fight insurgents. *Every operation undertaken should be planned and executed with an eye toward what intelligence can be collected.* In many cases, testing a theory about local insurgent activity or gathering important information may be the sole purpose of the mission. Unfortunately this happens too little in Iraq. Too few military operations are conducted with anything other than the immediate gratification of catching a few bad guys in mind because of the emphasis placed on the detainee account and the predilection for commanders at all levels to "go kinetic." U.S. soldiers must be taught patience and they must understand the importance of information dominance in this war. To a very great extent, *personnel in combat arms need to understand that, in COIN warfare, they are actually a supporting branch and that in many ways the supported branch must be the intelligence services.*

- *Soldiers must have realistic expectations about intelligence.* Military personnel typically expect intelligence to be provided from higher echelons, and while this should still be the case, they need to recognize that they likely will be providing as much or more intelligence to formations above them in the chain of command than they will be receiving from it. On the one hand, this cannot be paralyzing—units should not simply sit around waiting for complete intelligence. On the other hand, they must always keep in mind the injunction that violent operations should be avoided unless the intelligence and the purpose are clear and unassailable.

- *Platoons, companies and battalions should be provided with clear and specific information-gathering requirements for all missions.* Because all military operations should be conducted with an eye towards intelligence gathering, it is critical that higher echelons routinely provide subordinate formations with specific guidance and tasks beyond banal and useless admonitions to "look for signs of insurgent activity." Too often in Iraq, tactical formations are provided with no guidance as to what specific information would be useful.

- *A greater number of trained intelligence officers must be attached to lower echelons of command.* COIN and stability operations are practiced largely at the platoon-company-battalion level. Typically, U.S. Army and Marine units do not include intelligence personnel below the battalion level, and even at the battalion level, as the U.S. Army's military intelligence manual states, "Your battalion S2 section [the military intelligence section] is austere."[32] The result is that many platoons and even companies lack personnel trained to collect and interpret intelligence, with the result that they fail to pass on crucial pieces of information (because they do not see its utility) and act on poor information, needlessly alienating large numbers of Iraqis. Additional personnel should be detached from brigade, division, and higher levels and attached to lower formations to try to provide S2s at least for companies.

- *Intelligence gathering must be incorporated into the operations of soldiers at every level.* For soldiers who are holding territory, finding information is often their most important duty. Like cops on the beat, soldiers who know a territory well are often best able to anticipate any shift in support or identify suspect individuals. This also extends to training practices: if every soldier is meant to be a sensor—as the military intelligence credo argues—then every soldier must be trained in basic intelligence gathering, and this should start with basic training. This is the only way to ensure that every soldier and Marine understands the importance of intelligence gathering to fourth-generation warfare, and their role in performing this vital task.

- *Intelligence officers must be encouraged to have longer tours and otherwise develop their knowledge.* Even more than combat operations, effective COIN intelligence requires a painstaking awareness of local conditions, ranging from the complex web of family relations in a village to the number of medical personnel available in a particular town. As this knowledge is built up and disseminated, it enables collectors to become even more precise and helps avoid mistakes that engender more opposition.

- *Higher-quality (and higher-ranking) officers must be assigned to battalion (and company) S2 positions and both commanders and operations officers need to incorporate their intelligence personnel into all aspects of plans and operations.* At tactical levels, the U.S. Army in particular has a very bad reputation regarding its personnel policies and treatment of military intelligence specialists. S2s are often treated as useless, lesser beings and excluded from key decision-making. Frequently, S2s have a lower rank than S3s (operations officers), guaranteeing that their views carry less weight than the operations staff. For this reason, many of the finest officers shy away from military intelligence, and those who do so are often considered eccentrics. If military intelligence is to play the vital role that it must in fighting the counterinsurgent war in Iraq, the U.S. armed forces are going to have to start making it more palatable for its best and brightest to pursue intelligence as a specialization and encouraging those who do so with promotions and respect. Likewise, because intelligence must be one of the ultimate objectives of a great many tactical operations, intelligence officers must be trusted to participate in all planning and decision-making to ensure that they are able to shape the course of operations.

- *The U.S. military and the U.S. government must ratchet up their efforts to recruit and train Americans who can serve as Arabic translators.*[33] One of the greatest problems experienced by U.S. military units at all levels in Iraq is the dearth of Arabic interpreters, especially Arabic speakers that military officers can fully trust. Although the Defense Language Institute

---

32 United States Army, FM 34-8: Combat Commander's Handbook on Intelligence, September 28, 1992. Available at <http://www.fas.org/irp/doddir/army/fm34-8/ch3.htm#Chap3>.

33 Ideally, this would also include specialists in Iraqi culture; however, given the problems just finding people who speak the language, it would be excessive to in turn demand that the military also come up with large numbers of cultural specialists.

is graduating 600–900 Arabic speakers annually, this is nowhere near enough—especially since the DLI course provides students with proficiency, but not fluency. Consequently, U.S. forces in Iraq have been forced to rely on a huge complement of nearly 6,000 contractors, nearly 5,000 of them Iraqis, whose loyalty and reliability is unclear.[34] U.S. ground units require *at least* one English-Arabic translator per company or company-equivalent unit. In an ideal world, the U.S. would have one interpreter per squad, since COIN warfare rests heavily on the shoulders of the smallest tactical formations, and these units are "deaf and dumb" without interpreters, in the words of T.X. Hammes. Since translators get just as burnt out as infantrymen, it requires two to three times as many translators as are actually needed in Iraq at any given time to ensure an adequate rotational base. Therefore, U.S. forces in Iraq need somewhere between 10,000-15,000 translators in Iraq at any given time. At present, between contractors and military personnel, there are typically no more than 6,000 translators available.[35]

- *Programs like DLI's should be expanded by recruiting additional native Arabic speakers to serve as teachers as quickly as possible.* To their credit, both the U.S. Army and the Marines have inaugurated programs to attract Arabic language speakers through a variety of inducements. However, in both cases these programs try to convince Arabic speakers to enlist in special programs in the Individual Ready Reserve and have had the greatest luck recruiting non-citizens with the promise of citizenship. While this increases the number of Arabic speakers, they still come with strings attached; because they are not citizens they are often not trusted (and in some cases have proven untrustworthy) and do not always speak English as well as they speak Arabic. *To supplement this effort, the U.S. government needs to make a major effort to recruit American Arabic speakers to sign on for tours of duty in Iraq. A six-month or one-year program should be inaugurated with extremely high pay, huge bonuses, and other benefits (like educational incentives) to encourage Arab-Americans and others with Arabic language ability to serve as translators in Iraq.* The program should be designed specifically for Arabic translators and should be much easier both to get in to and get out of than actually joining the armed forces, either as active duty or reservists. While the cost of such a program could be very high, having adequate translators is absolutely vital to the success of the mission and minimizing U.S. casualties.

Personnel policy changes. Many U.S. military personnel like to complain that the nation is not at war, only they are. On the one hand, there is certainly some truth to that claim. Because the United States has an all volunteer army and the Bush Administration has asked the American people to make few personal sacrifices in the name of fighting the war, a great many Americans do not see it as a real presence in their lives. Only the military personnel deploying regularly to Iraq, their families, and the contractors who work with them feel the war on a constant basis.

On the other hand, it is disconcerting to see how little the war has affected a great many of even the military's

---

34 "Requirement for Contract Interpreters in Iraq and Afghanistan Climbs," *Inside the Army*, Vol. 17, No. 44, November 7, 2005; personal correspondence, Chief, Army Foreign Language Proponency Office (AFLPO) to Irena Sargsyan, December 30, 2005. It is worth noting that according to DoD, the U.S. Army (alone) believes it requires 7,200 contract interpreters for Iraq in FY 2006 and this does not meet the higher need of what would be preferable, as opposed to what is the bare minimum to allow U.S. forces to function. In addition, it is predicated on a system which does not assume as much embedding and joint operations between Iraqi and U.S. units as this report recommends. Thus part of the higher requirement stems from the desirability of changing American military methods of operation.

35 According to a U.S. Department of Defense (DoD) briefing, the U.S. armed forces had 3,686 Arabic speakers in mid-2004. Assuming that this number has probably increased thanks to recruitment and training, the number should now be well over 4,000, see Major B. J. Sanchez, "DoD: Our Language Capability," DoD Briefing, April 8, 2004, cited in Anita U. Hattiangadi, et. al., "Non-Citizens in Today's Military: Final Report," Center for Naval Analysis, April 2005. However, because of rotations, the demands of other missions, the fact that not all Arabic speakers can serve as translators, and other personnel matters, only 1,000-1,500 appear to be in Iraq at any given time, and fewer than that are actually serving as translators. In addition, DoD is employing 5,900 contract translators in Iraq, of whom 4,700 are Iraqis—personal correspondence, Chief, AFLPO to Irena Sargsyan, December 30, 2005.

practices. This is particularly true for personnel matters (and, until very recently, training and military education as well). Unfortunately, the armed services, and particularly the Army, are allowing careerism, ticket-punching, and time-serving to dictate a number of critical aspects of personnel policy regarding the war. Many serving and retired military officers rightly complain that personnel policies do not seem to reflect the fact that "there's a war on."

One key personnel issue for U.S. forces in Iraq is the length and frequency of tours. The military necessities of prosecuting the war argue for longer tours of duty, but the stresses of combat (and the potential for personnel to lose effectiveness through "burn out") in Iraq push for the opposite. The twelve-month (or less) tours of duty in Iraq mean that units barely have time to become proficient before they depart. The constant turnover of units means that a tremendous amount of accumulated knowledge is regularly lost. In a similar vein, it has been said that the United States did not fight a ten-year war in Vietnam, but a one-year war ten times over. Unfortunately some of this problem is recurring in Iraq. On the other hand, the pace of combat operations, the additional burdens placed on U.S. military personnel who often must also deal with all of the political and economic problems in their sector because no civilian counterparts are available (see chapter 2), and the strains inherent in counterinsurgency warfare—not being able to tell friend from foe, always being on your guard—mean that by the end of a year most military personnel have been stressed to the point where they are no longer effective and become a liability to themselves and their comrades. Unfortunately there is no perfect solution to this dilemma and adjustments will need to be made on both ends.

- *Promote those who perform well, remove those who don't.* To some extent, the military high command seems to regard the war in Iraq as an aberration, rather than what may well prove be the norm, at least for as long as the United States possesses unmatched conventional military capabilities.

Consequently, a failure to properly conduct COIN operations in Iraq seems rarely to damage military officers' careers, nor does the proven ability to do COIN operations appear to lead to promotion and other benefits. To some extent, the fault lies in the ignorance of COIN doctrine or the reluctance to employ appropriate COIN doctrine among many U.S. military personnel. As a result, some officers do not know what to expect from their subordinates, or expect the wrong things and praise it when they get what they expect. It is critical that those officers who understand and properly employ COIN tactics be promoted and given greater responsibility; while those who do not are relieved of their commands or have their careers suffer.

There can be no excuses made for those who fail to perform well in these operations in Iraq. The military is supposed to be a purely meritocratic society, success in the Iraq war is vital to the nation's interests, and COIN warfare is likely to remain a key mission for American forces for many years to come. Those who do well should be retained and given the opportunity to take a larger role in the fight. Those who do poorly have no business rising further or being rewarded with higher levels of command. Israel's experience with COIN operations in Lebanon and the Palestinian territories is an excellent example: initially, because the Israelis believed that their military should be principally oriented to handling conventional military threats, they indulged similar pathologies in their promotion system. However, over time, they realized that COIN operations against Lebanese, Palestinians and other foes were also vital to their security and they shifted to a system whereby promotion required demonstrated success in COIN warfare against these various groups.

- *Since Green Berets tend to be the most proficient in COIN warfare, they should also be given preference for key command positions, including Joint commands, in contrast to usual practices. The same should hold true for intelligence officers; since counterinsurgency is an intelligence-driven war, the military needs to put more senior intelligence officers in charge of operations.* This is one of the most important ways to ensure that operations are conducted based on proper intelligence work and with the goal of collecting or testing intelligence as major, if not the sole, purpose of the operation.

- *Embed the highest quality military personnel with Iraqi forces.* The U.S. has been doing a much better job recently of embedding U.S. personnel with Iraqi military units (and having U.S. and Iraqi units operating together jointly). This reflects the greater priority that senior American commanders have assigned to the training and readiness of Iraqi forces. However, one of many lingering problems hindering this effort has been the ambivalence of ambitious young officers about these assignments and the reluctance of commanders to assign their best personnel to these missions. Given how important these programs are, *the military must assign their best officers and units to them, and must be willing to develop a system of rewards and compensation to make these desirable assignments.*

- *Move to a system whereby units are rotated into and out of Iraq at battalion level.* Counterinsurgency warfare is inevitably small-unit warfare. Historically, every successful COIN campaign has prevailed, in part, by using smaller formations (battalions, companies and even platoons) as the principle units of maneuver. Because the most important task of military forces in a COIN campaign is area security, and because "presence" is critical to maintaining public safety and support, COIN forces must typically cover large areas. Since insurgents tend to lack large numbers and heavy firepower, they too tend to operate in small formations so that they do not provide the COIN forces with concentrated targets. For instance, in Algeria, the anti-French insurgents loyal to the Front de Libération Nationale never formed units larger than battalions and, as the war proceeded, increasingly learned to operate at company and platoon level. Moreover, since offensive operations requiring the concentration of large forces are often

counterproductive and therefore should be rare, there is little incentive for Coalition forces to do so—again, a mistake the U.S. has made repeatedly in Iraq.

Instead, divisions and brigades should be treated as nothing more than geographic commands because they should not be true units of maneuver except in extreme circumstances (because it should be a rarity that the U.S. is massing and maneuvering a full brigade, let alone a division). Moreover, divisions and brigades control huge areas in Iraq and by rotating them as whole units, the U.S. creates enormous problems with turnover, because the new units lack the institutional memory of those they are replacing. *Instead, the U.S. should move to a system whereby individual battalions are rotated in and out of Iraq, with each brigade always retaining at least one to two battalions that have been in country for at least six months.* In this way, the brigade commander will always have two battalions available with experience that can handle the hardest missions and back up inexperienced battalions if they get into trouble.

- *All U.S. Army and Marine battalions should be "paired up," with one of the pair always in Iraq in the same AOR and the other at home, resting and training for the next rotation.* The best way to deal with the problem of turnover, loss of institutional memory, and the need for frequent rotations to deal with "burnout," is to "pair up" battalions—such that one of the pair is always in Iraq while the other is at home and the two continue to swap for as long as our Iraq deployment lasts. Paired battalions are likely to become close and the officers can regularly exchange information about both friendly and enemy missions, as well as providing each other with lessons learned. Indeed, with modern technology, it should be possible for the resting battalion to listen in to discussions in the headquarters of the deployed battalion and participate in meetings via teleconference on a regular basis. The intelligence sections of the paired battalions should function as a "rear" and "forward" element, with constant exchanges of information over classified data transmission networks (like the

Secret Internet Protocol Router Network, SIPR-NET), whereby the stateside element will remain current on developments in Iraq and can function as a support center for the counterpart battalion in Iraq. Paired battalions will have a much greater incentive to do so. What's more, *by constantly sending units back to the same AOR in Iraq, the United States will minimize the learning curve of units being redeployed: they will go back to the geography, people, culture, and politics they already know.* Over time, they will build on that base of knowledge and become more proficient. In addition, it will be easier to maintain ties to the local community, to local allies, and even to informants if the same personnel keep coming back and switching off.

- *Consider lengthening some deployments of senior and staff personnel.* This is not nearly as cut-and-dried as the other recommendations. Another way to get at the problem of turnover is to retain some personnel in theater for longer. This is not practical for field-deployed combat units because the strains are too great. Indeed, the Marine Corps believes that its tours should be cut to six months, which squares with the British experience in Northern Ireland, where combat tours lasted just four months. However, it might be possible to retain more senior commanders and their staffs who do not have to deal with the stress of actual combat and deployment in the field. In particular, it would be highly advantageous to have intelligence officers serve longer tours, both because of the need for more such personnel in Iraq, and so that their intimate knowledge of the enemy is not regularly lost. It often takes six to twelve months for an intelligence officer to really gain an understanding of the enemy, only to head home just when he or she has become most valuable. Arguing against the need to have some personnel remain for longer to overcome turnover problems is the fact that even senior commanders and rear area headquarters staffs suffer from the stresses of war in Iraq. Because of the need to be always on guard, due to insurgent attacks on rear areas and civilians, and the determination of senior officers to take more responsibilities on themselves to alleviate those on their subordinates, levels of stress are very high even for these officers. Consequently, lengthening rotations in Iraq may not be a realistic solution to the problem of turnover.

- *Every effort must be made to augment the numbers of Green Berets in Iraq; likewise, they must be devoted entirely to the training of Iraqi forces, and not to other missions of secondary importance.* Special Forces (SF), particularly the Army's Green Berets, play a vital role in securing Iraq. These units have Arabic language speakers, they are masters of insurgent and counterinsurgent warfare, and they are skilled at training indigenous military forces. For all of these reasons they are invaluable for training the Iraqi armed forces in precisely the kinds of missions they will be called on to perform. In this way, they are considerably more valuable than conventional Army mechanized or even light infantry units. Although many Special Forces "A Teams" have been embedded with Iraqi formations to train them, it is still far too often the case that SF units are employed to gather intelligence or perform reconnaissance for offensive raids. Setting aside the point made previously that the Coalition is placing too great an emphasis on such raids, the use of such precious assets for such mundane tasks is almost criminal—like using a Swiss watch as a hammer.

To the extent that additional Green Berets can be spared, they should be sent to Iraq as quickly as possible. In particular, *SF personnel can and should be disengaged from other, less pressing missions to be made available in Iraq.* This should include other missions in the Middle East, south Asia (excepting the reconstruction of Afghanistan), and southeast Asia related to the Global War on Terror. It is critical to recognize that the demands and importance of the war in Iraq vastly outweigh all of these other assignments. Whether al-Qa'ida is able to hang on to its foothold in Yemen, for example, is of far less significance to American national security at this point than the war in Iraq. Therefore, SF missions in Yemen, and the like, should be discontinued or assigned to other forces, like Army Rangers, who are less valuable for training Iraqi security units, to ensure that the absolute maximum number of Green Berets are deployed to Iraq and embedded with Iraqi formations.

Structural changes. Another aspect of Coalition problems in Iraq relates to the structure of the U.S. relationship with the Iraqi government and its security forces, as well as the inability of the Iraqi government to take actions that could be helpful in counterinsurgency and stability operations. In every case, the needed changes reflect the consistent lessons of COIN and stability operations:

- *U.S. forces must allow the Iraqi security forces to take the lead in operations whenever possible.* The advantages of having mixed formations of Iraqis working with U.S. (and other Coalition) forces accrue largely from having Iraqis—with their language skills, knowledge of their own people and culture, and greater acceptance by many communities—perform most operations, leaving only major firefights (which should be rare) for the Americans. In addition, the more Iraqi forces are allowed to take the lead the more confidence they will have and the more pride in their jobs they will develop. Today it is still too often the case that American commanders simply decide to do things themselves because they do not trust either the skill or the determination of their Iraqi counterparts, which makes the Iraqis resentful and deprives them of valuable learning experiences.

- *Recreate something like the Iraqi Civil Defense Corps (ICDC), subordinate it to the Ministry of the Interior, and treat it as a locally-based paramilitary force or a gendarmerie.* In nearly every victorious COIN campaign of the past 100 years, a locally-based paramilitary force charged with protecting its own villages, towns and neighborhoods, has been a crucial element of success. The ICDC was just such a force for Iraq, but it has gone through several transformations and its units have now been incorporated into the army, although the mission for which it was created—local area security—remains largely unfilled throughout the country, creating the vacuum in to which the insurgents and militias have moved. Part of the process of filling that vacuum should be recreating an ICDC (or ICDC-like force) and training and equipping it for this mission. Since this mission is much closer to a gendarmerie-function (i.e., a more heavily-armed police force than the Iraqi police) than a conventional military function, it would be ideal for the recreated ICDC to serve under the Ministry of Interior (which will be less desirous of turning it into a conventional military formation, which is exactly what the Ministry of Defense did to the original ICDC) and be trained not by U.S. military personnel, but by European gendarmes, whose missions and operations are much closer to what the mission and activities of the ICDC should be. Italy's superb Carabinieri would make ideal trainers for this force and Rome might see this as a welcome change in Italy's role in Iraq.

- *Make the Department of State, not the Department of Defense (DoD), the U.S. advisor to the Iraqi Ministry of Interior.* Policing functions normally fall within the domain of the Department of State, not Defense. In Iraq, American leaders decided that because the Iraqi police needed to be an adjunct to the overall counterinsurgency effort, they should fall under the jurisdiction of DoD. First, as discussed below, the Iraqi police should not be part of the Ministry of the Interior, although a new Gendarmerie should. Second, DoD's advisory mission to the Ministry of the Interior is badly distorting the development of the Iraqi police towards both a more military culture and more military missions. Although it is true that policing is important to counterinsurgency operations, this is because the counterinsurgents require traditional police skills, not because the police need to serve as part of the military. In other words, the military forces need to be more like the police, not vice versa.

- *Military and civilian boundaries need to be brought into alignment.* This is a constant lesson from the history of COIN operations. Because of the necessity for civilian and military chains of command to work together intimately, it is critical that the same sets of people on the military and civilian sides be responsible for the same areas. When the two are not aligned, and officials constantly have to deal with different counterparts, unity of command inevitably breaks down badly. Thus, either Iraq's 18 provinces need to be grouped to align more closely with the Coalition divisional deployment or, if as seems far more pragmatic, the 18 provinces remain the most reasonable administrative layout, then U.S. and Iraqi forces should develop sub-divisional headquarters that correspond to the 18 provinces so that military and civilian officials (including the Iraqis) always have the same counterparts.

• *To facilitate population control, conduct a nationwide census and create a biometric identification card system.* Population control is another important lesson of COIN campaigns. Because the ability to mingle freely with the population is absolutely vital to insurgents, an important weapon of the government is to prevent such easy interaction. This requires a comprehensive system of population control, so that the insurgents will quickly be exposed by their inability to comply. A nationwide census would not only be useful for political purposes (see Chapter 2), but could also be invaluable in helping identify insurgents and their supporters—and dissuading others from becoming either. Because the goal of such a census should be merely to establish population by age and gender in each household—without any need to get into issues of socio-economic status, education, etc.—it should not be difficult to conduct quickly. (In Saddam's era, he conducted them by having all school teachers go out and canvas an assigned sector on a given day, which should still be feasible today.)

Similarly, a biometric ID card, that would be impossible to forge and useless to steal, would similarly be a major blow to the insurgency because it would make it extremely difficult for insurgents to hide their identities. Such a system could be relatively expensive (on the order of $1 billion), but this would be minor compared to the enormous benefit that it would bring in fighting both insurgents and organized crime, and would pale in comparison to annual American expenditures on Iraq. Many American field-grade officers consider this one of their highest priorities.

TRAINING THE IRAQI ARMED FORCES

The training of Iraqi security forces is progressing better than ever before, but there is still a long way to go before they will be able to shoulder the burden of providing security in Iraq alone. The Bush Administration appears correct in stating that there are a large number of Iraqi troops in various stages of readiness and various capacities to assist in security operations. However, even the 200,000 plus Iraqi security personnel in the field or in the training pipeline are inadequate to the task—as noted above, Iraq probably requires more than twice that number to address the security problems of a failed-state and an insurgency—and, at present, only about a quarter of the 200,000 considered "trained" are actually capable of playing a meaningful role in securing Iraq.

An important and related caveat is that the four-level rating system developed by Multi-National Security Transition Command-Iraq (MNSTCI) and regularly discussed in the media is unhelpful and unrepresentative. Every echelon of the chain of command in Iraq appears to use a different system to rate the readiness of the forces it is training, none appear to correspond easily to one another, and many personnel do not seem to understand the systems used by the echelons above or below them. One level will use colors to denote readiness, another letters, still others use numbers.

Moreover, the rating system used by MNSTCI itself sets the threshold for Iraqi security units too high. Counterinsurgent warfare requires only a small number of truly first-rate forces to serve as a strategic reserve and to conduct what should be rather limited and discrete offensive operations. The vast bulk of security forces are expected to conduct basic defensive missions, particularly area security, which requires far less capability—although it does require basic skills, effective leadership, and a high degree of unit cohesion. Thus, units do not need to reach the highest level of readiness (defined as the capacity to operate fully independently) to play a meaningful role in COIN operations. Plenty of units rated as level 2, or even some rated as level 3, are probably capable of handling their own battlespace while others can still be helpful when working closely with Coalition forces.

With all this in mind, it is probably the case that at this point, roughly 40,000-60,000 Iraqi security force personnel are capable of contributing in some meaningful way to COIN and stability operations in Iraq. Although this is a far cry from the roughly 450,000 that would probably be necessary to secure the country without U.S. military forces, it is not an insignificant number. It represents a very considerable increase over the past year, and since there are more in the pipeline, it suggests that Iraqi forces should be able to pick up more and more of the security burden in coming years.

U.S. military personnel and the MNSTCI must place a much greater emphasis on the selection and training of Iraqi military leaders, especially at tactical levels. Although many factors go into making a military effective, none is more important than the quality of its leadership at all levels. Unfortunately, the leadership of Iraqi security forces is very mixed. There are some intelligent, honest, brave, and patriotic officers, but there appear to be an equal number who are just the opposite. There are sadists, cowards, incompetents, thieves, along with too many whose first loyalty seems to be to the insurgents, the militias, or organized crime rings. The fact that so many unqualified Iraqis remain as leaders of companies, battalions, and brigades, is a major source of weakness. Moreover, it is often difficult to remove them—frequently, they received their commission and their command because they are important political figures or are related

to more senior officers. It is hard for U.S. military personnel to remove even those who do not fall into these categories because Iraq is now a sovereign state and the Americans must often negotiate serious political hurdles to have an Iraqi officer transferred or relieved of his command.

As hard as it may be, improving the quality of Iraq's military leadership is crucial to building Iraqi security forces capable of meeting the nation's problems on their own. *Consequently, the U.S. military command—including, but not limited to MNSTCI—must make it a priority for all Americans training Iraqi formations to identify competent personnel and see them promoted, while systematically removing from positions of authority those unqualified for their commands. All echelons of the chain of command must make this a priority so that lower level personnel will have the support of their superiors when pushing to remove unqualified Iraqi personnel.* Often times, it requires a very senior U.S. military officer to intervene to have an Iraqi company commander removed. Since it is currently not considered a high priority, most senior officers will not bother to intervene to have a lowly Iraqi major sacked, but the U.S. captain assigned to the company may lack the clout to do it himself. Only if the entire U.S. chain of command, up through the colonels and generals, are ready to assist that captain is it likely that the unqualified Iraqi majors will be weeded out.

At the same time, the U.S. training program which is now doing reasonably well at training the combat units themselves, must pay greater attention to the identification and training of Iraqi officers. True leaders take much longer to forge than the units they are to command. Additional training courses need to be added for officers, first to give them the basic soldiering skills that Iraqi officers typically lack; second to provide them with a better grounding in basic civics (and the role of military forces in a democratic society), which almost none of them understand; and last to teach them the art of leadership. At present, some training in all of these areas is provided, but not enough. Officer training is typically timed to the training of their units, so that both can be sent to the field as quickly as possible. As a result, Iraqi officers are not always able to fully absorb these lessons and employ their skills properly. Moreover, greater and longer training is also very helpful in allowing U.S. personnel to observe their Iraqi counterparts and identify both the best and worst among them.

The U.S. and Iraqi high commands must make a much greater effort to create integrated Iraqi security formations. Of the 30–40 best Iraqi battalions available at this time, virtually all are composed of soldiers from a single sect or ethnic group: these units are all Kurd, all Shi'i Arab, or occasionally all Sunni Arab. This has proven necessary because of the need to get some Iraqi formations out in the field and operating alongside Coalition forces promptly; however, it creates problems in the short term and risks in the long term. Many communities are angered by the presence of battalions entirely composed of members of another sect or ethnic group—in particular, Sunni Arab towns and villages react badly to the presence of all-Shi'i Arab units. Since the goal of the deployments is to make the local populace feel safe and supportive of the security presence, this is counterproductive. This is especially true because in many cases these units were simply militia units inducted *in toto* into the Iraqi security forces, given new uniforms and a new name, but little else. Over the long term, such single-sect units could not be counted on to remain loyal to the central government in time of great stress. The Iraqi armed forces must be one of the main centripetal forces to overcome the centrifugal forces that could push the country into civil war. These single-sect units might therefore make civil war more likely if, as seems probable, in a future crisis they chose to honor their loyalty to the leaders of their own sect rather than the central government.

Creating capable integrated units will take a great deal more time, effort and resources, but it is critical to the long-term success of the Iraqi armed forces and therefore the country:

- *Initially, the MNSTCI should concentrate on building up a small number of truly integrated units as élite formations, principally for psychological reasons.* The goal should be to make more Iraqi security personnel want to join these formations.

- *The best personnel must be recruited from all of the existing units of the armed forces.* They must be provided with higher pay and other benefits to coax them into volunteering for integrated units.

- *The integrated units should have longer periods of training with the best Coalition trainers.* It is critical for these units to feel confident in their abilities and to have the time for a sense of unit cohesion to develop. Both argue for a longer training period. Indeed, it might be particularly useful to train these formations outside of Iraq because isolation from the home country and all of the sectarian strife there typically helps breed a sense of "in-group" camaraderie that is important to unit cohesion.

- *Integrated units should be provided with the best equipment.* Indeed, they probably ought to be provided with the full suite of equipment, weaponry, etc., available to U.S. light infantry battalions. Again, it is imperative for the personnel of these units— more than for any other formations in the Iraqi military—to have confidence in their ability to execute their missions. Moreover, because inadequate gear is a constant complaint of Iraqi formations, the integrated battalions should be lavished with equipment so that they feel a degree of "eliteness" and so that other military personnel will want to join the integrated units.

- *Integrated units need to be put into operational situations, at least initially, only when their success is virtually guaranteed.* Although this should be true for all Iraqi security units as they are formed up, it is particularly true for these units. Their cohesion is likely to be fragile, so they need to be brought along slowly with stress applied only in gradual increments. Moreover, it would be disastrous if these units were involved in a military defeat early on, which could shatter the unit and dampen recruitment. By the same token, reports of their successes would likely strengthen their cohesion and improve recruitment.

Although it is not yet a priority, at some point, the United States will have to make building Iraq's military support infrastructure a higher priority if the Iraqi armed forces are to take over full responsibility for securing the country. At present Iraqi forces are wholly reliant on U.S. military forces for combat service support and most combat support functions. The Iraqis have taken the first steps toward eventually taking over their training and command and control systems; however, these are effectively the only areas where they have made any progress and even in these areas it has been very modest. The Iraqis have virtually no capacity to handle logistics, communications, intelligence, personnel, maintenance, medical, or transportation functions on their own, and these services are still almost wholly handled by the Coalition, in reality by the Americans.

This is not a criticism of U.S. policy: a decision was made early on to concentrate on Iraqi combat formations so that they could begin to participate in the fight alongside Coalition units, and this was the right decision. However, given the various limitations from both the American and Iraqi sides, it has meant that combat support and combat service support functions were relegated to very low priorities. Thus, the point is not to object to the current state of affairs, but simply to point out that an important gap exists in this area, and that this gap will have to be filled before the Iraqis are able to secure the country on their own. At present, if the United States (and the American contractors who currently perform nearly all of these functions for the Iraqis) were to withdraw from Iraq, even the 40-80 relatively capable Iraqi combat battalions would quickly be rendered ineffective because of the lack of any support.

Another reason to make support functions a secondary priority is that creating them will require dealing with the corruption and incapacity of the Iraqi ministries of defense and interior. These ministries will be responsible for providing many support functions directly, and controlling all of them after they have been established. However, at present, they are disasters—riddled by corruption, lacking many key personnel, plagued by inappropriate procedures, and manned by the wrong people, many of whom are probably guilty of human rights abuses. Indeed, the problems in the Ministry of Interior, headed during Ja'fari's transitional government by Badr Organization chief Bayan Jabr, are daunting. There have long been accusations that Jabr was bringing large numbers of Badr personnel into the ministry and using his control of it to wage a clandestine war against Iraq's Sunni Arabs, which evidence of secret prisons and torture coupled with reports of assassination squads would appear to substantiate. Consequently, creating Iraq's much needed military support system is going to require cleaning the Augean Stables of these two ministries, and that is unlikely to happen soon.

The training of Iraqi forces must be regularized across the force so that every Iraqi unit gets the right training to perform its mission and in effect the same training as every other unit. Although the creation of MNSTCI and its initial efforts have gone far to provide a standard level and type of basic training for Iraq units, this problem is not yet solved. In particular, in the field, some Iraqi units are trained by highly-qualified U.S. Special Forces personnel, while others are trained by largely unqualified U.S. conventional formations. The U.S. conventional formations often do not employ appropriate counterinsurgent tactics and doctrine themselves and, not surprisingly, therefore do not train their Iraqi charges in it either. Instead, these Iraqi formations get trained in the kind of conventional military operations (even mechanized combat) that are not just inappropriate but downright harmful to their performance in the COIN and stability operations needed in Iraq.

To correct this problem, MNSTCI should:

- *Issue clear guidelines for the procedures and content of field training for Iraqi combat units so that every*

American charged with training Iraqis will have an unequivocal statement of what the Iraqis are expected to learn and how they are to be taught. Obviously, this program should be geared toward proper COIN tactics and doctrine.

- *The U.S. military must make every effort to increase the numbers of Green Berets in Iraq; to use them for training rather than for reconnaissance, as noted above; and to put Special Operations Forces personnel in positions of authority over the various programs to train Iraqi military units.*

- Because of the limited number of Special Forces A Teams in Iraq, the United States has created Military Transition Teams (MITT) composed of conventional U.S. Army soldiers assigned to Iraqi battalions to supplement or substitute for the Green Beret teams. Most of the MITT personnel lack the proper training both in COIN techniques and in how to train Iraqi soldiers. Moreover, the ten-man teams that they are deployed in are far too small to have an impact (in part because rules regarding convoy sizes means that there are rarely enough MITT team personnel to take on more than one or two activities during any given day). *There needs to be a regular program to train the MITT teams before they are deployed and their size must be increased. The United States should establish advisor schools as we did for Vietnam that provide 6-12 month courses taught by officers and NCOs recently returned from serving as advisors in Iraq. All personnel assigned to the MITT teams should first attend one of these programs.*

- The U.S. Army and Marine Corps need to make training Iraqi military personnel highly rewarding for those of their personnel who do so and, especially, do it well. At present, training Iraqi troops is not a career-enhancing goal for ambitious young officers. Indeed, because it comes at the expense of other opportunities, like hunting down insurgents, which the military does reward, the best personnel attempt to avoid it. The result is that within con-

ventional units, it is often the case that the most competent soldiers and officers are not involved in training (and performing basic security missions with) Iraqis, even though that should be a much higher priority than chasing insurgents. *Starting immediately, American personnel should be evaluated for promotion and provided with other incentives to make them want to train and operate with Iraqi forces, and to make them want to help those Iraqi units become more effective and better able to protect their own communities.* Simultaneously, performance in offensive operations, and the misguided detainee counts, should be downgraded as criteria for promotion.

Iraqi units need better access to higher quality equipment based on integration and performance in the field. Another common problem for Iraqi military units is that they are typically deprived of access to first-rate equipment. There are two reasons for this. The first, and less important reason, is that in some cases U.S. units do not have adequate equipment and so their needs are being met before the Iraqis'. This is particularly true for body armor, M-4 carbines, and up-armored Humvees. The more important reason is that U.S. personnel face a dilemma when providing the best equipment to Iraqi army units: Iraqi soldiers frequently sell their equipment on the black market. The result is that they no longer have the equipment, and it generally ends up in the hands of organized crime, the militias, or the insurgency. Consequently, Coalition personnel must choose between properly equipping their Iraqi charges and risk having much of the gear disappear, or giving them lower-quality equipment that they will find it harder to sell (and will matter less if they do so anyway) but in so doing, deprive them of the wherewithal to succeed.

This is a very real problem. There is no silver bullet solution, but neither is it impossible to address. Three criteria should apply:

- *Make Iraqi NCOs responsible for the gear of their enlisted charges.* Good NCOs can make sure that their men don't lose their gear, in large part by making them wish they had never done so in the event that they do.

- *Issue the best gear to the best units.* Those that perform well in combat, that remain loyal to the state, and that don't lose their gear should be rewarded with better equipment.

- *Provide the best equipment to integrated units.* Again, this has more to do with providing incentives for high-caliber personnel to serve in integrated formations, but the point once again is to demonstrate to the Iraqis that the equipment is available to those who demonstrate that they merit it one way or another.

The importance of time. The single greatest problem with all American efforts to train a new Iraqi military has been (and to some extent, continues to be) political pressure to quickly produce more trained Iraqi units to show progress in Iraq. This has been disastrous. The first training program instituted by Maj. Gen. Paul Eaton's team was a perfectly reasonable program, and could have achieved its objectives had the Bush Administration not demanded that he both speed up the training course and increase the numbers of Iraqis trained. Even today, both the Bush Administration and its critics continue to press for accelerated training and a more rapid deployment of Iraqi forces to take over from American soldiers.

This is the worst approach we could take to the training of the new Iraqi armed forces. Our goal should be to expand and intensify the training of Iraqi forces, not accelerate it. *The quality of Iraqi forces is far more important than their quantity if our goal is for the Iraqis to shoulder a greater and greater share of the burden of securing their country in the years ahead. The only way to produce troops sufficiently capable of doing so is to give them the time in both formal and informal training to develop such quality.*

Although the MNSTCI has established a much-needed process of formal training, this alone is inadequate.

The U.S. military would never send its troops straight from basic training into combat. American units are given additional training in small unit tactics, they conduct field exercises, they engage in other forms of training, and are given other opportunities to participate in less-demanding operations before they are committed to battle. The same should be true for the Iraqis, and this has been an important failing of the Coalition, which frequently has taken units fresh from their initial training program and committed them to combat in the name of getting more Iraqi units out into the field. *Dr. Steven Metz has suggested that the United States develop Iraqi equivalents of the National Training Center and Joint Readiness Training Center where Iraqi units could be sent for rigorous field exercises as the capstone to a lengthy process of tactical training similar to that which the U.S. Army employs.*

Like all new military units, even after their formal training is completed, Iraqi formations need time to further gel. Unit cohesion needs to be formed in training, but it is inevitably tested by the first operations that a formation undertakes—so too with the confidence of Iraqi recruits, so too with the leadership skills of their officers. What's more, the process of vetting—weeding out those unsuited for the tasks at hand or those working for the enemy—is a lengthy one, and it is not unusual for soldiers and officers to do well in training but fail once placed in actual combat situations. *For all of these reasons, it is critical that Iraqi units begin their operational tours under the most permissive conditions. They need to crawl before they can walk.* (This is yet another reason to employ a spreading "oil stain" approach, because the secured areas of the oil spot offer exactly such a permissive environment for indigenous forces to gain confidence and operational experience under optimal conditions.)

At least twice since the fall of Baghdad, the United States believed that it had adequately trained and prepared Iraqi security forces only to have them collapse in combat. In April 2004, much of the security forces in southern and central Iraq melted away when confronted by the revolt of Muqtada as-Sadr's Mahdi

Army. Similarly, in November 2004, Coalition personnel believed that the Iraqi security forces around Mosul were doing fine—they had gone through the existing training programs, were deployed in and around the city, and seemed to be doing an excellent job maintaining law and order. However, that month, Sunni insurgents mounted a series of major attacks and these Iraqi security forces evaporated—all except one (mostly Kurdish) battalion that stood and fought with the Americans.

The nagging question plaguing Iraq's security forces is "how can we be sure that this latest force, which also seems to be fully capable and participating in combat operations, does not fall apart like its predecessors did in southern Iraq in April 2004 and around Mosul in November 2004?" The only answer to that question is "time." The more time we give Iraqi formations to train, conduct exercises and operate first in conditions that favor success, the more likely they will be to survive their first taste of real combat.

FIGHTING THE INSURGENCY BETTER

Although the threat from Sunni insurgents in western Iraq should be considered as a lesser priority than the threat from Shi'i and Sunni militias in central and southern Iraq, it obviously cannot be ignored. Similarly, although the U.S. and Iraqi governments have mistakenly made this their highest priority, their conduct of this campaign still leaves much to be desired. Many of the practices that need to be altered have already been discussed under "Tactical Changes" above, but a number of additional points are worth making.

Keeping in mind the bottom line. A large insurgency that commands the (passive) support of a significant portion of the population can only be defeated by a balanced strategy blending military, political, and economic elements. *It is critical to adapt a true COIN strategy that protects the people, trains indigenous forces, and disrupts insurgent operations. However, it is equally important that behind the protection of these military operations there is an aggressive political-economic pro-gram designed to eliminate the underlying grievances of those supporting the insurgency.* Without all elements of this strategy, the insurgency will persist, and might even prevail. Thus, none of the suggestions listed below will defeat the insurgency either by themselves or merely in conjunction with the others. There must be an integrated approach in which political, military and economic programs build off one another.

Harness Iraq's Sunni tribal patronage system. As noted previously, Sunni tribesmen acting as the Sunni equivalent of the Shi'i militias make up the bulk of the insurgency. Because they act out of more mundane motivations (fear, greed, anger) than either the Salafi Jihadists or the small number of hardcore Ba'thists still at large, it is possible to imagine ending their participation in the insurgency in the way that is not possible for the two smaller groups of fanatics. The best way to do this would be to essentially "buy-off" the Sunni tribal shaykhs.

Although our intelligence remains sketchy, it is clear that an important element of our problems with the insurgency comes from the active participation or passive acceptance by a huge range of Sunni shaykhs. In some cases, they appear to be ordering the young men under their authority to take up arms against the United States and the new regime because they feel politically and economically excluded from it (and they are well aware of the corruption of the new government), because they do fear a Shi'i dictatorship, and because no one is paying them not to. In other cases, they simply make no effort to stop their tribesmen and followers from participating because they have no incentive to do so.

However, for centuries, the central government in Baghdad successfully paid these shaykhs to cooperate with the regime rather than fight against it. This seems unpalatable to American ears, but it is part of Iraq's societal traditions. The tribes of the west and south were never fully under central government control and would often fight against it or simply ignore its efforts to establish law and order unless they were paid not to do so. But in return for such payments—which could come in the form of government contracts, infrastructure development, and other forms of aid, not just cash—the shaykhs generally were content to avoid attacks on the government and even to keep order in those areas effectively beyond Baghdad's control.

In the twentieth century, the shaykhs were often paid not to attack and even to police the roads, bridges, power lines, and pipelines the insurgency currently targets. When relations between the shaykhs and Baghdad soured, attacks on this infrastructure invariably increased.

Moreover, the shaykhs have shown a willingness to "do business" with a wide range of governments in Baghdad: the Ottomans, the British-backed monarchy, various Iraqi military dictators, and Saddam's Stalinist tyranny. Of course, all of these regimes were Sunni-dominated, at least on the façade, and it does remain to be seen whether they would give such fealty to a Shi'ah-led government, but there is every reason to expect that, coupled with an effort to increase Sunni tribal representation in the new government, the Sunni shaykhs would be willing to decrease or even end their support for the insurgency. To a great extent, it would mean giving this segment of the Sunni community a real stake in the success of the new Iraqi government and doing so in a very material way.

Indeed, anecdotal reporting indicates that whenever American military and political personnel have reached out to local Sunni shaykhs, and provided them with tangible incentives to cooperate, they have been willing to do so, at least on a selective basis. This too provides evidence that it should be possible to co-opt many, perhaps most, of the Sunni tribal shaykhs and get them to stop fighting us and instead help us.

Even if we were to successfully find ways of buying off the Sunni tribal shaykhs, we should not expect this to end the insurgency altogether. The Sunni shaykhs probably could convince a significant number of their followers to desist, either by using their authority, or by using the patronage they would in turn buy among their people with the resources we would be paying them. However, because the insurgency is so diverse, others would likely fight on: the foreign fighters, of course; homegrown Salafi Jihadists, of whom there is also a significant number; true Ba'thist (or, more properly, Saddamist) "dead-enders" who have so much blood on their hands that they could never expect anything but a hangman's noose from a new, democratic Iraqi government; and a number of others of diverse motives. But it is clear that this would be a greatly diminished cohort and that the insurgency would be much easier to manage without this vast core of support.

Inaugurate an amnesty program to make it attractive for insurgents who wish to give up the fight to do so. The amnesty program must be comprehensive, and cannot have any loopholes—nor should the government try to exploit any that exist. The benefit of the program comes from the propaganda value of making insurgents believe that their lives will be better by leaving the insurgency. For this to work, they cannot have any reservations about whether the amnesty pledge will be honored, which would only add to the fear that they would be caught and killed by their fellow guerrillas for deserting the cause. Ideally, as the Iraqi economy begins to rebound, the amnesty program should also include guarantees of job training and assistance finding employment and housing, so that the immediate material needs of those turning themselves in are met.

Expand the current catch-and-release program. Historically, counterinsurgency campaigns have benefited considerably from catch-and-release programs whereby low-level insurgents—and those whose guilt seems likely but not proven—are freed after an initial round of interrogation and an effort to recruit them to serve as informants. The goal of these programs is to breed distrust among the insurgents, making them wonder how many of those captured and released agreed to serve as spies. Because secrecy is vital to an insurgency, this kind of distrust, and the infighting and purges it breeds, can be devastating.

In Iraq, such a program exists, but it has not been employed to the extent that it should—far too many "little fish" or suspected insurgents are kept in confinement for long periods in hope of either convincing them to confess or preventing them from rejoining the insurgency. This approach is misguided in two ways. First, *it is far more important to avoid antagonizing the innocent than it is to catch the guilty; insurgencies are not defeated by killing or capturing all of the insurgents, but by turning the population against them.* Every false arrest turns too many Iraqis against us, and may even generate more new recruits for the insurgency than were taken into custody. Second, creating distrust within the ranks of the insurgency through a large scale catch-and-release program is a far more effective way to hamper the effectiveness of the guerrillas than the vast majority of military operations conducted against them employing whatever information might eventually be gleaned from these detainees. Anecdotal information suggests that it is frequently the case that far more insurgents can be eliminated by internal feuds and purges than by COIN operations. Consequently, Coalition forces in Iraq should not only try to minimize the numbers of Iraqis they detain, but should quickly release (after initial interrogation and an effort to turn any confirmed insurgents) all but high-level insurgents.

A Conditional Schedule for Withdrawal of U.S. Forces

Critics of the Bush Administration have proposed a variety of different methods of withdrawing American forces from Iraq. In general, this is not an optimal course of action either for the United States or for Iraq, but some proposals are better than others.

Establishing a firm *timetable* for withdrawing American forces from Iraq, especially one envisioning such a withdrawal within 6–24 months would be a tragic mistake. It is highly unlikely that Iraq's political or military institutions will be ready to hold the country together in that amount of time. Consequently, the most likely result would be civil war.

Moreover, were we to set a certain date for our withdrawal, the problem is not so much the reaction of our enemies (the idea that they would simply wait for us to leave and then resume their attacks seems unlikely since it flies in the face of the insurgents' various goals), but the reaction of our friends. We must keep in mind that Iraqi politicians are themselves extremely frightened about the possibility of civil war—and that is true even for those most committed to a secular, democratic Iraq. *If these leaders believed that the Americans would be gone at some point in the next few years, since they know full well that their political and military institutions are incapable of providing sustainable stability and prevent civil war, they would immediately try to cut deals with whatever insurgent group or militia was most likely to protect and reward them after the Americans left.* The result would be to make civil war a self-fulfilling prophecy.

One alternative is for a conditional schedule in which clear benchmarks would be established and, eventually, the achievement of these milestones would trigger various levels of American disengagement. The key difference is that no particular dates would be associated with any of the benchmarks, thereby preserving the freedom of maneuver that Washington and Baghdad need, and reassuring skittish Iraqi politicians that the United States will stay until they are in a position to effectively govern their country.

Ideally, the United States should refrain from taking even this course. Many of these benchmarks may seem reasonable when proposed but could turn out to be unrealistic later, which might lock the United States into doing something it realized it shouldn't, or else reneging on a deal made with both the people of America and the government of Iraq. However, there is at least one excellent reason to do so—if the Iraqis ask us to. In Cairo in November 2005, the Arab League endorsed just such a conditional schedule. While the Arab League counts for little, it is entirely possible that Iraqi politicians in the new government will feel pressure from their constituencies to assure them both that the Americans will be leaving and when they will be leaving. In this case, such a conditional schedule would be an excellent way to reassure the Iraqis that the United States did not intend to stay indefinitely, while likewise clarifying what steps Iraq would need to take to make such a withdrawal possible.

MEASURING SUCCESS

Congress and the press have an unenviable task during this war. Setting aside ulterior motives such as narrow political gain or financial profit, it is their responsibility to oversee the prosecution of the war and keep the Administration from squandering American lives through mistaken policy and strategy. However, guerrilla warfare is inherently difficult to quantify or otherwise keep track of. Members of both the legislature and the media have resorted to calls for "metrics" that they hope will provide them concrete standards against which to judge the success of U.S. military operations in Iraq, and so hold the Administration and the military accountable for "failure."

Although this is a perfectly understandable approach to take, it is also misguided. An emphasis on concrete metrics or benchmarks of success is impossible in warfare, and most impossible of all in insurgent warfare. History is lousy with examples of battles, campaigns, and wars in which numbers proved meaningless to victory or defeat. In conventional combat, some numbers can be useful for planning purposes, although they rarely hold up during the course of actual operations. In insurgent warfare, however, metrics are rarely even useful for planning.

Historically, only two sets of numbers seem to bear up as useful in thinking about COIN operations. The first is the "canonical" figure of 20 security personnel per thousand of population as the right approximate figure for how many COIN personnel are required to defeat an insurgency. The second is properly-asked and carefully-tracked public opinion surveys. Since the people's allegiance is the center of gravity in insurgent warfare, closely measuring popular sentiments and support for the war can be very useful in knowing

which side is winning. Of course, there are a great many potential pitfalls: questions can be asked improperly; the Iraqis often give misleading answers, either because they say what they believe the pollster wants to hear or they believe that this is their chance to speak truth to power and so overstate their answers; data can be sorted incorrectly; and samples can be inadequate or inappropriate. However, properly employed and properly interpreted, regular public opinion polling can be very revealing about which way the population is leaning. Beyond these two metrics, however, few numbers have any real relevancy to counterinsurgency warfare.

Moreover, placing too much of an emphasis on such metrics can be very harmful to the prosecution of a COIN campaign. The desire for a method of measuring progress in Vietnam led to reliance on the body count, among other wrong-headed numbers that were generated for the operations research offices of the Vietnam-era Pentagon. The same emphasis has produced the dangerous reliance on a detainee count in Iraq today. Such efforts create perverse incentives for military personnel, causing them to take actions like raiding and arresting whole villages or neighborhoods in the hope of pushing up their detainee count.

Thus the more that Congress and the media press the Administration for "metrics" of success in Iraq, admirable though this may seem, the more likely they are to actually harm the war effort. Unfortunately, victory in a counterinsurgency war is a lot like Justice Potter Stewart's famous definition of obscenity—you know it when you see it. And you can't know it any other way.

PREVENTING A "TOO LITTLE, TOO LATE" FAILURE

The prevailing scholarship of the Vietnam war holds that the critical failing of the United States during that conflict was that it refused to make anything but tactical changes to its strategic approach to the war until it was too late. Although the CORDS and Phoenix programs were highly effective counterinsurgency programs, the United States waited too long to adopt them, and by the time we did, the war was effectively over because the American people had already decided that the conflict was no longer worth the cost in lives and treasure.

Comparisons between Iraq and Vietnam are often more confusing than enlightening, but in this case the analogy is an apt warning. The Bush Administration and the U.S. armed forces have made numerous changes in Iraq over the course of the past two-and-a-half years, but they have been unwilling to make the kind of major reorientation that is required. In particular, as in Vietnam, they have refused to adopt a true COIN approach in all of its strategic and tactical dimensions. There is no reason that U.S. forces cannot quickly accept and prosecute a COIN strategy, as they did during that earlier conflict. The only question is whether they are willing to make the difficult political decision to admit that their earlier approach has not produced decisive results and is unlikely to do so—and whether the military commanders are willing to jettison the baggage of the U.S. Army's dislike of COIN techniques.

If America's leaders are willing to put aside these petty obstacles and embrace a realistic counterinsurgency strategy there is every reason to believe that we can overcome both the insurgency and the problems arising from Iraq's status as a failed-state—crime, the militias, and all of the economic and political problems that flow from them. If the United States is unwilling to do so, it seems unlikely that we will be able to create the kind of security environment that is a prerequisite for the successful reconstruction of Iraq.

II. Building a New Iraqi Political System

Securing Iraq is a necessary condition for success, but it is hardly sufficient. It is not sufficient because the goal of security is merely to make possible Iraq's political and economic reconstitution. That is the principal project of reconstruction. Thus it is vital that the United States help develop a new political system that will have the trust of all Iraqis. This new political system must convince Iraqis that there are effective, non-violent means to address their problems; that they will not have to fear that others will use violence against them; that they will have an equal opportunity to pursue a better life for themselves and their families; and that the state has institutions capable of addressing all of their country's needs. This is the foundation of the compact between a people and their government, and which defines the government's legitimacy.

In the specific circumstances of Iraq today, *these* requirements—not how many people turned out to vote in the election—will define the legitimacy of the new government. Any Iraqi government that cannot begin to deliver on them, no matter how many votes it may have won in elections, will be seen as illegitimate by the people. In the most immediate sense, it comes down to whether the new Iraqi government will be able to start improving the lives of the Iraqi people through higher employment, more constant electricity, more readily available clean water and gasoline, and the security that underpins all of these necessities.

Of course, the many missteps of the United States and the various Iraqi governments that followed Saddam's fall have left many Iraqis discouraged, and have opened the door for opponents of reconstruction, like Muqtada as-Sadr and the remnant of the Ba'th party, to propose their own alternatives. They are attempting to demonstrate that they can provide the necessities that Iraqis crave better than the Americans and the new central government can. Thus the risk we face is not just that political reconstruction will fail, but that in failing it will make it possible for chauvinist groups aligned with the insurgency and the militias to gain the support of large sectors of the Iraqi population, likely leading to eventual civil war.

This situation is hardly novel. Historian Richard Clutterbuck noted in his work on counterinsurgencies in Malaya and Vietnam that in Malaya the British realized that the key to the war was maintaining the support of the Malay people, and that this meant providing for them better than the Communists. As Clutterbuck notes of Britain's Lieutenant General Sir Harold Briggs, who authored the famous plan bearing his name:

> In his first directive, Briggs put his finger on what this war was really about—a competition in government. He aimed not only to resettle the squatters but to give them a standard of local government and a degree of prosperity that they would not wish to exchange for the barren austerity of life under the

Communists' parallel hierachy; in other words, to give them something to lose.[1]

Of course, America's goals in Iraq must extend beyond merely defeating the insurgents as the British did in Malaya, we must also stave off the risk of full-scale governmental collapse by creating a new political system that is capable of holding the country together without massive external assistance. However, the goal is ultimately the same: we and our Iraqi allies have failed to deliver on the promises of good government and prosperity, leaving Iraqis angry and open to the siren-song of fringe elements that can deliver on at least some basic necessities, and so are beating us in the competition for hearts and minds.

Of course, the failure to deliver on basic necessities is only one manifestation of the various problems besetting the Iraqi body politic. There are many others. However, for the sake of prioritization, and because this list is not intended to be comprehensive but rather to focus on what is most important (and how to address it), it is worth concentrating on four key problems in the realm of politics.

First, Iraq is now a deeply divided society and those divisions are creating animosity, fueling the violence, and preventing the efficient functioning of the Iraqi government. There were always divisions in Iraq, and it was always the case that after Saddam's fall the sectarian extremists were going to be the best organized and most willing to use violence, thereby giving them advantages. However, the United States exacerbated these problems by employing explicit quotas for the different denominations, allowing identity to become the dominant force in politics early on, and reaching out to many of the worst of the sectarian groups to serve in the new occupation-sponsored authorities. *Consequently, sectarian divisions have become far more prevalent and entrenched than they were in the past, and in the absence of a general program of national reconciliation or a broader power-sharing arrangement, they are*

tearing apart Iraq's large, peaceful, and integrated center—including allowing foreign Salafi Jihadists to turn the violent resistance of Iraq's minority Sunni community into a fairly deadly insurgency. Moreover, they have so far precluded the adoption of a workable constitution that might allow the Iraqi government to begin to address some of the country's many problems.

Second, Iraq's central government is now fully-constituted but essentially powerless. It lacks the resources or the governmental institutions to tackle any of the challenges facing the country without massive external assistance. Iraq's ministries are understaffed and eviscerated by endemic corruption of a kind that Iraqis believe compares unfavorably even with Saddam's despicable regime. Corruption has diverted much of Iraq's oil revenue from reconstruction to the bank accounts of government officials and their friends in organized crime. Iraq's local governments, originally founded by the U.S.-led Coalition in the immediate aftermath of the fall of Baghdad—and a critical element in a proper bottom-up approach to reconstruction—have largely been cut-off and neglected. The failings of Iraq's ministries have hamstrung the development of new military capabilities, reduced the amount of funding available, prevented the development of careful plans for reconstruction, and frightened investment capital out of the country.

Third, Iraq's political parties have only tenuous connections to the Iraqi people and mostly limit their interaction with their nominal constituents. This too is a product of American mistakes in the wake of the fall of Baghdad. By bringing to office political exiles and extremist groups neither of which truly represented the will of the Iraqi people (and in many cases were unknown to them), we created a political élite that did not come to power via a popular mandate and were, in fact, threatened by true leaders emerging from the people. As a result, Iraq's current leaders have mostly spent their time haggling over the division of power within the government and snuffing out any

---

1 Clutterbuck, op.cit, p. 57.

legitimate efforts by charismatic figures to organize new political movements that would genuinely represent the will of the Iraqi people. This disconnect has helped hinder the provision of basic necessities to the Iraqi people, warped Iraq's decision-making, and soured many Iraqis towards their own leadership.

Fourth, the United States, the principal occupying power and the driving force behind reconstruction lacks the personnel, the capabilities, the know-how, and even some of the resources to rebuild the Iraqi nation. Nevertheless, the Bush Administration's policy choices have effectively prevented the United Nations from playing a greater role in Iraq. That, as well as the security threats in Iraq, has also kept many Non-Governmental Organizations (NGOs) from participating in this effort. This is highly problematic because UN agencies and NGOs possess valuable skills and capabilities needed for nation-building.

POLITICAL REFORM IN IRAQ: A STRATEGIC VIEW

In the military and security realm, the United States developed a coherent strategy for tackling the problems of Iraq but, unfortunately, it has proven to be inappropriate. In the case of the political reconstruction of Iraq, the problem has been even more basic: the United States never developed a coherent political strategy capable of addressing the four basic challenges listed above. To a considerable extent, the failure of political reconstruction stems from the mistaken American prewar assumptions that nation-building would not be necessary in Iraq, which meant that no coherent plan for political reconstruction was available to guide the process from the beginning.

As a result, U.S. efforts have been disconnected, disjointed, scattershot, and have failed to accomplish even their highest priorities. *This is why the Administration is wrong to tout the elections that have been held in Iraq as constituting meaningful political progress. To date, none of the Iraqi governments born of these elections has been able to address any of Iraq's deep-seated problems.*

If the new Iraqi government, which is supposed to be the final product, is to do a better job in meeting these challenges than its predecessor governments, both the United States and the Iraqis are going to have to make a number of major changes.

This then must be the starting point for such a strategy for political reform in Iraq. However, there are several other critical considerations that must be considered. First, there is the increasing fragility of Iraqi public opinion and the threat that if Iraqis do not see their new government providing a material improvement in their daily circumstances—especially in those areas that matter most to them, unemployment, electricity, gasoline, clean water, sanitation, and security—they may begin to defect to the insurgents and militias in much larger numbers. (Most Iraqis probably would not cast their lot with the insurgents or militias in the belief that doing so would enhance reconstruction, but because it would be their only viable economic option or because the fear of imminent attack by rival groups pushed them to join in self-defense).

The second circumstance that must be factored into a strategy for political reform is the need to move to a revised military strategy employing traditional counterinsurgency methods. Such strategies demand the complete meshing of political, economic, and military activities at every level. In addition, it means that security and economic life will revive and progress very unevenly across the country with those areas where pacification is being applied seeing rapid progress and other areas experiencing less progress, or possibly even regressing because of a diminution of the security presence there.

Conceived broadly, a new approach to political reform in Iraq should consist of six interlocking processes.

1. National reconciliation. This is the one aspect of political reform where the U.S. government cannot be faulted for a lack of effort or creativity. That effort must be maintained. What needs to change, however, is the context in which national reconciliation and power-sharing talks are framed. It is hard to see what more the United States could do within this process; what we can change are other factors outside it but which impinge upon it because they shape the perspective of the various actors in terms of the costs, risks, and benefits of cutting a realistic deal.

2. *Decentralizing power.* Because Iraq's political leaders are consumed with their discussions over power-sharing, because many of them often care little about their constituents, and because Iraq's ministries are virtually powerless, it is critical to shift authority and resources away from the sinkhole of Baghdad and out to local governments that might be able to start delivering on the basic necessities Iraqis crave.

3. *Building central state capacity.* Decentralization can only ever be part of the solution. Ultimately, no matter how federalized Iraq becomes, only a central government will be able to handle certain key services—such as national security, foreign policy, and the direction of the nationwide oil system. Consequently, the United States must simultaneously help build the capacity of Iraqi governmental institutions, in particular by developing a comprehensive program to fight the corruption that is the single greatest factor crippling the central government.

4. *Reforming Iraqi politics and political parties.* Iraqi politicians have only ever known corrupt, predatory, and "winner-takes-all" politics. It is little surprise, therefore, that they are behaving in such a manner. Recognizing the dysfunctional norms with which the reconstruction period began should underscore even more boldly the need to create extensive oversight and institutions that enforce strong accountability. Iraqi institutions need to be structured so that they are continually oriented in the direction of the public good.

As noted above, there are two basic problems with the nature of Iraqi politics at present: Iraq's political élite is not terribly interested in the problems of the larger population, and the unhappiness of the masses adds an important edge to élite squabbles over power and wealth. Because most Iraqis are unhappy with their current lot, they encourage their political leaders to fight for more—thinking that this will ultimately trickle down to improve their lives. Of course, the leaders themselves do not need much encouragement to fight this battle, but being able to say that their people support them is very useful. Thus, the unhappiness of the people is an excuse that the political élites can use to justify pressing for unreasonable demands. To combat this, *Iraqi politicians need to have stronger incentives to be responsive to their constituents' priorities. This will help force them to spend more time providing basic necessities and less time scrapping among themselves.* To the extent that the Iraqi people are happier, this too should diminish the ability of the political leadership to rouse them to support extreme positions. Similarly, Iraqi political leaders need to see clear incentives for forging cross-ethnic and cross-sect coalitions. *Iraqi politics needs to shift from being identity-driven to being issues-driven,* which will allow a loosening of the deadlock among the current parties by introducing a new range of issues that could forge novel alliances and break up old, identity-based ones. Finally, fostering the emergence of new parties that truly represent the Iraqi people and are concerned about issues, not identity, can reinforce all of the above trends.

5. *Revising Iraq's oil distribution systems.* Iraq's oil can be a blessing or a curse. At present, it is mostly a curse because it simply fuels the vicious infighting among political élites who often are merely looking for a bigger (illegal) cut of Iraq's oil revenue. Iraq's oil revenue must be turned into a blessing by using it to create incentives related to the political reforms listed above: forcing Iraqi politicians to care about and be answerable to their constituents; allowing for the decentralization of power beyond Baghdad; and easing the process of national reconciliation by removing oil as an issue to be fought over.

6. Bringing in additional international assistance.
While this would always have been a positive, its importance has increased dramatically thanks to the failures of the past two-and-a-half years. The UN, NGOs and foreign governments have critical personnel and know-how to help build Iraqi political institutions and thus create more capable local and central government functions. Similarly, international organizations have highly relevant experience building political parties and guiding political processes toward becoming more transparent, accountable, and representative. Finally, as is now apparent, *the United States is increasingly wearing out its welcome in Iraq, and shifting to a more international approach would likely allow us to prolong the process of externally-assisted reconstruction longer than will a continuing U.S.-dominated approach.*

The Bush Administration will no doubt suggest that it has been pursuing some of these objectives already. There is certainly some truth to this claim; however, many of the specific efforts to achieve some of these objectives have left much to be desired, and there has been no effort to integrate these various efforts and guide them toward the implementation of a larger strategy. American implementation has been extremely uneven, demonstrating a lack of understanding at the highest levels as to how these various processes must work in unison if they are to have any chance of sparking real changes to the nascent Iraqi political system.

Caveat Number One: The Changed Political Environment. None of this would have been easy even if it had been planned for before the invasion and properly implemented afterwards. Unfortunately though, current conditions in Iraq are likely to make it that much harder to implement. Specifically, the December 15, 2005 elections have produced a new Iraqi government that is supposed to be fully sovereign, permanent, and capable of running the country alone. In truth, it is none of these—the last least of all. However, the reality may be less important than the perception. Many of the changes proposed below are

going to be painful for Iraq and even more so for Iraq's current political élite, which of course is both the product, and partial cause, of so many of the problems that must be solved. Moreover, the repeated failings and mistakes of the United States have considerably eroded Iraqi good will toward their liberators. All of which suggests that *U.S. representatives in Baghdad will face a very tough fight in having these changes (or any far-reaching reforms) adopted by the new government.*

This is an important consideration to bear in mind. Steering the development of Iraq's political system is likely to grow more and more difficult for the United States. This is particularly true if the United States follows the various recommendations contained in this report. Reforming Iraqi politics so that they provide the necessary framework for Iraqi security, stability and prosperity will mean taking a number of actions that will threaten the interests of many of Iraq's current powerbrokers—and they are likely to fight these U.S. initiatives. The further the United States is willing to push Iraq in positive directions, the harder the militia leaders, insurgents, crime bosses, religious fundamentalists, and corrupt politicians will push back.

Of course, the United States will not be powerless, especially not as long as there are upwards of 100,000 American troops in the country and Washington is providing billions of dollars in reconstruction aid. But the fight will be a hard one, even for someone who has proven as skillful as U.S. Ambassador Zalmay Khalilzad in directing this process. The United States will have to start treating Iraq as a sovereign, foreign government, threatening to withhold aid, or take other steps that the Iraqis dislike, to coax them to do the right things. Moreover, it may require frequent public remonstrations by Ambassador Khalilzad, Secretary Rice or even the White House, to expose which Iraqis are opposing measures that are for the best of the Iraqi nation as a whole. In general, it will require a far more sophisticated and nuanced approach to handling Iraq than we have needed in the past.

Caveat Number Two: Short-Term Expediency vs. The Long-Term Good. While critics like to mock the Bush Administration's grandiose visions of a utopian new Iraq, since the fall of Baghdad nearly all of America's mistakes have come not from reaching for the stars, but from a mistaken overemphasis on what was expedient. It is certainly the case that the Bush Administration badly misunderstood Iraqi society and what would be necessary to rebuild its political (and economic and military) systems after the fall of Saddam Hussein's regime. Unfortunately, the Administration compounded this original sin with a number of mistakes born of the opposite inclination—to find workable, short-term solutions that would create some degree of immediate stability in which to work out longer-term solutions. However, those short-term solutions have created countless problems of their own and have thus far succeeded in making it impossible to develop (let alone implement) the kinds of changes that would be necessary to create good government for the long-term.

For instance, in the summer of 2003, when it became evident that the United States had created a security vacuum and lacked the troops (or the orders) to properly fill it, the Administration imprudently rushed the creation of an Iraqi Governing Council (IGC) to quickly put an Iraqi face on reconstruction to deflect criticism away from the United States, bring in Iraqis who might know more about how to run the country than American bureaucrats, and delegitimize the fledgling insurgency. Although there should have been an Iraqi component to the U.S. occupation from the start, the creation of the IGC suffered from the hastiness of its organization. The Administration filled the IGC with the Iraqis it knew—exiled politicians (some of whom were well-meaning) without any constituencies in Iraq and Shi'i chauvinists who represented (in

many cases) the worst aspirations of their community.[2] We have been paying for this mistake ever since. It is no surprise that these groups have spent most of their time squabbling over the division of power (and spoils) in Baghdad, pay little attention to what is happening outside the Green Zone, have proven in many cases to be corrupt, and work relentlessly to prevent the emergence of more legitimate, representative and moderate leaders around the country. It is perhaps fitting that the only solution that many can now suggest to this problem is to bring in equally dangerous Sunni chauvinists to try to balance things out.

Today, a certain degree of expediency is absolutely essential, in large measure because Iraqi public opinion towards reconstruction has become fragile and therefore it is critical that the central government (and the Americans) be seen to deliver on their major concerns this year. Nevertheless, *we must do a much better job balancing short-term versus long-term needs.* Emphasizing short-term needs has not served us well so far. Most of the problems that this chapter discusses arose from earlier decisions based on expediency. Solving them will require undertaking a series of reforms that will be much more difficult, and require a much greater emphasis on what is best for Iraq over the long-term. Of necessity, they will require longer periods of time to make their impact felt, thus there is both a need, and an opportunity, to embark on broader programs of political reform to bring Iraq out of the doldrums into which it has drifted. Fareed Yasseen has wisely observed that the initial mistakes of the United States were to base decisions principally on general practices of management and governance without regard for the specifics of Iraq; since then, because these initial measures failed, the United States has swung in the opposite direction of treating Iraq almost entirely based on what seemed to work within its own dynamics. What is really needed is

---

2   Again, the Kurds should be mostly exempted from this list. Although there certainly are problems with the Patriotic Union of Kurdistan (PUK) and the Kurdistan Democratic Party (KDP), they cannot be lumped together with either the exiles or the Shi'i chauvinists who still largely dominate Iraq's political leadership. Unhappiness over corruption and the slow pace of true democratization aside, the vast majority of Kurds accept Massoud Barzani and Jalal Talabani as their principal leaders. Thus the Kurdish leaders had precisely the kind of political support among their communities that the others largely lacked, especially at the time of the creation of the IGC. Indeed, even in the case of SCIRI, most Shi'ah voted for them because they were well known, not necessarily well-beloved. Moreover, the Kurdish leaders have shown a willingness to fight for what is best for their constituencies (and for Iraq) that is often absent among most other Iraqi political figures.

a proper balance of the two—general practices of good governance, tailored to Iraq's specific circumstances.

POWER SHARING AND NATIONAL RECONCILIATION

Iraq's political problems start with the many differences among, and within, its different communities and the paralysis this has injected into the process of creating a new Iraqi political system. Like security, some form of national reconciliation coupled with a new power-sharing arrangement is a necessary precondition for any progress in Iraq. As Raad Alkadiri has repeatedly warned, like security, national reconciliation will not solve all Iraq's problems, but the absence of national reconciliation will make it impossible to solve any of Iraq's problems.

Iraq's power brokers have so far defied two-and-a-half years of efforts by Iraqis, Americans, and international representatives to forge a new political compact among them. Thus, while it is true that this is one area where the Bush Administration has made an effort commensurate with the importance of the issue—and Ambassador Khalilzad has demonstrated that he is a master of precisely this sort of political maneuvering—it is still the case that the United States is far from having achieved its objectives.

Iraq has no Nelson Mandela or Vaclav Havel—a figure so universally admired that he could become a unifying force and help the various factions to make compromises. Ayatollah Ali Al-Sistani, for all his stature and well-meaning efforts, is not such a figure. While he is probably the only figure who can transcend the differences among the various Shi'i groups, he cannot do so for the Sunni Arabs, the Kurds, or Iraq's other minorities. Consequently, it would be foolish to go fishing for such a personage, as some commentators have suggested. Unfortunately, the United States is going to have to find another solution to the current impasse.

Typically, there are two ways to deal with difficult negotiations. The first is to find a solution within the negotiations by convincing one side or the other to make a salient concession and then using that to squeeze a corresponding concession out of the other side. That is the approach the United States has tried so far and it has borne some fruit, but it has not succeeded in producing the kind of national accord on power-sharing that is needed. The other method is to try to change the position of the parties themselves by changing the external context in which they are negotiating. *This is where the United States now needs to make a much greater effort.* Given current circumstances, none of the parties in Iraq appears willing to budge on its bottom line—and these bottom lines appear to be mutually incompatible. The key, therefore, is to change the circumstances for each of the parties to make them willing to accept less than the maximal positions they have so far clung to. In every case, the parties have been unwilling to budge from their positions because they fear that their situation will worsen dramatically by doing so. The best way to break this logjam is to make them less fearful and find other ways to meet their demands outside of the power-sharing negotiations.

Bringing the Sunnis back in. The Bush Administration has made its greatest effort in trying to co-opt Iraq's wayward Sunni Arab community, and their efforts have certainly paid some dividends, most notably in the high Sunni participation in the December 2005 elections and their likely role in the new Iraqi government coalition. However, these accomplishments need to be seen in their proper context. As President Bush correctly observed in November 2005,[3] the insurgency is composed of a number of different groups, and while the media (and the military) tend to focus on the most virulent groups—the Salafi Jihadists and the former Ba'thists—the largest and most important group are the Sunni tribals who are participating in the insurgency largely because they were deprived of

---

3 Speech by President George W. Bush, "President Outlines Strategy for Victory in Iraq," The White House, November 30, 2005, available at <http://www.whitehouse.gov/news/releases/2005/11/20051130-2.html>.

their privileged position by the U.S. invasion, and who fear that the Shi'ah and Kurds (whom they believe the United States is determined to leave in control of the country) will use their position within the Iraqi government to oppress Iraq's Sunni community just as they were oppressed under Saddam's Sunni-dominated regime. In addition, the tribal Sunnis have thus far felt completely shut out of the process of government and deprived of the patronage that they typically received from Baghdad in the past. Over the past two-and-a-half years, they have seen Shi'ah and, to a lesser degree, Kurds running Iraqi ministries very much for their own benefit and that of their families, friends, tribes, etc. The decision by many Sunni leaders to participate in the December 2005 elections stemmed as much from a desire to get control over at least some Iraqi ministries both as a weapon to prevent the Shi'ah and Kurds from oppressing them and as a vehicle for patronage (i.e. graft) so that they can get a piece of Iraq's pie and not allow it to be devoured entirely by the Shi'ah and Kurds. This is far from the progressive realization that violence does not serve the Sunni community's purposes that the Administration would like to portray it as.

At the heart of the matter is the fact that many Sunni Arabs feel alienated from the process of political reconstruction by the Shi'ah, the Americans, and, to a lesser extent, the Kurds. The arbitrary and excessive U.S. edicts regarding de-Ba'thification; placing the de-Ba'thification program in the hands of Ahmed Chalabi, who has reportedly used it in arbitrary fashion to advance his own interests; and the sudden disbanding of the army and the security services, all struck deeply at tribal Sunnis. These measures had their greatest impact upon the officers and senior bureaucrats of the old regime, who were generally important members of Sunni tribes. They once had dignity, power, wealth, and patronage—and were suddenly stripped of all that. Not surprisingly, many went home and either joined the insurgency or encouraged their sons and nephews to do so. In addition to humiliating many once-powerful Sunni officers, the disbanding of Iraq's army and security services also put a

lot of lower-class Sunni tribesmen out of work. Although the Shi'ah dominated the rank and file of the Iraqi Army, Sunni tribesmen dominated the lower rungs of the Republican Guard and the internal security forces, and these men are now unemployed and easy recruits for the insurgents. What's more, after forcing the tribal Sunnis out of the old government, the United States largely excluded them from the new one. There was only one Sunni tribesman on the IGC, and he was not well respected among his peers. Moreover, the tribal shaykhs formerly depended upon power and payments from Baghdad, which have not been forthcoming from the United States.

Regardless of these grievances, the Sunnis are going to have to make some major concessions to reality if Iraq is to have a workable power-sharing arrangement. The Sunnis are going to have to accept that they are not the majority (as many passionately insist), and that the Shi'ah are. They are going to have to accept that they will only get to enjoy a portion of Iraq's resources proportionate to their numbers, and will not enjoy the excessive rewards they received under Saddam's tyranny. They are going to have to compete for jobs in Iraq's security forces and civil service on an equal footing with everyone else, and without the privileged positions they occupied under Saddam. They are going to have to turn in the worst of the insurgents—including the foreign-born Salafi Jihadists and unreconstructed Saddamists—and agree to help the government and the Coalition against any Sunnis who continue to reject reconstruction even after a National Reconciliation accord has been signed. They are going to have to make a host of other adjustments to life in a democracy that they have so far been unwilling to make.

In return, there are a number of concessions that Iraq's Shi'ah and Kurdish communities should be willing to accept to assuage some of the fears of the Sunni community and thereby make it easier for them to soften their position in the negotiations:

• *A revised program of de-Ba'thification.* This is probably the most significant and certainly the most obvious grievance of the Sunni community. Huge numbers of Sunnis, especially tribal Sunnis from western Iraq, from where Saddam drew his power, were Ba'th party members of one sort or another. While many were brutal thugs with blood on their hands, many more were just ambitious men and women who saw party membership as nothing but a chance to make a better life for themselves and their families. The United States began these problems by declaring that all party members who had achieved the top four ranks of the party hierarchy were disqualified from service in the public sector. Although, this was a perfectly reasonable step to take, the CPA failed to take the next logical step of declaring that no one below those four ranks would be deprived of work or otherwise prosecuted. To make matters worse, the United States handed the de-Ba'thification portfolio to Ahmed Chalabi, who numerous Iraqis claim employed it to eliminate rivals and marginalize leading Sunnis. Together, this pattern of behavior led to numerous other instances of "private" de-Ba'thification, both in terms of citizens barring Sunnis or former party members from working or taking part in various social activities, or in extreme cases murdering those held responsible for crimes committed under the former regime.

While some of this was probably inevitable, it has gone too far and is now a primary source of the alienation, anger and fear among tribal Sunnis, which in turn feeds their support of the insurgency. *The new government must begin a dramatic overhaul of the de-Ba'thification process, starting by placing it in the hands of a committee of respected, well-regarded judges, lawyers, and human rights experts, preferably with the participation of foreigners from neutral countries or human rights NGOs to ensure that a new system is respectful of the victims of Saddam's oppression, fair to Iraq's Sunni community, and is not manipulated for private aims.*

- *A formal truth and reconciliation process.* Another matter closely related to de-Ba'thification is the failings of Iraq's efforts to deal with those guilty of heinous crimes under Saddam's regime and to reconcile the rest of the country. Most Iraqi Sunnis understand that there must be a process for bringing the guiltiest to justice for crimes they committed under Saddam's regime, and that this burden will fall overwhelmingly on their community. What is unnecessarily exasperating is the opacity and arbitrariness of the process so far. The Sunnis need a clearer sense of who will be held accountable and when the process will end so that they can stop holding their breath in fear that they or someone close to them will suddenly be arrested. It is a reasonable request, one that would probably benefit the Shi'ah as well, as the Shi'ah are also looking for a sense of what kind of justice they will receive from this process and how soon they will get it. Once a process for trying those guilty of egregious crimes has been reformed accordingly and a parallel process to reconcile the victims of Saddam's reign with those who only marginally abetted his crimes, much of the country may be able to start moving on to other business. Truth and reconciliation processes inevitably take long periods of time, so the goal cannot be to have such a process inaugurated and wrapped up quickly but, as Joseph Siegle suggests, to simply send "a clear signal as to what types of crimes will be prosecuted and that the process is being undertaken in a competent and just manner."

- *An amnesty program for insurgents.* Although it seems hard to countenance now, it will be necessary at some point to offer an amnesty to all those who participated in the insurgency to try to bring them back into the political process. Just as Israel negotiated with the PLO, and the British eventually chose to negotiate with the IRA, so too are Americans and Iraqis going to have to find ways to negotiate with and then live peacefully with the current crop of insurgents, and an amnesty that effectively says "the past is forgotten" is the only way to do so. Of course, this amnesty program should only be undertaken as part of a larger process of national reconciliation and, preferably, in conjunction with a major shift in military strategy toward a traditional counterinsurgency approach.

- *Reintegration of Sunnis into the armed forces and civil service.* Not unexpectedly, Sunnis have largely been excluded from the military and civilian bureaucracy.[4] In many cases, the fact that they were Ba'th party members has been used to justify wholesale purges in another example of how de-Ba'thification has been taken too far. Although it will be unappealing to many Shi'ah and Kurds because of the way that many Sunnis abused their positions under Saddam and participated in his many crimes against humanity, there is no alternative other than to allow most Sunnis back in to public life, at least to the extent they want it. Although it would be preferable to bring in younger Sunnis who were not Ba'th party members under Saddam, true National Reconciliation is going to require allowing some former party members—principally those who joined only to get ahead—to resume their places in Iraqi society. Iraq's public sector simply cannot be entirely closed off to an important segment of the population.

- *Job retraining.* As part of the amnesty program, former insurgents motivated by their dire financial status are going to need to receive immediate job training or other educational benefits, and possibly even assistance finding a job, so that they can expect to have a better life in the future. Again, this will be galling for many Shi'ah (especially if they are still plagued by unemployment when this program goes into effect) but numerous historical examples demonstrate that this is key to making an amnesty program effective in convincing a potentially sizeable component of the insurgents to give up the fight.

- *Oil distribution based primarily on population.* The Sunni population is going to have to be guaranteed that it will receive its fair share of Iraq's oil revenues. This means that the current provision in the consti-

tution suggesting that the localities in which the oil is pumped will receive some additional consideration must be reduced to the absolute minimum. This also requires a national program for the distribution of Iraqi oil revenues. (Such a system is described below.)

- *Protection for minorities.* Even more than the Kurds, Iraq's Sunni Arabs will need stronger guarantees than the constitution currently provides that they will not be oppressed as Saddam once oppressed the Shi'ah and Kurds. Iraq needs a more redundant system of checks and balances, such as making it necessary for a super-majority in parliament to authorize the armed forces to take action against any internal threat. Putting the local police forces under the jurisdiction of local officials and creating a new gendarmerie under the Ministry of Interior (MOI, to balance the armed forces under the Ministry of Defense) would be another helpful measure. *Iraq also needs a more stringent application of the rule of law across the country* so that every person can feel secure that he or she will not be subject to arbitrary violence either from private groups or from a government that runs amok. Along similar lines, *Iraq's judicial system must be reformed to the point where the average person can seek redress for grievances through the courts, including grievances against the government itself.* (All of these measures are described in greater length below). *These measures should be accompanied by an ongoing public relations campaign that helps articulate and strengthen norms for minority rights.*

- *Electoral laws that prevent true chauvinists from running.* As part of protecting minorities, Iraq might consider revising its election laws such that candidates for national office must not only win a majority of the vote, but also must win a certain percentage of the votes of every segment of society. This would ensure that major political figures are at least minimally acceptable to all groups, including

---

4 See for instance Richard A. Oppel, Jr, "Iraq Vote Shows Sunnis are Few in New Military," *The New York Times*, December 27, 2005.

minorities, and tends to promote figures who unite, not divide.

- *Help the Sunnis develop new political institutions.* For the Sunnis this need may actually be even more pressing than it is for the rest of the country. The Kurds have their two great parties. For the present, the Shi'ah at least have Ayatollah Ali Al-Sistani and the Hawza of Najaf—although these too are imperfect vehicles for expressing their true political aspirations. But the Sunnis have nothing. Their principle political institution was the Ba'th party and it has been proscribed, along with all of its senior members. Consequently, the United States is going to have to help them create new, progressive political institutions that will allow their voices to be heard. Even in these, the Sunni tribesman cannot predominate, and should have no more political power than their demographic weight, but they cannot be excluded entirely as they effectively have been so far. As Daniel Byman has warned, if the United States and the new Iraqi government do not help them create new political institutions, it is likely to be that they will flock to various Islamist movements as their only alternative.

- *Conduct a census.* To reiterate a point made in Chapter 1 in a different context, Iraq needs a new, accurate census. In the Middle East, knowledge has frequently been sacrificed to politics, most notably in Lebanon with the decision not to conduct a census for fear that such knowledge would upset the compromises worked out among the political élites. This cannot be allowed to happen in Iraq, and so a first census as part of a regular process of census taking, should be conducted as soon as possible. In addition, it is important to national reconciliation because a census will establish the actual population and its composition—religious, ethnic, and geographic. (The inevitable charges of fraud can easily be dispelled if proper procedures are followed, and perhaps even handled by an international organization). This will put to rest Sunni claims that they are the majority, and ensure that Iraq's parliamentary seats and oil revenues are distributed fairly.

- As described in Chapter 1, *offer to provide Sunni tribal shaykhs with resources if they will "assist with security"—i.e. stop attacking the roads, power lines, oil pipelines, and Coalition forces in their territory and prevent other groups from doing the same.* These payments do not necessarily have to be cold cash, like Saddam's, but Baghdad and Washington need to find ways to provide resources that will give the tribal shaykhs and their people an incentive to cooperate with us. This can come in the form of goods, construction equipment or project funding, or even the projects themselves. *It can come by "deputizing" tribal military leaders, enlisting their personnel in an Iraqi security force and then paying them for their service.* (Since we have done far worse by allowing the MOI to bring whole units of the Badr Organization into the Iraqi police, this is a rather minor concession in comparison). The key is to start meeting with the shaykhs and convincing them that if they cooperate, there will be resources and other benefits for them and their followers.

- *Begin a process of education among Sunni tribesmen (indeed, all across Iraq) that will make them understand the nature of the new Iraq and their role in it.* For instance, they need to understand that in a system where the rule of law prevails they will not have to fear being oppressed by the Shi'ah. Similarly, they need to be persuaded that while they will no longer enjoy the privileged position they had under Saddam, and so will no longer be relatively better off than the rest of the country, if reconstruction succeeds, Iraq will be so much more prosperous than it was under Saddam that, in absolute terms, they will be much better off.

Reining in the Shi'ah. The problems with the Shi'ah, naturally, are mostly the opposite of those with the Sunnis. The Shi'ah feel empowered and, in some ways, too empowered. They are now finally in control of Iraq and, unfortunately, it has gone to some of their heads. It is the Shi'ah who are responsible for many of the problems that the Sunnis now face. Again, this is perfectly understandable given what the Shi'ah went through at the hands of Saddam's regime, but it is not helpful to the future of Iraq.

Obviously, all of this behavior on the part of the Shi'ah needs to be removed or at least reined in to make the Sunnis feel comfortable enough to engage in a process of national reconciliation. However, there are a set of other problems as well. First, there are a number of problems related to natural tendencies to create a dictatorship of the majority. The best example of this lies in the realm of the mixing of religion and politics. Many of the Shi'i leaders are far more religious either than their own constituents or the Iraqi population as a whole, and they have shown a willingness to use their majority in parliament to push for laws favoring Islam and religion in politics in ways that other Iraqis (Sunni Arab, Kurd, and secular Shi'ah) have disliked.

Second, although many Shi'ah do share broad agreement on a range of issues, there are deep divisions among them that also hinder national reconciliation. Americans tend to talk of "the Shi'ah" as if they were a monolithic bloc (we make the same mistakes about "the Sunnis" and "the Kurds" as well, but the sin is particularly egregious among the Shi'ah, whose differences are often the most pronounced).There are large numbers of secular Shi'ah who do not care for SCIRI, Dawa, and the Sadrists whom they (rightly) regard as religious fundamentalists of one kind or another. Likewise, there are deep divisions even among these parties, with SCIRI staunchly supporting Shi'i regionalism and the Sadrists opposing it just as adamantly. This adds a further set of complications to the mix by making it difficult for the various Shi'ah groups to agree on a common position and acceptable compromises.

The third set of problems derives from the advantageous geographic position of the Shi'ah and the aspirations of some of their new leaders. The Shi'ah dominate southeastern Iraq, with its good agricultural lands; access to the sea, the Gulf states, and Iran; and roughly two-thirds of Iraq's oil production (and probably a larger percentage of its remaining

reserves). These fortunate geographic conditions make it attractive as a statelet of its own, and some Shi'i leaders are beginning to advocate this. Led by 'Abd al-Aziz al-Hakim, the leader of the SCIRI, these Shi'i leaders increasingly talk about the desirability of splitting off all of southeastern Iraq to form an autonomous region of their own, very much like Iraqi Kurdistan. Indeed, provisions for the creation of such a region—with its own security forces and government—have been included in the current version of the constitution. There are many disquieting signs that these leaders fully intend to exercise these powers and split off the south from the rest of the country. They probably also mean to keep the oil revenues from the southern oil fields for themselves, and will expect the Kurds to do the same in the north, leaving the Sunnis with nothing.

This would be a disastrous development for Iraq if it were pursued. It likely would spark two different civil wars in Iraq, the first within the Shi'ah community. Although Hakim appears to believe that he has both the muscle (in the form of the Badr Organization, the largest of the Shi'i militias) and the popular support (SCIRI won overwhelmingly in the 2005 municipal elections everywhere across the southeast, except in Basra), he is almost certainly mistaken. While SCIRI's Badr brigades are probably the strongest of the Shi'i militias, Muqtada as-Sadr's Mahdi Army is a close second and would be a very formidable opponent, as clashes in 2005 in the Najaf-Karbala area demonstrated. Moreover, there are a great many other local militias, some of which are quite strong. With a force of probably only about 25–30,000 men, Badr could not conquer the entire south without a protracted fight. Thus, any bid to control the south would probably cause it to fragment instead.

At the same time, a Shi'i move to create an autonomous zone in the southeast would probably unite the Sunni community and drive them into open warfare with the Shi'ah. The Sunni heartland in western Iraq has nothing of any real worth, and sits in the empty desert, landlocked and distant from any area of economic value. If only to prevent themselves from becoming an isolated backwater, the Sunnis would fight to keep their share of Iraq's wealth. Moreover, it is a common mistake to think of Iraq's communities as discrete and occupying well-defined geographic enclaves. In fact, precisely the opposite is the case. Nearly one-third of Iraq's population lives in mixed areas. In particular, much of the Shi'ah and Sunni Arab populations live in heavily-integrated areas, making it almost impossible for the Shi'ah to break away from the Sunnis cleanly. If the Shi'ah ever tried to create such an extreme-form of autonomous (let alone independent) region in the southeast, there would be a great deal of territory that would require the spilling of blood to determine who controlled it. So far, the Bush Administration has been able to prevent the Shi'i leaders from moving too far in this direction, and they will have to redouble their efforts in the future, especially if negotiations over the constitution, power-sharing and national reconciliation remain paralyzed.

Although at present the greatest risks from the Shi'ah remain the potential for them to overreach and discard the considerations of the Sunnis, making national reconciliation impossible, it is important to keep in mind that they still have legitimate fears and grievances left over from their traumatic experience under Saddam. Many Shi'ah remain fearful that they are going to be deprived once again of their demographic right to dominate the Iraqi government. Many still do not trust the United States—which did nothing for them in the past, and is the long-time ally of the Sunni states of Saudi Arabia, Kuwait, Jordan, and Turkey. Many fear the Salafi Jihadist groups that have taken root in Iraq's Sunni tribal community and preach worse punishment for the Shi'ah (whom they consider apostates or heretics) than for Westerners (who are merely infidels). And many Shi'ah continue to think in traditional Middle Eastern patronage terms, whereby those who dominate the political system get to apportion the country's economic wealth to their followers. The Shi'ah suffered under such a system for 80 years (arguably longer) and they believe that now is their turn at the trough.

Keeping the Kurds on board. No group has conducted itself as intelligently and conscientiously in recent years as the Kurdish parties, although this is a relative statement. Since the fall of Baghdad, Kurdish political leaders have been Iraq's greatest statesmen. Barham Salih and Hoshyar Zebari (among others) have played arguably the most positive role in inter-Iraqi politics throughout the post-Saddam period. Remarkably for the leaders of a people who make no effort to hide their desire for independence, it is these men and their comrades who have most consistently put the interests of Iraq first. This is not to say that they have not jealously guarded Kurdistan's prerogatives, only that they have been the most willing to argue for actions that are in the best interests of Iraq, and have frequently put the interests of the whole country ahead of those of the Kurds. Indeed, this has caused some considerable intra-Kurdish tension, especially because more and more Kurds favor a prompt declaration of independence as a way of extricating themselves from the morass of Iraq. In January 2005, over 95 percent of Kurdish voters declared themselves in favor of independence for Iraqi Kurdistan in an unofficial referendum. Many Kurds will say in private, "You [the United States] are making a mess in the center and the south. Why would we want to be part of that?" Unfortunately, they have a point.

Nevertheless, the Kurdish leadership has recognized that the time is not propitious for them to declare independence and they therefore must do everything to make Iraq secure and stable. Kurdish leaders understand that unilaterally declaring independence today would leave them with a small, land-locked country amid neighbors who hated them for doing so. Nor would the diminishing production of the Kirkuk oil fields be enough to offset such animosity. Thus, this would not be an advantageous beginning for a new Kurdistan. They also recognize that declaring independence could easily spark either a war with Iraq's Sunnis and Shi'ah (who might unite against them) or a civil war among Iraq's divided Arab communities.

Moreover, Kurdish leaders seem to have a sound appreciation for the dangers that civil war in Iraq would hold for them. While civil war would seem to justify their declaring independence, it would immediately present them with a series of dreadful dilemmas. There are large Kurdish populations in Kirkuk, Baghdad, Mosul, and other multi-ethnic cities of northwest and central Iraq. These would immediately be vulnerable to attack by various Arab groups and would doubtless demand protection from the *peshmerga*. The question that the Kurds would then face would be whether to mount military campaigns to take over these cities to protect their brethren. If they did, it would mean occupying major pieces of Iraq inhabited by large populations of Arabs, Turkomen, Chaldeans, etc., which would doubtless provoke the ire of Iraq's Arabs, and of those neighboring countries that undoubtedly would become embroiled in a civil war in support of their co-religionists: Iran in support of the Shi'ah; Saudi Arabia, Jordan, Kuwait, and Syria on behalf of the Sunni Arabs; and possibly Turkey on behalf of the Turkomen. On the other hand, if the Kurdish leaders did nothing, they could well be leaving as many as a million Kurds to become the victims of ethnic cleansing. Neither of these courses would be good for the Kurds, and their leaders seem to be trying to avoid having to make such a choice.

Instead, the Kurds have demanded maximum autonomy, which both Sunni and Shi'i Arabs appear to have grudgingly accepted. As Massoud Barzani has put it, the Kurds want "whatever is just below full independence." This is a helpful decision on the part of the Kurds and has meant that their leaders have played a more constructive role than anticipated in trying to solve the many political problems that currently beset Iraq because they too recognize that failure to resolve them peacefully will lead to the civil war they fear.

For the moment, the Kurds seem politically secure and, because the other parties appear to have accepted their demands for autonomy, their position is not the central problem in the effort to hammer out a new power-sharing arrangement. As long as the Kurds do not decide to push for maximalist demands (immediate secession, full ownership of all revenues from the northern oilfields, or an arbitrary solution to competing property claims in Kirkuk in their favor) the *status quo* on issues related to the Kurds should not preclude finding solutions to Iraq's other political problems.

However, Kurdish concerns about issues such as war crimes and de-Ba'thification do reinforce the Shi'ah position, while their definition of autonomy feeds into questions about the status of militias and oil revenues that exacerbates the negotiations on all of these issues between the Sunnis and the Shi'ah. Thus, it is likely that they too will have to make some concessions. The easiest to convince the Kurds to make are likely to be those regarding the extent of de-Ba'thification and how oil revenues are shared with the community in which the oil is pumped (on this, see the section on the distribution of oil revenues below).

Of course, the Kurds are going to want something for making these compromises. Moreover, Kurdish leaders have another problem they must deal with—a population of their own that does not understand the merits of remaining a part of Iraq (at least for now) and trying to help stabilize it to prevent a civil war. This is where the United States comes back into the picture. Washington has been rather niggardly with its aid to Iraqi Kurdistan in the belief that the Kurds don't need it as much as other parts of Iraq.

This approach on Washington's part is short-sighted and should be reversed. First, while Kurdistan is relatively better off than the rest of the country, it is not rich by any means. Kurdistan has major shortcomings that could be remedied by U.S. aid. Second, denying Kurdistan aid because it is safe and doing modestly well runs counter to good COIN practices, a key principle of which is that reconstruction funding should be devoted to those areas that are the most supportive and secure, both because that is where the money can do the most good and to make other communities desirous of receiving the same treatment and therefore support the "oil stain" of security protection when it spreads to them. Indeed, taking money away from the Kurds to sink it into the "Sunni Triangle" is a waste of precious resources that could do real good in Kurdistan. Third, *the Kurdish leadership needs to demonstrate to its public that there are real, tangible benefits of remaining a part of Iraq and foreign aid is an obvious benefit.* If the Kurds are consistently deprived of aid, the separatists among them will argue that they would do better by seceding and taking the Kirkuk oilfields with them. The fact that this will not work out to their advantage is likely to be lost on a people imbued with nationalism and deeply fearful of the quagmire burbling to their south.

National reconciliation and traditional counterinsurgency strategy. As set out in some length in Chapter 1, the "oil stain" approach of a traditional counterinsurgency strategy has a great deal to recommend its adoption in Iraq today. Indeed, it is the only military approach that has any realistic likelihood of succeeding. However, it is hardly a perfect strategy, especially because the circumstances of Iraq have become so difficult that no strategy will be without problems. In this case, the greatest problem with applying an "oil stain" approach to Iraq is that it could exacerbate some of the tensions enumerated above. By pacifying major parts of Iraq and tying the north in better with the south and the center, it should take the edge off of Kurdish popular demands for autonomy. However, it could have the opposite effect in the west and south of the country.

Sunni leaders, especially the most chauvinistic among them, will doubtless claim that the "oil stain" is proof that the Americans, the Shi'ah and the Kurds all intend to exclude them from any share in Iraq's wealth. This is already a principle fear among many Sunnis, and an improperly drawn "oil stain" could easily add substance to these fears, no matter how inaccurate. It is for this reason that it is vital that the initial "oil stain" include all of Baghdad (with its large Sunni neighborhoods on the west side of the Tigris), and a number of Sunni towns north, west, and/or south of the capital to demonstrate that Sunnis too will reap the benefits of

this strategy, even if most of the Sunni tribal population will have to wait before they do so.

Among the Shi'ah, figures like Hakim might use the exclusion of the Sunni triangle from the initial "oil stain" to advance his own preference for a Shi'ah region with its own security forces and control over the oil revenues of southern Iraq. Indeed, he might embrace such an approach regardless of how much of the southeast were part of the initial "oil stain." If most were excluded, Hakim and other regionalists could claim that the Shi'ah have to establish their own autonomous region—and use "their" oil resources to pay for security and social services since the central government would not be doing so. On the other hand, if most of the southeast were part of the initial "oil stain", regionalists could establish regional institutions to address their needs alone, and press for the creation of an autonomous Shi'ah region to protect their gains before the "Sunni Triangle" was brought into the pacified zone. Of course, since many other Shi'ah oppose the idea of a southern autonomous zone, moves to advance this based on opportunities created by the initial application of the "oil stain" strategy could provoke further conflict among various Shi'i groups. Unfortunately, this is probably inevitable and so U.S. officials will have to work hard to prevent either outcome as they pursue the "oil stain" and reconstruction in Iraq in the future.

DECENTRALIZATION

Reducing the power and influence of the Iraqi central government in Baghdad is both inevitable and necessary. It is necessary because Baghdad has become a major obstacle to reconstruction in all aspects. Iraq's central government is dominated by political leaders many of whose legitimacy, in the sense of actually representing a significant segment of the population, is dubious and who have largely spent their time squabbling over the division of power and spoils, leaving the rest of the country to fend for itself. To make matters worse, they are so jealous of their power and prerogatives that they regularly attempt to prevent those outside of Baghdad (and especially those outside Baghdad who owe them no allegiance) from exercising authority or getting things done. This is not to suggest that there are not some good Iraqi political leaders trying to do the right thing for their country and their people, only that these are too few in number. Iraq's ministries are crippled by corruption, lack many key personnel, are generally undermanned, and largely remain tied to sclerotic bureaucratic practices inherited from the former regime. Baghdad has always been something of a bottleneck in Iraq, but this was greatly exacerbated during Saddam's regime because he wanted every decision to be referred to Baghdad to preclude the emergence of independent centers of power elsewhere in the country.

The result of all of this is that the Iraqi capital is incapable of doing much for the Iraqi people but still prevents the rest of the country from providing for itself. This state of affairs is intolerable: it is one of the main reasons, along with the persistent security vacuum, that Iraqis do not have the basic necessities they so desperately desire (and deserve). Thus *the overwhelming requirement to begin materially improving the lives of average Iraqis within the next 6–12 months demands that the United States pursue this goal vigorously, both through its own foreign aid efforts and by pressing the Iraqi government to begin a major effort to decentralize power and resources away from Baghdad and out to local governments that may be able to use them more effectively.*[5]

An important part of this process will be building the capacity of local governments so that they can employ the authority and resources to be devolved to them. At present, because they have been so badly neglected, few Iraqi provincial or municipal governments can do so. Thus, this process also demands a major emphasis on capacity building at the local level. This is critical for the development of pluralism and good government in Iraq (both of which grow best from the bottom up),

and in many ways should be easier than dealing with the incapacity of the central government (which cannot be neglected either, see below). Local governments are, by definition, smaller and dealing with the needs of fewer people, which makes them easier to reform. Moreover, it will be much easier to build capacity at the local level than at the national level as part of a traditional counterinsurgency strategy: simply put, the Coalition should focus on building capacity only in those areas that begin as part of the initial "oil stain", which is far more feasible when considering sub-national governments than when dealing with national-level ministries that are designed and intended to serve the entire country. As the "oil stain" spreads to new regions, the Coalition should in turn set to work reforming local government in those areas as well.

Federalism is another part of this equation. Whether the United States likes it or not, federalism is inevitable in Iraq. It is possible that had we handled the early days of the post-Saddam era differently, we might have moved Iraqis down a path that would have allowed for the re-creation of a more centralized state, but that is impossible today. The Kurds were always uneasy about a centralized system and having seen all of the chaos and violence unleashed by the Shi'ah and Sunni Arabs against each other, they want even less to do with what goes on there. Unfortunately, the same is now true of many (but hardly all) of the Shi'ah, as noted above. A number of Shi'ah leaders have decided that it would be better for the Shi'ah also to preserve a considerable degree of autonomy from Baghdad so that they can live their lives as they see fit without fear of being told otherwise, or the need to get Iraq's other communities to ratify it. The Sunni Arabs are the most uniformly opposed to federalism, largely because they fear that it will leave the Kurds and the Shi'ah with the vast bulk of Iraq's oil resources (which they assume those two groups will attempt to control locally), but also

---

5 Joseph Siegle points to another value of decentralization, which is that it invariably leads to greater experimentation as different localities try different methods of accomplishing a given task, which in turn accelerates learning across the country. This too could only benefit Iraq in its drive to build a new society.

because they are the most ardently devoted to Iraqi nationalism. But even some Sunnis are beginning to approve of federalism in the realization that the new Iraqi government is likely to be dominated by the Shi'ah for many years to come, and they fear that this could mean that they would be oppressed by the Shi'ah just as Saddam's Sunni regime oppressed them.

To the extent possible then, the United States and the new Iraqi government should begin moving toward a federal system in which the central government retains control of the armed forces (but not the police, see below), foreign policy, monetary policy and currency, national standards including the regulation of the media, and the regulation of the oil sector (but not its distribution, see below). Most other powers should be allowed to devolve to local governments and the process of filling in the gaps in the constitution should be used to assist this process.

Thus, decentralization is inevitable and necessary, but its course is not set. This creates a very dangerous set of conditions and it is crucial for the United States not to attempt to impede that process, but to foster it and guide it in directions that will assist reconstruction. Some of the most important initiatives that the United States should pursue include:

- *Enhance the political authority and economic and security power of local government.* Wherever possible, the United States and members of the Iraqi government must look for ways to shift various economic, political, social, and even security responsibilities from the central government to local government and provide them directly with the resources necessary to accomplish them. This is the heart of decentralization. It should include the provision of funds directly to local government to be spent at their discretion. These funds should include money from Iraq's oil revenues (discussed in greater detail below), foreign aid, and eventually the raising of local taxes. Similarly, Iraq's various police forces should be transferred from the Ministry of the Interior (MOI) to the control of local officials (also

discussed in greater detail below). *Without control over money and even limited security forces, Iraq's local governments will be powerless.* Indeed, the central goal of decentralization should be to shift as much control as possible over funding and security forces from Baghdad to the rest of the country.

- *Establish local taxes.* Initially, it would be preferable for local governments to raise revenue via foreign aid, transfers from the central government, and a direct apportionment of Iraq's oil revenues. However, taxation is a very important element of good government as it mobilizes the community to care about politics, to participate in and monitor the activities of the government, and to think about the common good. Thus, taxing should be seen as a means of community-building and political reconstruction, in addition to the economic benefits of raising taxes to pay for infrastructure development and other community needs.

Of course, most Iraqis have never had to pay taxes thanks to Iraq's oil wealth, and introducing heavy taxation too soon could be the "straw that broke the camel's back" for a population that is already frustrated by how little reconstruction has benefited them. However, there are still approaches that could eventually be introduced and be seen as providing immediate benefit. For instance, Joseph Siegle has suggested that *Iraqi communities could voluntarily establish targeted taxes for specific infrastructure repair and development projects that the community at large identified as a priority.* Setting the precedent of communities taking ownership over the use of local resources has potentially far-reaching implications for local government accountability. Once communities are confident their taxes will be used for beneficial ends, they may choose to make them permanent. Taking this a step further, Frederick Barton has suggested a system whereby *international agencies, foreign donors, or the central government could establish pools of money to provide matching funds for money raised by Iraqi communities through local taxes to pay for these specific projects.*

Moreover, the establishment of very progressive local taxes could be seen as helping to redistribute wealth from the rich to the poor. Thus, *property taxes, automobile taxes, and luxury taxes, when coupled with public spending to benefit the poorest segments of society could also have some immediate appeal.* Finally, as part of the privatization of Iraq's oil industry, *the central government should impose a national tax on petroleum* to remind Iraqis that consuming oil means burning Iraq's most precious export commodity.

- *Respect the decisions of local governments.* Both the U.S.-led Coalition and the Iraqi central government have a deplorable record of running roughshod over local government. The United States effectively created all of Iraq's local councils, and then just as quickly left them powerless by transferring authority to the IGC and CPA. Even today, many American personnel continue to ignore the requests and decisions of local governments. This is corrosive to the necessary process of decentralizing power in Iraq. It also continues the pattern established under Saddam and previous dictators, whereby Baghdad made all significant decisions and local government, to the extent it existed, did nothing but serve as a conduit for decisions that Baghdad did not think important enough to have implemented by the ministries, the military, or other assets of the central state apparatus. All societies are status-conscious and Iraqi Arab society more than most. Thus, ignoring local governments materially affects their ability to rule because signs of disrespect are quickly recognized by the public. *It is critical that U.S. and Iraqi government personnel abide by the decisions of the local government on all but clearly delineated national policies to allow them to establish their authority to rule.*

- *Diminish the role of Iraqi ministries by allowing considerable implementation, contracting and even some elements of regulation to be set by local governments.* Iraq's ministries are too heavily involved in implementation of policy. For a variety of reasons, including the fight against corruption (see below), this needs to be changed. Doing so will allow many of the prerogatives currently exercised by the central government to be transferred to local governments. The ministries need to be reoriented toward setting broad policy, national standards and practices, and for holding both private firms and local governments accountable for implementation, but not for handling the actual implementation themselves. This approach, furthermore, would emphasize the technocratic rather than financial rationale for joining government service.

- *Encourage greater transparency in local government.* Another method of empowering local government is to inject transparency into its procedures. Doing so makes the public more aware, confident, and interested in government decisions. Transparency is both easier and more intimate for local government, where the audience often knows the people and the issues much better than they would know what is going on in Baghdad. *Iraqi local governments should be encouraged (or directed) to have regular, open public meetings where members of the public should be able to engage either the local legislature or executive figures directly.* While this could take the form of New England town meetings, it might take a form more traditional for Iraqi Arabs such as the *majlis* of a tribal shaykh or the *shura* of an Arab government. In addition, *local councils should be encouraged to broadcast their meetings and publish their proceedings to make it easy for people to learn about their activities.* Of course, transparency is also important because if greater power and money is going to be delegated to the local government, greater controls and oversight must also come along with it.

- *Distribute resources and authority based on performance.* Although some degree of funding and control over local security forces should accrue to every locality, there should also be incentives for local governments to exercise power prudently and implement their responsibilities effectively. Moreover, because of the neglect first under Saddam and later under the CPA, the abilities and popularity of Iraqi local government are highly uneven. Iraqis need to see real benefits for improving local government on all counts and the best way to do this is by rewarding those localities that are doing well. Simply put, *the better-run provinces should get more funding and other resources.* Objective criteria focused on transparency and effectiveness must be developed both by the central government, foreign donors or the international community, and those that meet the standards should be rewarded. Conversely, those governments found to be misusing public funds should be subject to cut-backs, prosecution of responsible officials, and additional external scrutiny. Some pools of money might be set aside for localities that met election deadlines, standards and thresholds for participation. Likewise, foreign aid providers would want to continue using some subjective criteria to reward those governments doing best because objective measures would likely fail to capture some issues, no matter how well-designed the metrics.

On a matter closely tied to performance-based resource distribution for local governments, it is important to keep in mind the relationship between decentralization and the traditional counterinsurgency strategy (the spreading "oil stain") outlined in Chapter 1. Part of decentralization is intended to reward communities within (and supportive of) the "oil stain." As noted previously, resources committed to unsecured areas of Iraq are in effect wasted because whatever they build cannot be protected from destruction or corruption. Thus, it only makes sense to pump resources into those parts of Iraq that are truly secured, and the goal of the spreading "oil stain" approach is to create large regions of the country where that is the case. By the same token, it is vital to commit massive resources to those parts of the country that are secure to allow political and economic systems to begin to revive to create areas of good government and prosperity. Thus, the "jurisdictional

variation" in apportioning resources that Joseph Siegle and others have advocated is closely tied to the selective pacification approach of a traditional counterinsurgency strategy. Those areas that should be rewarded for practicing good government should also be those within the "oil stain."

THE POLITICAL DIMENSION OF IRAQI OIL REVENUES

Like so many other developing countries, Iraq's massive oil reserves have been both a blessing and a curse. A blessing because Iraqis are (relatively) better off today and potentially much better off in the future because of the possibilities created by their country's oil wealth. A curse, because oil has brought rampant corruption and is a major source of internal conflict. Indeed, it is probably the case that the success or failure of political reconstruction in Iraq hinges on (among other things) getting the distribution of Iraq's oil revenues right. This issue is critical to a number of the biggest problems facing Iraq today:

- *National reconciliation will only be possible if all groups believe that an equitable distribution of oil revenues has been put in place.* The lure of Iraq's oil wealth is so vast that any number of Iraqi groups—political parties, militias, insurgents, etc.—would fight if they believed they were being denied their fair share.

- *Rebuilding central government capacity and convincing elected officials in Baghdad to try to improve the lives of their constituents is probably a will-o'-the-wisp until a scheme for distributing and accounting for Iraqi oil resources has been developed.* As long as there is no fixed system for apportioning Iraq's oil revenues, all of the sub-groups in Iraq will continue to fight over the division of the spoils rather than bothering to govern or rebuild the country.

- *Distributing Iraqi oil revenues directly to the provincial and municipal levels of government is key to decentralizing power and resources.* Indeed, for most local governments money is power and is the most important resource. Thus, breaking Baghdad's lock on oil revenues is also vital to breaking the logjam created by the capital's corrupt and incompetent bureaucracy.

- *An important element in reforming Iraqi politics is to use Iraq's oil revenues to make the Iraqi people interested in the goings on in Baghdad by tying their own material rewards to the actions of the Council of Representatives.* When there is money involved, people pay attention.

- *One way to help galvanize people against both organized crime and the insurgency is to give them a direct stake in Iraq's oil revenues.* If they know that a system has been created which will result in more of the oil money going to their benefit—both directly and indirectly—they will be much more motivated to actively oppose both the criminals who steal the oil and the insurgents who attack the oil production and export systems.

- *Similarly, since a great deal of the corruption in Baghdad stems from misappropriation (or outright theft) of oil revenues, developing a system that makes it harder to steal oil or oil money is also an important part of dampening corruption.* This could be a logical area of engagement by the International Monetary Fund (IMF) and World Bank. The IMF has recently established some standardized financial practices for the accounting of extractive sector revenues. On a similar point, given the growing recognition of the myriad of dysfunctions stemming from the "oil curse," Great Britain has championed the Extractive Industries Transparency Initiative (EITI),[6] which sets out a protocol for the disclosure of revenues/royalties paid. While currently voluntary, there is growing pressure to make such practices the norm. *Iraqis should be convinced to sign on to the EITI protocol and to implement it.*

- *Iraq's oil revenues are vital to Iraq's economy for growth, employment and ultimately diversification.*

What all of these imperatives make clear is that Iraq must have a relatively fixed system for the distribution of its oil revenues. Without such a fixed plan, it is impossible to imagine real national reconciliation because all of the parties will continue to fight over who gets how much—and anyone who doesn't like the results will be tempted to resort to force to try to have their way. All of the fighting for oil revenues will distract elected officials and technocrats from the job of running the country, let alone rebuilding it. And varying constituencies could feel alienated by a particularly inequitable division of the pot, possibly pushing them to rebel.

Moreover, a fixed distribution plan is necessary to ensure that not all of the revenues simply go into central government coffers, there to await redistribution. Having all oil revenues go to the central government as simple revenue (and pure discretionary funding) breeds corruption, because it becomes very difficult to keep track of the money and where it is supposed to go. In addition, it also centralizes power in the hands of the federal government, to whom local governments must apply for funding. This would undermine the critical objective of decentralizing power.

A plan for a new distribution of Iraqi oil revenues. If it is self-evident that Iraq requires a relatively set distribution scheme for oil revenues, it is harder, but not impossible, to stipulate what that scheme should look like *a priori*. Dollar figures can really only be set based on the price of oil, the actual costs of governance (which are not yet available and vary from year to year), and the needs of various projects. However, it is possible to describe the basic features of such a plan and its essential workings. The basic schematics are shown in graphic 1, opposite page. Its key features are:

- *Ensure that there are multiple "baskets" into which Iraq's oil revenues are poured.* Fewer, larger pools of money are always easier to rob than more, but

---

6   Details on EITI are available at <http://www.eitransparency.org/>. A list of countries that have implemented and signed the EITI principles is available at <http://www.eitransparency.org/countryupdates.htm>.

Iraqi Oil Revenue Sharing Plan

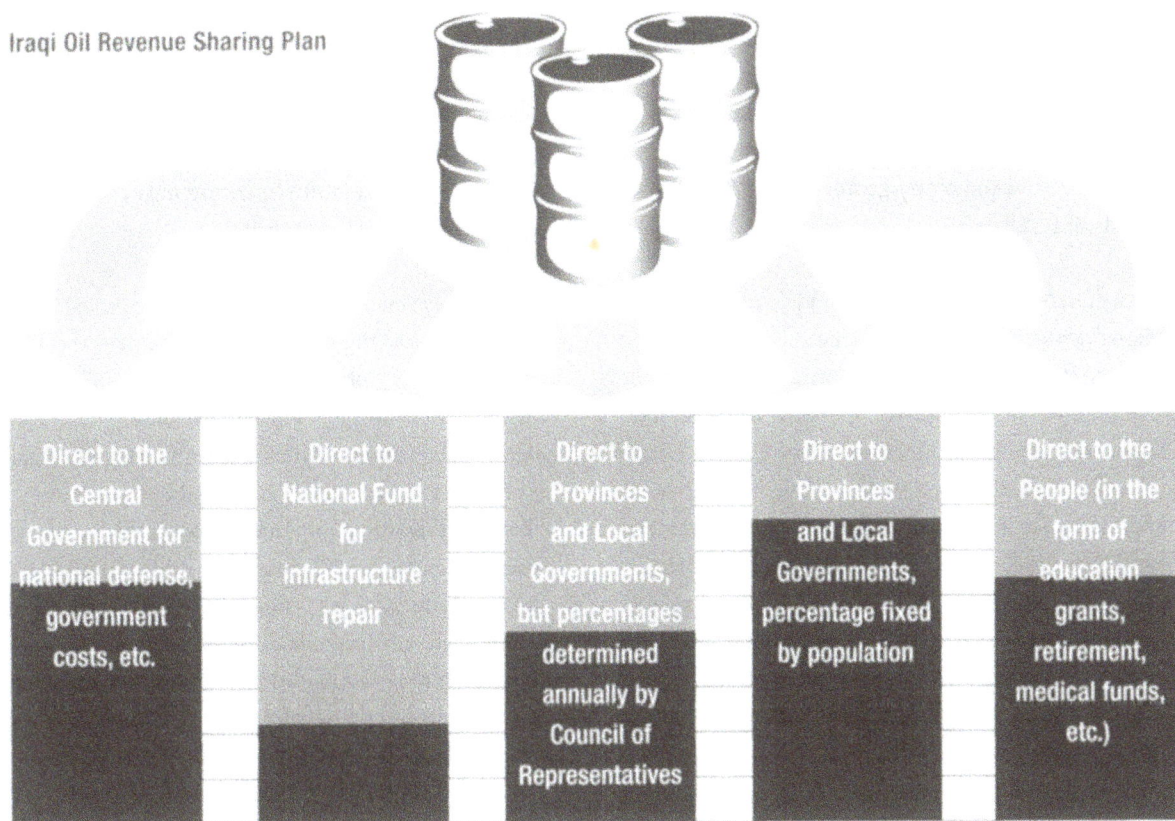

| Direct to the Central Government for national defense, government costs, etc. | Direct to National Fund for infrastructure repair | Direct to Provinces and Local Governments, but percentages determined annually by Council of Representatives | Direct to Provinces and Local Governments, percentage fixed by population | Direct to the People (in the form of education grants, retirement, medical funds, etc.) |

smaller, pools. This plan proposes five separate such "baskets."

- *Basket 1: Some funding of the Iraqi federal government is critical.* In particular, the salaries of federal employees and all members of the nation's armed forces (including the reconstituted ICDC/Gendarmerie which will be part of the Ministry of the Interior) could all reasonably be funded from oil revenues. However, between cutting corruption, ending subsidies, and shifting many former central government tasks to local government or the private sector, it should be possible to greatly decrease central government expenditures leaving more oil revenue for spending on other sectors.

- *Basket 2: Fund infrastructure development directly.* Iraq's infrastructure is in a woeful state and it would be ideal to have a pool of money available to directly fund local, municipal, and provincial-level projects to repair and build new infrastructure. Likewise,

infrastructure projects are often major opportunities for corruption and an independent entity charged with distributing the funds, overseeing the project, and then reporting on its outcome to the Council of Representatives could help deal with this problem.

- *Baskets 3 and 4: Create a mixed system for wealth distribution to provincial and municipal governments to promote popular interest in local government and national representation and in turn make both local and national-level representatives more accountable to their constituents.* This is a critical aspect of the proposed system. Just as it is important that some revenue be used to continue to fund the federal government, so too is it important that a portion of oil revenues also go directly to lower levels in the Iraqi governmental structure to ensure the decentralization of authority, empower local governments, and diminish the amount of resources that must be directed from Baghdad.

As shown in graphic 1 above, there are two different

baskets of money that would go to the local governments. Basket 3 would provide oil revenues directly to local governments based on the population in their municipality thus ensuring that every government has some oil money available to it to meet the needs of its citizens.

Basket 4, on the other hand, would provide an additional pool of revenues that could be divided up among the provinces on an annual basis by the Council of Representatives. As Noah Feldman suggests, the idea behind this second pool would be to give the average Iraqi a very tangible interest in the performance of his or her national representatives and encourage deal-making across party and sectarian lines. Since the division of this second pool is variable, and its ultimate distribution would be publicly known, every Iraqi would want his or her representatives to fight for as much of that money to go to their province as possible. It thereby creates a concrete standard by which voters can measure on an annual basis how well their representatives are doing for them. For example, if during one year the average division of this basket were 6 percent per province, then any representatives who delivered over 6 percent would be lauded by their constituents, and any who delivered under the average would be derided—and possibly voted out of office at the next election.

Similarly, since Iraq is now voting for the Council of Representatives based on provincial lists (still not as beneficial as direct geographic elections, discussed below, but much better than the single-district system used in January 2005) such a system would encourage candidates from different political parties but from the same province to work together to get as much of this pool of money as possible for their province so that they all could stay in office. In mixed provinces (and roughly one-third of Iraq's population does live in mixed provinces) this would force Council of Representatives members to associate with their geographic comrades, even though they might be ideological rivals, thereby building up

the cross-cutting alliances that are vital to diminishing sectarian cleavages in the Iraqi system. It is similar to how the entire Congressional delegation from a split state in the United States works together to ensure the maximum government expenditures (including pork) for their state.

- *Basket 5: Provide funds directly to the people themselves.* One of the best ways to stimulate the Iraqi economy is by putting money in the hands of the people. This would help reconstruction in several ways. First, this money should not simply be paid directly to every Iraqi household, but would be better deposited in individual bank accounts earmarked for specific purposes—education, retirement, healthcare, etc., that could either be determined on a country-wide basis by the Council of Representatives or left up to individual Iraqis themselves (preferably the latter). *Putting the money into special bank accounts would capitalize Iraq's banking system; re-capitalization is desperately needed to inject liquidity into the Iraqi economy and to create funds for investment.* Second, *by giving the Iraqi people a direct stake in oil revenues it will energize Iraqis to oppose both organized crime and the insurgents who steal the oil and its revenues and destroy the oil infrastructure.* Third, *by putting money in Iraqi hands and then giving them a choice on how to spend it, market forces are able to operate more efficiently*—if the people want to use the money for healthcare, the demand will stimulate the growth of clinics and hospitals and make it more profitable for doctors to stay in Iraq rather than fleeing to the West. On the other hand, if they want education, the demand will inevitably spur the building of schools and increased pay for teachers, which will in turn entice more qualified people into teaching.

Alternatively (or perhaps additionally), revenues directly to the people could be used to eliminate the food rations that Iraqis still receive from the central government. This is a horribly inefficient use of resources, and it would be much better to put the money in the hands of Iraqis and allow them to decide what they want to eat, thereby removing the corrupt and inefficient central bureaucracy from this necessity of life.

Two additional points are worth making about this oil revenue distribution plan. First, *it is critical not to under fund the various baskets.* If Iraqis only get a few cents per month from direct distributions, it is likely to be seen as a joke, and probably as proof that the system is still deeply corrupt. Thus, in setting the proportions to go to each basket, it is important to keep in mind both percentages and absolute minimum figures. It may be that for some of the baskets—particularly the infrastructure development fund in Basket 2—they will not be funded at all unless the country brings in a certain level of oil revenue (a level which should be inflation indexed) so that if oil revenues are particularly low one year, that basket is not funded at all so that more of the revenues can go to the other baskets, which are more important. Second, *ensuring an equitable distribution of the oil wealth is yet another reason why Iraq needs an accurate census, and the sooner the better.*

TACKLING CORRUPTION

Corruption has become one of the most important issues facing Iraq today. Like the problem of insecurity, with which it is intertwined in many ways, corruption undermines nearly every aspect of reconstruction directly or indirectly. In public opinion polls, it consistently ranks with security and unemployment as the top three issues that Iraqis believe have the greatest negative impact on their lives.[7] And, unfortunately, they are right. Billions of dollars are being siphoned away from reconstruction through corruption. Along with the security vacuum that made it possible, corruption has been a major impetus to the massive growth of organized crime in Iraq—from crime rings that steal and sell oil to assassination teams that kill uncooperative Iraqi officials or business rivals. Corruption is one of the

problems that has hindered the restoration of Iraq's infrastructure, the creation of capable Iraqi security forces, the provision of adequate supplies of fuel, and the acceptance of a new power-sharing arrangement among Iraq's various ethnic and religious groups. In particular, *corruption is probably the single greatest factor inhibiting the creation of Iraqi political institutions (especially for the central government in Baghdad) capable of governing Iraqi society and supporting an independent military and a prosperous economy.*

Corruption has always been a problem in Iraq, but since the fall of Baghdad, most Iraqis believe that it has reached astronomical new proportions. Part of the problem was the unpreparedness of the United States for postwar reconstruction, resulting in many haphazard and *ad hoc* decisions made without any safeguards, a situation that created enormous opportunities for graft. Another, related, problem was the shortage of Coalition personnel to oversee, audit, and supervise Iraqi activity. The result was problems across the board, which set terrible precedents and created entrenched interests that cannot now be easily removed. As one important example, the UN International Adivsory and Monitoring Board "found gross irregularities by CPA officials in their management of the DFI [the Development Fund for Iraq, set up to hold Iraq's oil revenues and foreign aid to pay for reconstruction needs] and condemned the United States for 'lack of transparency' and providing the opportunity for 'fraudulent acts.'"[8] Moreover, the lack of formal controls on Iraq's interim and transitional governments meant that thousands of government officials at all levels were profiting illegally from Iraqi oil revenues, contracts, and the illegal sale of government assets in ways that they would never have dreamed of doing under Saddam.

There should be little doubt that the United States must place the highest priority on fighting corruption in Iraq in all of its manifestations. We will never see the creation

7   See for instance, International Republican Institute, "Survey of Iraqi Public Opinion, November 1–11," November 2005, p. 36.
8   Diana Rodriguez, Gerard Waite and Toby Wolfe, eds., *Global Corruption Report 2005*, Transparency International, London 2005, p. 85.

of military and political institutions capable of holding Iraq together without massive external assistance unless corruption is brought down to a level where it is no longer hollowing out every Iraqi ministry. Moreover, there is no "silver bullet" solution to the problem of corruption. The United States and the international community have confronted corruption in nearly every exercise in nation-building undertaken in the past 60 years and no one has ever discovered a way of eradicating it quickly or completely. However, there are a wide range of tactics which, if prosecuted collectively, energetically and on a sustained basis, can produce a real diminution in corruption.

General principles for fighting corruption. There is no government on the planet without some degree of corruption, and given the history of Iraq it is outlandish and unnecessary to believe that it could be completely eliminated there. However, corruption can be dramatically reduced by adhering to a general set of principles devised over time and proven effective in a range of cases. The primary goal of all anti-corruption efforts must be to increase the costs and risks while simultaneously diminishing the incentives for graft. In simple terms, this means making it harder for people to cheat, making the penalties for getting caught more painful, and raising the compensation for officials at all levels so that they have less need for extra income and more to lose by getting caught. A comprehensive approach focusing on all three aspects can reduce corruption to the level where it is a nuisance and an embarrassment, rather than the current national emergency. In practice, this amounts to:

• *Creating a process of comprehensive re-education to make people understand that corruption is wrong and harmful to everyone; to help them identify corruption, and to explain how they should react when confronted by acts of corruption.*

• *Paying good salaries to public officials across the board.*

• *Imposing severe fines, jail time, and other punishments for those convicted of corruption to deter all but*

the most determined from committing acts of graft. This is of particular importance in Iraq, because its cultural system sees many acts of corruption as "normal" behavior—like people ousting qualified personnel to be able to move their unqualified relatives into more lucrative positions. Thus, while the process of education changes norms about corruption over time, heavy penalties are needed as simple deterrents in the short term.

• *Making sure that those who must enforce the laws governing corruption are themselves honest people, well paid, provided with adequate resources, employing proper techniques, and protected from retribution by those whom they must prosecute—especially organized crime, insurgents and militias.*

• *Creating incentives for those who want to get rich to pursue their fortunes in the private sector, rather than by the lure of graft in the public sector.* Ideally, over the long-term in Iraq, a prosperous economy will make it far easier to make money outside government than in it. However, because Iraq's economy remains hobbled by overcentralization, undercapitalization, and insecurity at present, the cleverest (and greediest) recognize that they can make far more by robbing from the public coffers than by making risky investments in the private sector.

• *Recognizing that the quantity of anti-corruption measures is as important as their quality.* Because there is no "silver bullet" solution to the problem of corruption, and clever and determined crooks will always find ways to cheat, it is important to have as many anti-corruption measures as possible. The more that anti-corruption measures complicate the efforts of the criminals, the more they impose costs and risks. With such a heavily "layered" approach, even if each only complicates corruption slightly, the combination can create a deterrent effect that is far greater than the sum of its parts.

• Finally, in Joseph Siegle's memorable phrase, *it is important to separate positions of public authority* from opportunities for private enrichment. In particular, this requires a comprehensive set of government regulations concerning personnel, financing, procurement, contracting, and accounting to make illegal all of the various practices that Iraqis have been indulging in for decades—and over-indulging in for the past three years. Everything from nepotism to preferentially awarding contracts to accepting bribes must be carefully defined and unambiguously prohibited.

Minimizing opportunities for graft. When considering how to minimize graft, it is important to start by reducing the opportunities, to make it more difficult and more costly for determined crooks, and to reduce temptation for those who might otherwise stay on the straight and narrow path.

- *Privatize the implementation of policy.* As noted above, the Iraqi government is already far too centralized, controlling far too much of Iraq's political and economic activity. A plan for gradual privatization is an important element of decentralization, but it is equally important to curbing corruption. The more that the government and its ministries control the means of implementation, the more opportunities for graft. For instance, ideally, Iraq's ministry of energy would set guidance, guidelines, standards, and practices for electricity provision—as well as overseeing the activities of the providers—but would not run the generators and sub-stations themselves. Private industry is far better able to deal with graft than government, and the more that the government can allow the provision of services to be handled by industry and the market, the more likely that they will be supplied with minimal corruption. Moreover, privatization introduces additional actors into the equation, and the more actors, the more difficult it is to organize graft and the more opportunities for the corrupt to be caught (because more people have to turn a blind eye or participate in the corruption).

The area most in need of privatization is Iraq's refining,

distribution and sale of petroleum products (what is called "downstream" oil production). Huge amounts of Iraqi oil is lost to smugglers and black marketeers who have connections to, bribe, blackmail, or threaten with violence, everyone from truck drivers to guards to gas station attendants to steal Iraqi petroleum products. This is a piece of the Iraqi economy that is ripe for privatization and desperately needs it.

- *Regulate privatization carefully.* Of course, in addition to other problems of overly-rapid privatization, there is the risk of increasing corruption if it is done wrong. If industries are privatized too quickly—before there are entrepreneurs organizationally, psychologically, and financially ready to buy them—they often end up in the hands of organized crime, which is always ready and able to come up with the cash. Moreover, if privatization is not properly regulated, including having the time to properly vet the procedures, industries often get sold to those connected to (or paying off) government officials. This is precisely how privatization in Russia led to the massive enrichment of Russian organized crime.

- *Gradually end Iraq's subsidies on oil and food.* Subsidies interfere with the efficient functioning of the market, which by definition introduces opportunities for graft. In particular, the ridiculously low price of gasoline in Iraq (about 2 percent of the cost in neighboring Jordan) creates enormous temptations for corruption. Those associated with Iraq's state-run oil industry can sell oil to black marketeers for several times what it would be sold for on the domestic market, and the black marketeers can in turn sell it in neighboring countries still below market rate, but well above the Iraqi subsidized price.

In the case of oil, the United States has prevailed on the government of Iraq to begin this process, with the price of premium gasoline being raised from $0.13 per gallon to $0.64 per gallon this year. It is fine for this to happen in a gradual fashion, both to mitigate the anger of the average Iraqi and to allow markets to adjust.

However, it is absolutely crucial that the process continue and that this first price hike not be the last.

With food, the story is not even this good, with little change in the provision of monthly rations to Iraqi families. On the one hand, because of the depredations of unemployment, underemployment and inflation, most Iraqis can't afford to buy what they need to survive. On the other hand, the food rationing system is highly corrupted, having been created under the UN Oil-for-Food program—now finally exposed as having been riddled with graft and a principal method by which Saddam starved recalcitrant members of his population into submission. At the very least, *the United States should press Iraq to instead provide food stamps or a similar program to those in need* (and, like food stamps, a determination of need should be required before the food stamps are provided) so that money is pumped into Iraq's economy to improve liquidity and market forces can be allowed to work.

- *Reduce the monetary size of aid and reconstruction contracts.* The bigger the dollar amount of any contract, the easier it is to hide graft in it and allow both sides to skim off the finances. Smaller contracts are less efficient in many cases, but are harder to corrupt. Moreover, for the simple reason that smaller contracts mean smaller amounts of money, more but smaller contracts means that it is harder for an individual or group to steal large amounts of money, and there are more opportunities for them to get caught doing so. As an added benefit, smaller contracts are generally within the reach of most Iraqi contractors, making it more likely that money will flow into the Iraqi economy rather than the bank accounts of the international shareholders of Bechtel and Halliburton. USAID has taken some very important steps in the right direction on this matter, but it is not the only aid provider and there are still too many giant contracts on offer.

- *Emphasize the funding of small businesses.* For reasons similar to the need for smaller contracts, so too funding smaller business is a better way to reduce graft. This would also stimulate the development of a broader entrepreneurial middle-class in Iraq that would be a major source of employment generation and economic dynamism for the country.

- *Physical impediments to corruption.* Iraq can also raise the costs and risks involved in graft through various physical (and organizational or accounting) methods. Checkpoints at key border crossings used by smugglers, random checks on gas stations, and the physical capture or even destruction of known storage facilities (especially for oil) are examples of some of the many measures that should be implemented or augmented.

With reference to the oil industry, it is vital that the United States and the Iraqi government make a major effort to *eliminate the gaps in the tracking of Iraqi oil production.* Although it has been over a year since the UN's International Monitoring and Advisory Board condemned the United States for failing to ensure that Iraqi oil production was properly metered, problems still remain. Moreover, gauges on Iraqi oil storage facilities frequently do not work, either through neglect or tampering. As a result, it remains very difficult to account for all of Iraq's oil as it moves through the production, refinement, and export (or distribution) systems making it easy for corrupt officials to sell off barrels on the side. Another problem is that *the oil ministry has woefully under funded the office charged with inspecting these facilities*—likely because officials in the ministry are reputed to be among the most corrupt in Iraq and so have no incentive to retain adequate numbers of inspectors who might uncover their illicit activities. According to some reports, the ministry has only 10 percent of the number of inspectors it needs.[9] This must be rectified immediately.

---

9   Alex Rodriguez, "Graft Holds Back Economy; But those Trying to clean up Corrupt Oil Industry Risk Lives," *The Chicago Tribune*, September 25, 2005, p. 3.

Transparency. Another method of fighting corruption closely related to the need for physical impediments is the need for transparency. Corruption needs darkness to thrive, so shedding light on the procedures of Iraqi ministries and their personnel can only make corruption harder, costlier, and riskier. Some suggestions for improving transparency include:

• *Full disclosure of all governmental revenues and expenditures.* This is the simplest, most obvious and most important of all elements of transparency. In any democracy, the people have the right to know how much their government took in (including from what sources) as well as how much it spent (and on what). The best way to begin to uncover corruption is to know what the government claims to have brought in and what it claims to have spent and on what items. At this point, Iraq's revenues and budget remain lost in a fog of incomplete and partial information. It is in effect impossible to know the answers to these questions, yet they are a critical starting point to allowing legislators, opposition political figures, watchdog groups, and the press— and through them, the Iraqi people—to trace the flow of revenues through the government's coffers.

• *Reveal the finances of Iraqi officials and prevent them from profiting while in government.* Under U.S. pressure, Iraq adopted a requirement for all public officials to disclose their wealth and financial assets upon taking office. This is an important first step, but it needs to be expanded so that Iraqi officials must make the same declarations on an annual basis. Likewise, it would be useful for Iraqi law to mandate that senior leaders, and/or officials connected with key ministries (oil, finance, trade, interior, defense), or even all officials, may not have any private business interests. *Those they have upon entering government should have to be placed in "blind" trusts.* This helps separate public authority from opportunities for private enrichment.

• *Cut time and steps needed for business licensing.* Throughout history and across the globe, business licenses are prime vehicles for graft, creating opportunities for bribes and blackmail. The more that the process can be simplified and accelerated, the less the temptation for corruption.

• *Local community leaders should participate in monitoring reconstruction contracts.* In addition to helping decentralize authority by empowering local leaders, bringing in local community leaders to assist with the oversight of reconstruction projects can greatly reduce corruption. Local leaders often have an incentive in having contracts completed properly— because they will benefit or suffer in a very immediate sense—and can keep track of a project in ways that external auditors generally just can't. The locals are there on the scene on a constant basis, and usually have good information as to whether the terms of the contract are being properly met.

• *Government contracting offices (and foreign countries providing aid) must have the resources and personnel to conduct regular but random follow-up inspections to ensure that the contract is being properly executed.*

• *An independent entity should be responsible for issuing "report cards" on Iraqi budgetary, fiscal, monetary systems, on an annual basis and the results made public.* Because report cards are so easily understood by the public, they are a very effective way to focus unwanted attention on corrupt (and/or inefficient) agencies and offices of the Iraqi government. Since no agency would want to come out at the bottom, at the least they would create incentives for ministries to come out relatively better than their counterparts. Because it would be difficult to keep this process entirely untainted if the entity issuing the report cards was part of the Iraqi government, it might have to be an external actor that did so. The IMF might be willing to take up the task, given both its capabilities and its other missions, and if so, this might be ideal.

Aggressively "watchdogging" Iraqi officials. Along with the need for transparency so that corruption can be exposed is the need for someone to do the looking and the exposing. As with all anti-corruption measures, the more watchdogs there are over the public sector, the better. Frederick Barton has made the point that because corruption is so widespread in Iraq, U.S. and Iraqi officials need to "flood the market" with individuals and groups looking to expose and eliminate corruption. These groups would sharpen the teeth of any anti-corruption effort. The goal would be both to catch as many of the guilty as possible, but also to deter the tempted innocent. Some of the most important include:

• *Multiple, reinforcing oversight agencies overseeing governmental procedures, especially contracting, accounting, financing, and disbursing.* Under U.S. tutelage, every Iraqi ministry now has an Inspector General's office with the mission to monitor the ministry for corruption, among other things. Although this is a positive move, all of them remain badly under resourced and many are manned by cronies of the minister, making them unwilling to actually pursue corruption. Others are fearful that they will be killed by the corrupt officials or their business partners, who are often members of organized crime. These offices are complemented by the Commission on Public Integrity and a Supreme Audit board, but these too are understaffed, under funded, and reportedly heavily penetrated by organized crime and corrupt Iraqi politicians themselves. Likewise, the UN's International Monitoring and Advisory Board serves as a super-Inspector General with the writ to oversee the government as a whole. However, it too lacks the resources to conduct this function comprehensively or aggressively. Finally, Iraq has several narrowly-focused anti-corruption committees (including one charged with looking into the oil ministry), which lack the purview to make more than a marginal effort, and are actually staffed by some of the most corrupt people in the Iraqi government, who use them merely to attack their political enemies and economic rivals.

Consequently, there is still much to be done in this area. The Council of Representatives, in particular, needs to create committees with real oversight functions and the resources to do so. To this end, it would be extremely helpful *to create an Iraqi equivalent of the General Accounting Office,* which performs an independent, non-partisan oversight role for the U.S. Congress in addition to that exercised by Congressional committees. The Supreme Audit Board might grow into this function, but it so far has failed to do so. Likewise, Iraq should also have its own *"super-inspector general" office within the executive branch, with the powers to delve into any ministry or agency and investigate it for corruption.* Finally, considerable effort should be committed to instilling generally accepted accounting standards and ensuring that there is adequate private sector auditing capability. Government agencies, in turn, should routinely *hire one or more private accounting firms to serve as independent external auditors.* Frederick Barton has suggested that the Iraqi government hire large numbers of unemployed college graduates to snoop around the country looking for signs of governmental corruption, both to fight corruption and rein in unemployment. Again, the idea is not that any one of these groups will uncover all of the corruption in the system, but that by having so many—and encouraging them to compete with one another—Iraq would greatly increase the likelihood that the guilty would be caught, and others would simply be deterred from ever heading down the crooked path.

• *There must be legal (and physical) protection for whistle-blowers and it must be easy for people to report corruption.* Iraq should create anti-corruption "tiplines" where people can call in with reports. Likewise there should be both national level and ministerial ombudsman's offices where employees can go to report corruption without fear of retaliation.

• *Those who successfully expose corruption should be rewarded.* Personnel in anti-corruption agencies need to be paid well for their efforts (because their work will be unpopular and potentially dangerous, and to raise the threshold for them to become corrupt) and need to be rewarded for their successes. Likewise, whistleblowers should receive monetary rewards if the target of their tip is convicted of corruption offenses.

- *All of the anti-corruption mechanisms must be properly funded.* In particular, the Iraqi government has done a very bad job of paying people regularly and punctually. This practice has to be fixed across the board, but especially for those people charged with stamping out corruption. The more a person has trouble with his or her paycheck, the more they are likely to engage in graft. Funding of anti-corruption mechanisms may make the ideal avenue of support for donors that have been reluctant to support the reconstruction effort thus far.

Accountability. The next aspect of Iraq's war on corruption that must be beefed up is its willingness and ability to hold those guilty of corruption accountable for their actions and punish them. A substantial part of any anti-corruption program involves deterring people from engaging in corruption and a key aspect of deterrence is the threat of significant punishment—loss of money, loss of employment, or loss of freedom through imprisonment—for those caught. If corruption is not punished when it is discovered, it will run rampant. Iraq's efforts to punish corruption are worse than non-existent, they are generally counterproductive, with those few groups empowered to root out corruption generally being so corrupt themselves that they punish their political enemies rather than those most guilty. Consequently, there are any number of steps Iraq should take:

- *Prosecute high-profile cases.* It is absolutely essential to effective anti-corruption measures that examples be made. Moreover, these examples must be very important figures to send the message that *anyone* found guilty of corruption will pay a price no matter who they are. (This is also important for establishing the rule of law and the notion of impartiality in governance throughout the country). In some ways, this is the biggest problem with corruption in Iraq today,

and the issue most in need of immediate reversal. Iraq's most corrupt officials have not paid any price for their malfeasance. In particular, stories abound of the corruption of Iraq's oil and interior ministers under Ibrahim Ja'fari's transitional government—the one for theft, the other for use of his ministry to pursue a political agenda through violence, including reports of assassinations and ethnic cleansing. Yet little to nothing has been done even to investigate these charges. In both cases, no one has taken action because those allegedly involved are extremely important political figures. However, if ministers are not held accountable (at least to investigate the accusations, which could very well be groundless) it will embolden every petty thief in the government.

- *Because of both the importance and delicacy of handling these cases, there should be a special court for cases of corruption,* especially those of high-ranking and otherwise well-connected officials. The judges, prosecutors, and other personnel assigned to this court, in particular, must receive generous salaries, considerable protection, and perhaps even anonymity to allow them to perform their duties objectively and impartially. The judges and other personnel should also be very carefully screened. Noah Feldman has suggested that *these cases should be decided by a panel of judges, and that it might be helpful to have at least one foreign judge (who must be an Arabic speaker, see below) on each panel to ensure impartiality.*

- *Members of Iraqi anti-corruption organizations of all kinds must be thoroughly vetted by multiple agencies,* preferably including by several of the judges of the special corruption court. This is more about choosing good, honest people from the beginning, but in current circumstances would likely play an important role in accountability; this vetting process would probably result in the ousting of a number of currently serving officials.

The role of the Iraqi media. The Fourth Estate is critical to any aggressive anti-corruption campaign because of its power to expose and embarrass both the corrupt and those who failed to take action against them.

- *The Iraqi press must be pushed to report on corruption as aggressively as possible.* Iraqi investigative journalists should be encouraged and assisted in pursuing these stories, even though they might also be embarrassing to Americans. This is the quintessential role of the media in fighting graft in a democratic society.

- *The members of the press must be educated in government administration, politics, civics, and economics so that they know where to look for corruption and recognize it when they see it.* It is important to keep in mind that Iraqi journalists are very new to their craft and as a result, do not always know enough about the function of government to know where to look for corruption. This would be an excellent venue for universities, schools of journalism, institutes of politics, or politically-focused NGOs (like NDI and IRI) to make a major contribution by *setting up programs to teach Iraqi journalists the basics of how government functions, how democracies work, what constitutes corruption, and a bit of economics so that they understand how mechanisms of corruption (like "arbitraging" oil prices) work.*

- *Along similar lines, the media must be employed by the government, watchdog groups, and donors to inform the public about the anti-corruption campaign.* The government needs to take out advertisements on radio, television, and print media condemning corruption, explaining what constitutes corruption (again, because much of what is considered corrupt by democratic standards is considered "normal" behavior in Iraqi society), and alerting would-be whistleblowers and other concerned citizens of opportunities to report corruption. In particular, *the government needs to use all forms of media to publicize the corruption "tip lines" and the rewards to be gained for the successful conviction of corrupt officials.* Saturation campaigns involving huge numbers of brief, repetitive radio advertisements worked well in both Brazil and Thailand in this respect.

Education. Transparency, watchdogs, and accountability are all designed to create structural incentives (or disincentives) to keep Iraqi officials from acting corruptly. However, of equal importance is changing Iraq's educational system so that it teaches against graft, defined broadly, so that Iraqis will be less likely to act corruptly based on their own moral compass and more likely to act against corruption where they see it in others. Again, as noted above, most Iraqis do not understand the norms of a democratic society and consequently view many aspects of corruption as perfectly normal.

- *Teach civics.* For twenty-four years, the Iraqi people lived in the perverse world of Saddam Hussein's totalitarianism. Before that, they lived under other forms of autocracy, benignly neglected though they were at times. At no time did they live in a true democracy and therefore their ideas about behavior are derived from these other systems of government, and are rarely consistent with behavior in a democracy. Iraqis need to learn new values—particularly what constitutes corruption, that it is wrong, and how to take action to stop it. Certainly civics needs to be introduced into Iraqi educational curricula at all levels so that future generations will understand these principles. However, it is vital that their parents and grandparents learn it now.

In particular, members of the Iraqi security services should be subjected to lengthy courses on civics and the role of the armed forces and police in a pluralistic society. These courses are just as important to the future of Iraq as training in weapons handling or small unit tactics. *Courses where students get no more than a couple of hours of civics, or even a couple of hours a week, as part of a larger curricula mostly focused on other things (as is our current practice) are unlikely to have any meaningful impact.* Only by constantly reinforcing these lessons and giving Iraqi personnel the chance to discuss, debate and internalize them are they likely to begin to reshape public attitudes.

- *Provide training courses and opportunities for officials* already in government to learn about civics in a democratic society. Another important aspect of education is to provide training and other opportunities to learn for those already in government. This can take the form of *classes in civics in each ministry, educational programs either in Iraq or in foreign countries where democratic norms are strong, and participation in international fora where Iraqi officials can see and learn from representatives of foreign governments.* For instance, Transparency International has recommended, that it would be helpful "to grant the Iraqi Supreme Audit Board a seat on the International Monitoring and Advisory Board, to familiarize it with international auditing standards and improve Iraq's local expertise."[10]

• *Explain how corruption undermines democracy, reconstruction, and prosperity.* Especially for Iraq's older generations, simple insistence that corruption (above all concerning nepotism and other forms of favoritism) is wrong is unlikely to convince them of anything. They are likely to see such efforts as an attempt to impose Western cultural values on them and will reject them. Consequently, all civics education must be rooted in a rational explanation of *how* corruption hurts all Iraqis.

Another important lesson to teach in these programs is *the difference between public and private resources.* In Iraq's traditional system where patronage is accepted and expected, it is commonplace for officials to use their position to help themselves, their family, and their friends with jobs, contracts, and other forms of government favor. When the corruption reaches grotesque levels the people may grumble, but they are typically objecting to the extent of the favoritism, not the practice itself.

• *The United States and other foreign governments should loudly and repeatedly condemn corrupt practices uncovered in Iraq.* Part of inculcating new norms is to reinforce them by constantly calling attention

to unacceptable behavior. Indeed, because the United States has often chosen to ignore or downplay instances of Iraqi corruption for its own purposes, this has sent the wrong message to many Iraqis.

Reforming Iraq's police and judiciary. It is self-evident that another important element in fighting corruption is to ensure that Iraq has a strong police force capable of deterring, investigating, and uncovering graft, and a judiciary capable of prosecuting the offenders. Without a determined, capable police force and impartial, dedicated judges, corruption will rage unchecked. Unfortunately, in present-day Iraq neither institution has yet reached a point where it can play the role that it must. In addition to their failings as a counterinsurgent force (discussed in Chapter 1), Iraq's police are riddled with corruption; deeply penetrated by the insurgents, militias, and organized crime; poorly equipped; undermanned; and the principal target of attack by various armed groups. Likewise, Iraq's judiciary is understaffed, the target of pressure and even attack from all sides, and still includes far too many judges appointed under Saddam's reign whose loyalties, values, and capacities are suspect.

Iraq's police suffer from many of the same problems as the other Iraqi security forces and therefore many of the changes recommended in Chapter 1 regarding the training of Iraqi security forces should be seen as applying to them as well. However, a number of other points are worth making because of the different, additional missions of the Iraqi police force.

• *Make fighting crime and keeping public safety the first job of the police.* One reason that the police have performed so poorly over the past two-and-a-half years is Washington's harmful pre-occupation with the insurgency. As a result of this, the United States has emphasized the need to have a capable police force to help fight the insurgency, and has curtailed and skewed recruiting, vetting and training in the name of getting more police officers on the street to help Coalition forces combat the insurgents. This is one

---

10 Diana Rodriguez, Gerard Waite and Toby Wolfe, eds., *Global Corruption Report 2005*, Transparency International, London 2005, p.87.

reason that Iraqi police officers have generally neglected to aggressively pursue crime, both random and organized. The police need instead to be trained, equipped, and directed to make keeping the peace their highest priority, with fighting the insurgency a secondary concern.

- *Leave fighting the insurgents and organized crime to the Gendarmerie (and the armed forces).* Of course, counterinsurgent warfare does require considerable police assistance—in terms of detective work, information gathering, protecting the people against insurgent attack, and a host of other missions. In Iraq, many of these "policing" functions of counterinsurgency strategy should be left to a new Gendarmerie (addressed in Chapter 1) with the equipment, training, and specific mission to handle these tasks. Likewise, the Gendarmerie should be deployed to support the police with added firepower whenever they come up against groups of insurgents, militias, or heavily-armed mafias. Indeed, because organized crime is often a nation-wide phenomenon, because of their heavier armament, and because of their relationships with various insurgent and militia groups, it makes the most sense to leave this problem to the Gendarmerie altogether. Ultimately, the main role of the police should be establishing safety through presence (the "cop on the beat" role) and the pursuit of ordinary crime.

- *Revise police training and education with emphasis on civics.* The single greatest problem with the Iraqi police force is that it remains manned largely by officers who served in the same capacity under Saddam Hussein. The Saddam-era police force believed that its job was to oppress and to steal; the new Iraqi police must learn that its job is to protect and to serve. This will not come easily. As the Kurds learned when they took over Iraqi Kurdistan in 1991—and inherited part of Saddam's police force in so doing—*the only way to change this problem is through a process of lengthy re-education.* The Kurds put their police officers through repeated courses in civics, teaching both new recruits and old hands the basics of democratic governance, the relationship of a police officer to his community, and the role of the police in keeping order and peace. As could only be expected, the Kurds found that there were basically three types of personnel in their police force: those who understood and adopted this credo readily, those who could be persuaded over time, and those who never "got it." These training courses became invaluable for them to identify which personnel fell into which groups, allowing them to put the best officers out on the street quickly and remove the worst from the force altogether. It took nearly a decade, but the Kurds now have a competent and trustworthy police force that we should hope that the rest of Iraq will someday emulate.

- *Transfer control of the Iraqi police to their local leaders.* Although it is common practice in the Middle East, *it was a mistake to allow the Iraqi police to come under the control of the Ministry of the Interior in Baghdad. Instead, it is imperative that control of Iraq's police forces be transferred to their local municipalities and have the new gendarmerie support the police against the insurgents and the militia* (as described above). By placing the police under the command of the MOI, they became an arm of the central government, rather than of the people themselves. Making the police part of the local municipal government structure means that police officers are responsible to local magistrates, and ultimately to the people of the community in which they serve. Even within this structure, the police must be accountable to elected, and not just appointed, officials. This is the best way to ensure that the police come to learn that their job is to protect and to serve. It is also the case that local leaders are more likely to know about problems of corruption in their local police than that the MOI in Baghdad would. Finally, because the MOI in Baghdad is itself both rife with corruption and largely incapable of actually serving the state, turning Iraq's police forces over to the communities that they serve would mean a far greater likelihood that they would be able to do their job, unhindered by the problems crippling the MOI.

- *Mandate internal investigative units for every police force of even moderate size.* Just as every ministry needs a well-funded and fully empowered Inspector General, so every police force needs an equivalent service (akin to the Internal Affairs Bureaus of large American police forces) to ensure that there is a system for the people to complain about the police and know that their charges are being investigated seriously.

- *Give them the equipment they need.* Like all Iraqi forces, the police are without much of the equipment they need to perform their jobs, especially in the risky security environment today's Iraq. As noted in Chapter 1, the problem of corruption makes the United States wary of providing Iraqi forces in general with equipment that could end up in the hands of the insurgents within hours. However, it is important to do so, at least as a reward for units who demonstrate commitment and ability.

- *Harsh responses to those who kill police or members of their families.* A constant problem for the Iraqi police is that insurgents, militias, and criminals may target them or their families for violence if they do not do as the bad guys want. This is one of the most important of many reasons why the Iraqi police remain compromised by corruption. One way to address this is to instill in every part of Iraq's governmental system the idea that those who harm policemen or their families have crossed a red line and are deserving of the harshest treatment under the law. The police and other security personnel must be encouraged and enabled to pursue cop killers to the maximum extent legally possible. Judges and prosecutors must also be convinced that those guilty of employing violence against the police or their families should be punished to the full extent of the law.

- *Empower the police.* Under Saddam, the Iraqi police were the lowest rung on Iraq's security ladder. As a result, they had little confidence in themselves which in turn undermined their capabilities. Today, this same perspective towards the police is resurfacing among Iraq's other security forces and, especially,

among U.S. military personnel who know that the Iraqi police are not well-regarded. As a result, it is rarely the case that the Iraqi police are allowed to take on any assignment that is in any way challenging. *Iraqi and Coalition forces must make a determined effort to work with the Iraqi police and allow them to take the lead in as many operations as possible—even recognizing that doing so could jeopardize the specific mission.* It is of great importance that the Iraqi police believe that they will be permitted and are considered able to handle all of their responsibilities, or else they will remain unable to do so.

Considerable progress has already been made with Iraq's judiciary, and large numbers of courts are up and running. Needless to say, there is still more to be done.

- *Make the selection process for judges transparent and merit-based.* So far, the Coalition and the Iraqi Ministry of Justice appear to have done well removing the worst offenders from Iraq's bench. However, the process has not been transparent and, at least so far, it has focused on removing those most loyal to the Ba'thist regime as well as the most corrupt, rather than retaining the most competent. This set of priorities is entirely understandable and commendable. However, now that the initial purges are completed, it is important to start building a system for selecting judges that will focus as much on picking the right people as excluding the wrong ones.

A related matter is the question of promotion, which is important for maintaining the integrity of judges once they have been elevated to the bench. The process for receiving promotions should include a committee that vets judges by looking over their record of decisions for any signs of corruption. Indeed, *it might be ideal to include well-regarded judges from foreign countries on these panels to ensure an outside and, hopefully, unbiased perspective in the process.*

- *Insulate judges from external pressure.* Again, real progress has been made in this regard with judges receiving significantly higher salaries than other civil servants of equivalent rank and being afforded security details for themselves and their families. Even the currently high salaries should be examined closely to ensure that judges are compensated well enough to make it unlikely that they would succumb easily to bribery. Beyond this, the tenure of senior judges (including the Court of Cassation, Iraq's "Supreme Court") should be lengthened to inure judges to political vicissitudes. The Iraqi government has generally done well physically protecting its judges and their families and this must be maintained.

- *Make examples of corrupt judges.* Just as the most important corrupt ministers and other officials need to be investigated and prosecuted, so too should corrupt judges.

- *Create and fund an Iraqi NGO as a watchdog group over the judiciary.* In addition to a strong Inspector General to look for corruption on the bench, this is one of several areas where it would be beneficial to organize and fund a private entity dedicated to watching the decisions of the judiciary to try to uncover corruption. Iraq has a great many skilled lawyers, and it would not be difficult to convince a number of them to work for such an organization where they could scrutinize both the cases and the judges looking for suspicious patterns of behavior.

- *Demand maximum transparency.* Neither the public, nor the legislature, nor an NGO dedicated to sniffing out corruption is likely to have much success unless Iraq's judicial proceedings are transparent and easily accessible. In some cases, the extreme demands of national security might make some aspects of transparency impossible, but neither the Iraqis nor their U.S. advisers should err on the side of greater secrecy: as noted throughout Chapter 1, the key to defeating the insurgency and dealing with Iraq's other security threats is to create a strong state through a process of good government. Transparency in the judicial system is a foundational element of good government and should not be sacrificed in the name of what are typically ephemeral threats to national security; threats that would be vastly outweighed by the long-term damage to national security by a judicial process that is seen by the public as arbitrary or corrupted. Consequently, in all but the most extreme circumstances, *Iraqi trials should be open to the public and a C-SPAN-like network should be established so that the general public can regularly watch important trials* (another good way of teaching civics). *Judges should be required to submit written decisions so that there is a public record* and these should be posted immediately on the internet for all to see. *Video tapes of the trials, as well as transcripts, should also be readily available.* In all of these ways, judges will have to make a well-justified argument in support of their decisions, and those decisions and the proceedings will remain on the public record for many years to come, creating a track record that should reveal corrupt practices—and deter other judges from ever going down that path.

- *Employ panels of judges, possibly including foreign judges, for key cases.* For capital offenses; high-profile cases; and those involving members of Iraq's insurgency, militias, organized crime, and senior former Ba'thist officials, it is important for Iraq to employ panels of judges (as it is in some of the highest profile cases, such as the trial of Saddam Hussein and his chief henchmen). Having multiple judges makes it harder to bribe or blackmail them, and makes it more likely that the verdict will reflect the law rather than fear, greed or some other bias. Similarly, Noah Feldman argues that Iraq should follow a practice employed successfully elsewhere of asking at least one foreign judge to be a member of these panels to ensure that at least one objective outsider is present to further diminish the likelihood of improper behavior. Feldman stresses that these outside judges must be Arabic speakers to ensure that trials do not become overly cumbersome, and recommends attracting the most highly-regarded members of the bench from Egypt, Jordan, Morocco and other states for stints in Iraq.

- *Revise judicial education.* In Iraq, judges are produced by an established educational process, very different from the U.S. practice. However, this also means that it is relatively easy to teach Iraqi judges new sets of practices and norms. The key is to thoroughly revise the curriculum and vet the faculty of these programs to ensure that they are teaching appropriate legal and civics lessons to their charges.

REFORMING THE IRAQI POLITICAL PROCESS

Iraq's current political system is not helping the process of reconstruction either—quite the contrary. Here as well, the early mistakes of the United States—first among them allowing a group of exiles and Shi'i chauvinists to determine the shape of Iraq's democratic process—have resulted in a political structure that is exacerbating or even creating many of the problems plaguing the country. There is little evidence to suggest that those parties currently in power really represent the aspirations of the Iraqi people and a good deal to the contrary, their electoral victories notwithstanding. Not surprisingly, the leaders of these parties have few incentives to make the kinds of compromises necessary to achieve the national reconciliation that most Iraqis ardently desire. They have little incentive to make the government work more efficiently, and every incentive to pocket as much public wealth as they can. Likewise, few of Iraq's political leaders pay much attention to addressing the needs of the Iraqi people.

For instance, Phebe Marr, the doyenne of American Iraq experts, interviewed a wide range of Iraqi political leaders in 2004–05 and while she noted that every one of them recognized that the main concerns of the people were security, employment, and electricity, she also observed that few spent any time working to obtain those benefits for their constituents. In her words, "One rather surprising conclusion to emerge in these interviews was the relative lack of emphasis on economics. Economic development did not appear to be of paramount concern either among the Kurds or the shi'ah

[sic] Alliance leaders. While all gave lip service to the necessity of economic development and jobs, few put it at the top of their list. Nor did they dwell on it, or indicate much thought on the direction the economy should take.... At local levels, however, both in Baghdad provincial and local councils, and in the south (Basra and neighboring provinces) leaders put much more emphasis on economics and the need to get the economy moving. Clearly they saw their interests and their ability to hang on to power more closely tied with the economic well being of their constituents. Almost all random polling of Iraqi citizens shows that they put security, jobs and delivery of services such as electricity and water, at the top of their priorities. These interviews may indicate a disconnect between the political leaders at the national level and their constituents."[11]

The only reason that the situation is not worse is that the United States has managed to curb some of the worst excesses of the current leadership, and a small number of those serving in the Iraqi government have turned out to be both morally upright and committed to the notion of a safe, prosperous Iraq. However, we cannot count on a few good apples curing the bunch. Instead, key features of the Iraqi system need to be reformed so that the country has a better chance of solving its many problems.

Revise the Iraqi electoral system. Because of the instability that has plagued the country and the mistakes of the United States when it created the original IGC, the process of allowing viable representatives and political parties to emerge has been greatly delayed. Many of the exiles used their positions on the IGC and their access to U.S. decision-makers and Iraqi resources to prevent potential rivals from securing resources or public support. This is a problem that is ongoing in Iraq, with new parties hamstrung in every way, including with the threat or use of violence by the ruling parties. In addition, the problems with security have made those who can promise Iraqis safety because of their

---

11 Personal correspondence, Phebe Marr to Kenneth Pollack, January 9, 2006.

control over irregular military forces unduly popular. As a result, few of those we would consider Iraq's true democratic élite have been able to emerge, gain public attention, acquire experience as candidates or public servants, and develop a network that would allow them to get elected, let alone represent a constituency in a genuinely democratic parliament.

Iraq's current electoral system employs a modified form of proportional representation which is hindering the emergence of many key features of democracy and could eventually prove disastrous for Iraq. All party leaders want proportional representation because it rewards party loyalty and favors weak national parties over strong individual candidates. It is only natural that Iraq's party leaders favored it, especially so given how little popular support most of them had when they first took power. Proportional representation has made every election a choice among these various parties—because they were the best organized—even though Iraqis might not have voted for any of the individuals on their party slates if the candidates had had to run on their own in local elections. This is also one of the reasons for the growth of sectarianism in Iraq: since the United States empowered a number of chauvinistic and religiously-based Shi'i parties and most Iraqi Shi'ah had few other choices for whom they could vote (and Ayatollah Sistani urged them to vote for these parties), they garnered a huge percentage of the vote, in many cases by default. Once in power, those Shi'i chauvinists proceeded to act, unsurprisingly, like Shi'i chauvinists. This alienated the Kurds and Sunni Arabs, and marginalized the secular exile parties, the most important of which had already been discredited by the inability of Ayad Allawi's interim government to live up to its promises during the period June 2004–January 2005.

There are two problems associated with proportional representation as an electoral system. The first is that *it polarizes the political system and therefore hinders the national reconciliation Iraq so desperately needs.* By requiring would-be leaders to get elected on party slates, it reinforces party loyalty and encourages parties to highlight their differences, thereby pushing them to the extremes. It also rewards the fringes of a society at the expense of the moderates: because voting is not done locally, a would-be radical simply needs to find enough radical supporters across the entire population (or in the Iraqi case, across the population of an entire province) to get elected, rather than having to find a concentration of them in a narrow geographic area. Fringe voters can vote for fringe candidates who represent extreme views, or simply single issues. This is why proportional representation results in badly fragmented parliaments where tiny extremist parties can pull larger moderate blocks to their extreme. The moderates often lack the parliamentary majorities necessary to rule and so must build coalitions that include radical groups.

The second problem created by proportional representation is that *it distances parliamentary representatives from the people.* Members of parliament are elected as part of a party list, and therefore their loyalty is to the party, not to their constituents. Individual parliamentarians lack a true constituency that they must serve. Only the party has constituents and this diffuses the imperative to work for the voters. It also reinforces the worst qualities of Iraq's current political élite, allowing them to largely ignore the population and concentrate on scheming for a greater proportion of power and graft for themselves and their party.

The best system for Iraq would probably be some sort of direct, geographic representation, as in Great Britain and the United States, because this would encourage parliamentary compromise (and national reconciliation) and force legislators to pay close attention to the needs of their constituents.[12] Geographic representation favors

---

12 This is not to suggest that the Anglo-American system is the "best" overall only that given the particular needs of Iraq today, that system is best suited to help Iraqis overcome their problems. Other systems do better at addressing other problems, but in Iraq's case these other electoral systems would exacerbate Iraq's particular difficulties.

the individual candidate over the party, thus allowing the emergence of strong, popular figures. And because every parliamentarian is elected by a specific district, he or she must care deeply about the well-being of those voters. Moreover, a geographically-based "winner-takes-all" system emphasizes compromise within the legislative process. Candidates from districts representing mixed populations have a tremendous incentive to find solutions that will secure the support of all of their constituents. Thus, while proportional representation pushes parliamentarians toward the extremes (to demonstrate the differences between the parties) geographic representation pushes parliamentarians toward the center. And Iraq desperately needs a political system that will encourage compromise across party and sectarian lines.

Because of how deeply entrenched the current parties are, it will be extremely difficult to have them give up their current form of proportional representation. *One solution would be to encourage the Iraqis to adopt a hybrid system like Germany's, with half of the seats in the Council of Representatives being decided by proportional representation and half by geographic direct election.* At the very least, having half of the Council of Representatives directly elected would place an important curb on some of the worst tendencies of proportional representation for the Iraqi system. If the Council of Representatives were to agree to it, they could pass such an electoral change in a matter of weeks or months, dissolve parliament, and have new elections very quickly.

Other methods of connecting Iraqi politicians to the people. As noted several times, one of the more deleterious traits of current Iraqi politics is the disconnect between the political leaders in Baghdad and the rest of the country. It is critical to create structural incentives for Iraqi national figures to pay more attention to the needs of their constituents. In addition to changing the electoral system to employ a geographic "winner-takes-all" method, several other options suggest themselves:

• *Reduce the period between mandated elections from four to two years.* The more frequently parliamentarians have to run for re-election, the more attentive they must be to their constituents.

• *Create formal feedback mechanisms whereby voters can make their grievances known to those who represent them.* For example, Council of Representatives members could be required to attend regular public meetings in their district where they could be questioned by anyone who showed. (Or in the event proportional representation is retained, the parties could be required to send one or more of their Council of Representatives members to such meetings all across the province from which they were elected). At the very least, this would force parliamentarians to hear the complaints of their voters, which might make them more responsive, if only so that they won't hear so much criticism at the next meeting.

• *Make it mandatory that in either the 2009 or 2013 elections all (or even just half of all) candidates for Council of Representatives must have served on either a local or provincial council.* This could be a very powerful method for injecting the needs of local populations into Iraq's rarefied national politics. If every member of the Council of Representatives has to have been elected to local and provincial councils it forces the political parties to pay a great deal of attention to elections for the lesser assemblies. Even if only half of their election lists must meet this requirement, that too would force them to care more about what goes on in the local governments.[13] What's more, because candidates will take with them a reputation from their time on the local and provincial councils—which will inevitably play a role in later elections—the candidates themselves

---

13 If Iraq were to adopt the German system of having half of its parliament elected by direct geographic election and half by proportional representation, then it would be ideal to couple this with a requirement for the half of the Council of Representatives to be elected by proportional representation to have proven themselves by having first served on local or provincial councils. This would ensure that every Iraqi representative felt at least some incentives to act on behalf of their constituency.

and the parties to which they are beholden will have a tremendous incentive to do well on the local and provincial councils. These, by their very nature, are far more concerned with practical matters like improving local irrigation and assessing property taxes—basically about delivering what the voters need and want, which is so lacking in Baghdad today.

Other methods of diminishing sectarianism. Because so many of the problems facing Iraq today are exacerbated or caused by the deepening sectarianism in the country, reversing this trend is also crucial. This is difficult but not impossible, especially with enough time to undo the damage of the past two-and-a-half years.

- *Foster civil society groups that focus on issues.* Governments (including the U.S. government), international organizations, and NGOs should all be encouraged to help establish and fund private citizens' groups within Iraq dedicated to specific issues or sets of issues relevant to the public interest —improving education, improving health care, improving the quality of life for women, etc. Because these issues invariably span sects and ethnicities, they can help connect people from across Iraq's religious and ethnic spectrum. *The goal is to create what political scientists call "cross-cutting cleavages,"* which means that the population can be divided in multiple ways depending on what the issue is, which makes compromise possible across issues and weakens identity as a defining feature of the Iraqi political landscape. For example, if all of Iraq's women can line up on the issue of *shari'a* law, that weakens each ethnic or religious bloc because now half the members of each bloc have something in common with one another that they do not have in common with the other half (the men) of their bloc.

- *Support political parties that run on issues—even single issues—rather than identity.* It is vital to change Iraq's political discourse from a debate over identity to a debate over issues, both because doing so would further weaken the strength of the sectarian blocs

and because differences over issues can more easily be solved through a democratic political process than can fundamental clashes between sects. The United States, foreign governments, international agencies, and NGOs should encourage groups of Iraqis particularly passionate about specific issues to form political parties and run for office based on those issues. An Iraqi "Green" party dedicated to environmental concerns, an Iraqi feminist party dedicated to equal rights for women, or an Iraqi farmers' party dedicated to supporting Iraq's agricultural workers would all be positive developments. There are conservationists, women and farmers in every ethnic group, and the more that they could be linked and convinced to make politics about issues, not identity, the better off the state will be.

- *Education, both for voters and candidates.* Education is always an important element in solving political problems and teaching Iraqis that elections should be about issues rather than identity can help discredit those who try to run based solely on their identity, or try to attract voters by advocating ethnically divisive policies. Similarly, it would be useful to create and fund NGOs to train would-be Iraqi candidates in democratic practices that would include defining a political platform based on what you stand for, not who you are.

- *Support an independent media.* Iraq needs its own television, radio, newspapers, and news magazines divorced from political parties. To some extent this exists in the U.S.-funded *al-Iraqiya* network; however, *al-Iraqiya* has suffered from poor management and direction and is not quite the Iraqi BBC that it was envisioned to be. *Thoroughly overhauling al-Iraqiya and transferring its control, direction, staffing, and content to an independent agency funded and staffed by the Iraqi government (on the BBC model), could help greatly.* Capital should also be made available to support private media enterprises. Given their independence, authenticity with the target audience, and prospects for sustainability, private media are potentially highly effective means by which to increase openness and foster critical debate in formerly closed societies.

Help new parties and leaders to emerge. This is an obvious point, but one more easily said than done. The United States needs to make an aggressive effort to allow new political parties and new Iraqi politicians to emerge who will be more representative of the views of the Iraqi people, if only to force the existing parties to move in the same direction.

- *Punish Iraqi parties that prevent new parties from emerging.* This is probably the most important step that the United States can take to advance this goal. There are widespread allegations of established parties using every method available to them, including violence and murder, to prevent rivals from emerging that could challenge them for power. Washington should obviously press the Iraqi government to investigate such charges, and prosecute those believed to be responsible. However, the Iraqi government has a poor track record on this matter and so it would behoove us to pursue it independently as well. *The United States should attempt to investigate charges of suppressing political rivals independently, and if the investigation finds another Iraqi political party guilty, the United States should impose its own sanctions against that party.* These sanctions could include barring the party or its members from receiving any U.S. aid (including reconstruction contracts), barring U.S. diplomatic or military personnel from meeting with members of the party, or barring them from traveling to the United States. To be clear, the United States should be focused on supporting democratic processes and institutions—not getting behind particular individuals. It is not our role to pick winners.

- *Fund start-up parties.* The United States is already providing a fair degree of support to Iraqi political parties. This simply needs to be continued and expanded.

Media training. A strong, independent and competent Iraqi media is a critical element of a healthy Iraqi political system. The Bush Administration has made a considerable effort to advance this goal. However, there is at least one area where more can clearly be done:

- *The United States should provide education to Iraqi journalists in basic civics, the functioning of democracy, bureaucratic procedures, and some basic economics to enable them to play their role of public watchdog better. The United States should create programs to teach these subjects in Iraq and provide six-month or one year fellowships for Iraqi journalists to study these subjects outside of Iraq.*

REFORMING THE AMERICAN EFFORT

Not all of the problems that need remedying in Iraq lie within the Iraqi political system. Unfortunately, a fair number reside with the U.S. government. The U.S. military can be faulted for certain important aspects of its handling of the war in Iraq, but the civilian side of the bureaucracy has, in many ways, performed far worse. And the problems start at the very top. So far, the White House has not pushed as hard or as consistently as necessary to ensure that things are getting done, and has done a poor job managing the federal bureaucracy. The interagency process has broken down. There is too little direction from the top or coordination of effort, and too little coordination with efforts in the field. (There have been some important bureaucratic changes in recent weeks, but it is too soon to tell if they will reverse these trends).

An important aspect of this problem has been that the Bush Administration has not conveyed a sense of priority for Iraq issues to the bureaucracy. As a result, key items have frequently been snarled by petty bureaucratic hurdles. One of the most vexing problems facing the disbursement of monies appropriated for Iraq has been federal contracting and anti-corruption guidelines. Too many would-be Iraqi contractors are unable to get through this web: they lack the language skills, they do not have the legal education to understand most of what is required, their organizations often do not meet U.S. standards, they operate in a cash economy (whereas U.S. contracting practices are set up for a credit economy), they do not have auditing mechanisms, and they operate in a world where some degree of graft is part of doing business. This is a principal reason that so few of these funds are going to Iraqi firms and so much to Halliburton, Bechtel, and other U.S. conglomerates—who know exactly how to submit a contract, and have everything needed to pass muster under U.S. regulations.

- *The United States must streamline its existing bureaucratic procedures to ensure that money gets quickly into the hands of Iraqis.* This will require a major push by the Executive Office of the President to make clear both the importance that the President attaches to it, and to ride herd over the bureaucracy to see that it is applied.

This is an effort that needs to be extended to the entire bureaucratic process of managing Iraq. At present, both in Washington and Baghdad, there are too many layers of red tape. Some of the problems are caused by draconian security procedures that make some work virtually impossible. Improving the security situation will help alleviate this problem. But it may be necessary to insist on U.S. personnel accepting a slightly higher degree of risk to get their jobs done because we likely will need to start knocking down these bureaucratic walls long before the security situation has been improved dramatically.

Devise a new, unified chain of command to be established across the country for the prosecution of the counterinsurgency campaign and for reconstruction more broadly. The current bureaucratic system that the United States has been employing to manage reconstruction with the new Iraqi government is hopelessly inadequate. Devising a more effective structure must therefore be a high priority. Chapter 1 introduced the idea of a hierarchy of joint committees

Schematic Diagram of Proposed Iraqi Reconstruction Hierarchy

that would integrate military, political, and economic decision-making. This change is vitally needed both to better run reconstruction in all its dimensions, and to help increase the effectiveness of the Iraqi governmental system. Moreover, it is a system that has worked well whenever employed, from the Briggs plan in Malaya through the CORDS program in Vietnam.

The key to this reform is to put in place a hierarchy of committees consisting of all key players in reconstruction and governance. At the highest level, there should be a Supreme Reconstruction Council (SRC), which should include the American reconstruction "chief" (described in Chapter 1), the Commander of Coalition forces in Iraq, the U.S. ambassador, the British ambassador, the highest ranking international official in Iraq, along with the Iraqi Prime Minister, National Security Advisor, and the Ministers of Defense, Interior, Oil, and Finance. The SRC would set broad guidelines for policy and all of the subordinate committees would ultimately report to it.

Beneath the SRC would be 18 Provincial Reconstruction Councils (PRCs)—one for each of Iraq's 18 provinces—and each modeled on the SRC. Each PRC would include the local Coalition military commander (and every province would have its own division-level or sub-division-level command staff, as stipulated in Chapter 1, to bring them into alignment with the political hierarchy), a representative of the U.S. State Department charged with the political aspects of reconstruction in that province, a member of USAID charged with the economic aspects of reconstruction in that sector, representatives of any UN agencies working in that province, a representative of the NGOs working in that province, along with the Iraqi governor and members of the governor's staff responsible for local security, politics, and economic development. The PRCs would regularly report to the SRC and seek guidance from it, while simultaneously managing the work of the next rung in the ladder beneath them, the Local Reconstruction Committees (LRCs).

Like the SRC and PRCs, the LRCs would consist of the local Coalition military commander, representatives from State and USAID, at least one representative of the major NGOs working in the locality, along with the most senior Iraqi official in the area, the local chief of police, along with the senior officials responsible for specific sectors of reconstruction in that area like agriculture, industry, education, health, oil, infrastructure, human rights, trade, etc. There should be scores, perhaps even hundreds of LRCs all across Iraq, taking the guidance passed down from the SRC and the PRCs and turning it into practical efforts on the ground. The LRCs should be given considerable autonomy and encouraged to take the initiative in solving local problems, because every locality will have unique circumstances and the higher level committees should mostly be responsible for directing resources and providing broad guidance, with the LRCs responsible for adapting them to their specific circumstances. The LRCs should also provide constant feedback to the PRCs (and from there to the SRC) regarding what is working and not working, what problems they are facing, and what solutions they have devised. *Both the PRCs and the SRCs should be explicitly tasked with constantly developing lessons learned and formulating "best practices" that can then be passed back down to all of the PRCs and LRCs in hope that they might be able to adopt and adapt some of the solutions devised by other LRCs elsewhere in the country.* Indeed, this function is so important that it might warrant the creation of a distinct inter-committee staff explicitly tasked with this responsibility.

In some cases, the LRCs might be the lowest rung of the ladder, representing the governance/security/economic development team charged with running reconstruction efforts in smaller towns and their environs. For big cities, however, the LRCs would themselves control a series of Neighborhood Reconstruction Committees (NRCs) that would be composed of similar groups, but at a lower level than the LRCs, and would perform the same functions for parts of large cities that the LRCs would perform for towns and rural areas. *The key is to ensure an adequate distribution of such committees based on population density.*

Ideally, there would be either an LRC or an NRC for every 50-100,000 people in Iraq. This is the best, and really the only way to ensure that the immediate needs of the Iraqi people are met, that reconstruction starts at the grass roots and builds upwards, that reconstruction is carried out equitably across the population—at least within secured areas, because the committee structure really should only apply within the "oil stain", where it should be safe enough for the civilian members of these teams to operate and to make real political and economic reconstruction possible—and that reconstruction is able to seep into every part of Iraq. These principles are vital to the success of reconstruction and it is hard to imagine another system that would be able to address this requirement.

What's more, this system, over time can allow the disengagement of foreign personnel, particularly the U.S.-led military Coalition. As an area is secured, becomes politically stable, and then economically prosperous, Coalition personnel can be withdrawn from the relevant committees, leaving only the Iraqis, the international personnel, and the NGO representatives. Eventually, even the international and NGO members might also become superfluous, leaving only the Iraqis.

The Bush Administration's nascent plan to deploy Provincial Reconstruction Teams (PRTs) to Iraq is a good start in the same direction, but falls far short of what is needed because it will not erect an integrated hierarchy reaching from the bottom to the top of Iraqi government. Although the PRTs in Iraq are intended to be different from those employed in Afghanistan, it is still the case that PRTs rely too heavily on military personnel and so are better suited to helping with security sector than civilian sector reforms.[14] Of greater importance still, PRTs are teams who work with local Iraqi officials; they are not a hierarchy that integrates the reconstruction effort both horizontally and vertically, which is what Iraq desperately needs

(and is a well-tried method of addressing the problems of both insurgencies and failed states). Finally, PRTs are teams of Americans and/or other foreigners who are supposed to assist the local Iraqis—they are not part of a structure that integrates Iraqis, Americans and other personnel (including international and NGO members) into a single decision-making entity to coordinate the work of all and ensure that decisions are taken in common with the backing of all of the various groups.

Increasing civilian personnel in Iraq. Another important failing of the U.S. effort has been the dearth of civilian personnel from State, USAID, CIA, Energy, Agriculture, and other key agencies. At present, there are barely 1,000 American civilian officials in Iraq, of whom roughly 90 percent are based at the embassy in Baghdad.[15] As noted in Chapter 1, it is frequently the case that American military personnel are the only Americans present in a town or other part of Iraq. Very few of Iraq's 18 provinces have more than a half-dozen American civilian government personnel working in them, and even fewer American military units have civilian advisers attached to them. The most basic problem is that it is not safe for American civilians to travel in Iraq outside Baghdad's Green Zone. However, it is absolutely vital that they do so. A great many of the changes recommended in this report require increased contact between Americans and Iraqi personnel at all echelons in the Iraqi governmental structure and across the pacified sectors of Iraq. This, of course, is part of the solution to the problem: by concentrating security forces to create safe zones, the United States would be opening up much larger swathes of Iraq to the free movement of American (and other foreign) civilians. However, this is only part of the problem.

The other part of the problem stems from the failure of the White House to put the government on a true

---

14 For an assessment of the experiences and problems with the PRTs in Afghanistan, see Robert M. Perito, "The U.S. Experience with Provincial Reconstruction Teams in Afghanistan," United States Institute of Peace, Special Report 152, October 2005.

15 "Iraq: Assessment of Progress in Economic Reconstruction Governmental Capacity," Staff Trip Report to the Committee on Foreign Relations, United States Senate, December 2005, pp. 23–24.

war footing, mobilize all resources to prosecute and win the war, and notify all personnel to be ready for deployment to Iraq to perform the services their country requires of them. It is worth noting that in Vietnam the highly-successful CORDS program employed over 1,200 American civilians alone, virtually all of whom were deployed to the field to work with the Vietnamese at every level of society.[16] Many members of the State Department opposed the invasion of Iraq, and were further angered by the, admittedly foolish and arrogant, behavior of some DoD officials in handling the immediate postwar period. It is true that a number of senior DoD personnel acted in an unprofessional fashion, barring some of the most knowledgeable and capable people at State from participating in reconstruction activities either in Washington or in Iraq. Nevertheless, many at State responded in a similarly unprofessional manner by refusing to take ownership of Iraqi reconstruction in return. Even today, when the Secretary of State has nominally taken over principal responsibility for the Iraq project, there are far too few State Department and USAID personnel serving in Iraq. Like it or not, the war in Iraq is the most important effort of U.S. foreign policy in the world today by far, and its outcome will have a profound impact on America's place in the world for many years to come. It is time for all U.S. government agencies and their personnel to start acting accordingly.

- *State and USAID must commit far greater numbers of personnel—particularly those with Arabic and knowledge of the Arab world—to the reconstruction of Iraq, even if this means reducing the manning of posts elsewhere.* As was the case in Vietnam, State Department officers sent to Iraq should serve 18-24 month tours. *In particular, there need to be sufficient State and USAID personnel to fill the various slots assigned to them on the SRC, as well as the PRCs, LRCs and NRCs described above.* Fully staffing this integrated hierarchy is non-negotiable; it is vital to the success of reconstruction in Iraq, and it will

only work if the requisite personnel are assigned to it.

- *Although they need to be deployed in safe environments, far more personnel need to be assigned to missions outside of the Baghdad Green Zone.* Again, it is particularly important that sufficient civilians be deployed throughout the country to fill out the various PRCs, LRCs, and NRCs, that will serve as the new nervous system for the reconstruction program as it slowly spreads across Iraq. Without the civilian component, this hierarchy will be just as irrelevant as the present all-military chain of command.

- *Civilian agencies must consistently send their best people to Iraq.* While certainly some of our best technocrats have served in Iraq, this is not always the case. Unfortunately, with many of the civilian agencies, when they are called on to provide personnel for Iraq, because they do not consider it their highest priority, they typically give up those personnel they are most willing to lose—who are rarely their most capable. In this case, State and USAID have been much better than other agencies, but even they could do better. Once again, the issue here seems to be the failure of the White House to impress upon these other agencies that there truly is a war on, and they are expected to make winning that war their highest priority.

- *To complement this effort, civilians in the government must be given greater incentives—both positive and negative—to serve in Iraq.* Those who served there should not only receive higher pay and bonuses, they should also get preference for promotions, choice assignments, and other perks. Those who refuse to serve in Iraq without a very good reason should be penalized in the same manner. The bottom line is that the agencies of the U.S. government need to start conveying to their personnel that service in Iraq is a priority for the agency and their careers could perish or flourish based on it.

16 Perito, op. cit.

INCREASING INTERNATIONAL ASSISTANCE

Although it has largely faded from the op-ed pages as a topic in the debate over American policy toward Iraq, there are still important roles to be played by the United Nations. This is particularly the case now, after the December 2005 elections have ushered in what is to be Iraq's permanent and fully sovereign new government. This is a moment of transition and it would be a fitting moment for the United States to begin handing over some of the burden of guiding Iraq's reconstruction to an international body. This would be beneficial to Washington because of the high risk that the new Iraqi government will be less willing to follow U.S. political guidance than its predecessors. There is still a tremendous amount of work to be done to create a stable Iraqi political system and at this point, it would be much easier for the United Nations or some other international actor to take the lead in pushing the Iraqis on this issue than the United States. Thus, a greater international role would both reinforce the Bush Administration's claim that the elections mark a significant point of departure from the past and bring in new figures and institutions that could help press what is likely to be an increasingly recalcitrant Iraqi government that it must thoroughly reform itself. What's more, greater UN involvement could help pave the way for greater allied contributions, albeit not necessarily in terms of large numbers of combat troops.

At the most basic level, it remains the case that the United Nations, through its various agencies, can call upon a vast network of personnel and resources vital to various aspects of nation-building. One of the greatest problems the United States has faced is that we simply do not have enough people who know how to do all of the things necessary to rebuild the political and economic system of a shattered nation. The United Nations has worked with thousands of people who have such skills in Cambodia, Bosnia, Kosovo, East Timor, Afghanistan, and elsewhere. If the United Nations ask those people to help in Iraq, they are quite likely to come, whereas they have largely been unwilling to answer the same call from the Bush Administration so far. The ability to tap into a much bigger network of people with desperately needed skills, by itself, is a crucial virtue of the United Nations.

Indeed, many of the recommendations of this report either require or would be improved by an increase of skilled personnel from international organizations, NGOs, and foreign governments to perform much-needed functions. For instance, the greater numbers of police instructors needed to provide Iraq's police with longer, more intensive and more frequent training; the foreign judges who are to sit as part of judicial panels for key cases including those involving corruption; and the teachers needed to train Iraq's media in the functioning of a democratic government and free-market economy, can and should all be provided by sources other than the United States of America.

Is greater international participation feasible? The reticence of the international community to participate more fully in the reconstruction of Iraq stems from two separate issues. The first of these was the stubbornness that Washington initially indulged in before and immediately after the invasion of Iraq. The Administration's often-perfunctory diplomatic efforts, its insistence that third parties act fully in accord with U.S. preferences rather than per widely-accepted norms for conducting nation-building operations, its refusal to place the operation under some form of UN chapeau and its undiplomatic conduct toward a number of countries and international organizations alienated a great many who initially showed themselves willing to participate in postwar reconstruction, even though they may have disagreed with the decision to mount the invasion in the first place.

The other stumbling block to garnering greater support through the United Nations has been, once again, the security situation. After the bombing of the UN headquarters in Baghdad in August 2003, the UN Secretary General, Kofi Annan, has been disinclined to put large numbers of additional UN personnel into the country. This provides still another incentive to deal with the security situation quickly—by shifting to a true COIN strategy that would begin by making key sectors of the country safe enough for civilians to perform their missions. As with the greater number of U.S. civilian officials, discussed above, creating safe zones in Iraq should make it much easier to bring in larger numbers of foreigners as long as they are retained in the secured areas. This should make it easier to convince Secretary General Annan to send people to Iraq, which should make it easier to secure support from international NGOs, which should then allow the security situation to improve in a virtuous cycle. And historically, post-conflict reconstructions generally follow either a virtuous cycle (with each positive development reinforcing other positive developments, which in turn reinforce the original positive developments) or a vicious cycle in which failures and problems feed off of one another to make everything progressively worse.

With regard to the political problems, the United States will not only have to change its tone to our allies, to international organizations like the United Nations, and to the NGOs (something that is already improving under the changed personnel of the second Bush 43 Administration) but will have to be willing to allow the United Nations and foreign countries to play a leadership role—particularly on the political and economic tracks—in the reconstruction of Iraq.

• *The Bush Administration should meet with the P-5, other UN Security Council members, and the Secretary General, and make clear that the United States is willing to cede real control in return for the United Nations providing real resources and real leadership.* We should specify areas where we would like greater assistance from the United Nations in the political, economic, and social spheres, discuss what assistance and resources the United Nations could provide, and even agree to allow them to take the lead if we are convinced that doing so will be helpful. It would be preferable to have all of this codified in a new UN Security Council resolution and the functions stipulated as responsibilities of a new high commissioner.

The need for a UN-authorized High Commissioner for Iraq similar to the High Commissioner for Bosnia. There is also the need for UN cover at the top of the reconstruction pyramid. The new Iraqi government and the U.S. embassy have not yet publicly clashed on anything of real significance, and so the current arrangement has "worked" so far. But it is unclear that this will always be true: one can postulate a multitude of scenarios in which an Iraqi government—this one or another—will disagree with the United States, and then the U.S. ambassador will be in a weak position to try to prevent the Iraqis from doing as they please, even if it is deleterious to Iraq. A UN-authorized High Commissioner for Iraq with the power (as the Bosnia High Commissioner has) to veto orders by the Iraqi executive and legislation from the Iraqi Council of Representatives could solve this problem by cajoling or coercing Iraqi leaders in ways that the U.S. ambassador probably cannot and will not want to. To put it bluntly, given the composition of the current Iraqi political leadership there is a high likelihood that someone will have to step in at some point to stop the Iraqis from taking some action that would be very harmful to the future security, stability, or prosperity of Iraq. In such instances, it would be much better for both the United States and Iraq if that "someone" is a UN-authorized high commissioner, and not the U.S. ambassador.

In addition, another reason ("excuse" may be more accurate) offered up by our European and other allies is that they cannot, politically and/or legally, participate in an occupation not under UN jurisdiction. Washington's willingness to accept a UN-authorized High Commissioner, as part of a new U.S. approach to the United Nations, an approach that agreed to allowing the UN Security Council (and/or the Secretary General) a genuine role in Iraq's reconstruction, would effectively remove that obstacle. It might be enough to persuade some governments to join the coalition, and might make it impossible for others not to do so. In the end, some countries might still balk, but because it would be so useful to secure as many additional allied contributions as possible, it is critical for the United States to be seen as going the extra mile to meet the conditions laid out by these various countries for their support, and for most of them, the insecurity and the meager UN role have been their principal complaints. It still may not work, but we must be willing to try.

Engaging the neighbors. All of Iraq's neighbors have considerable influence with different groups inside the country—especially the most problematic groups that are looking to pursue extreme or unilateral courses that would undermine stability and unity and could help push the country into civil war. What's more, many of them have real resources that could be of value to the process of reconstruction. Consequently, the United States would do well to make a greater effort to engage them in the reconstruction effort. In particular, Iran's support is vital to the success of reconstruction and we must find ways to restore the backchannel cooperation that Washington and Tehran engaged in to their mutual benefit during Operation Enduring Freedom.

• *Creating a contact group for Iraq.* The United States should institutionalize a conference with representatives from the United States, Great Britain, Iraq, and all of Iraq's neighbors—conducted under the auspices of the United Nations. In this forum, the United States, Great Britain, and Iraq should all regularly brief the other members on key developments, short and long-term plans, and key requirements. All of the neighbors are deeply concerned about developments inside Iraq, and being more forthcoming with information would be an important first step toward assuaging their fears. In addition, they should be encouraged to make suggestions regarding future developments in the country: it will be impossible to prevent them from doing so under any circumstances, they may actually have some good ideas, and the more we and the Iraqis can be seen as solicitous of their opinions (let alone actually adopting some, even minor, suggestions) the better we will be in a position to secure their assistance in every sense of the word.

In return, we and the Iraqis should make clear that we expect the neighbors to provide support to the reconstruction. The Iraqi people tend to dislike all of their neighbors for one reason or another, thus we should avoid requesting large numbers of troops if at all possible. However, it probably would be reasonable to ask for smaller numbers of personnel from Jordan, Saudi Arabia, and Kuwait to serve as translators in Iraq, and to increase their financial contributions to reconstruction. Likewise, these three and the Syrians should be encouraged to lean on Sunni tribal leaders to end their support for the insurgency and instead back the reconstruction. Similarly, the Iranians need to be encouraged to remain supportive of reconstruction. We need to reassure them both that the United States will succeed and that we will not use a stable new Iraq as a base for future operations against Iran. And we need to encourage them to continue to encourage their various proxies in Iraq to continue to work peacefully in support of reconstruction, and not against it.

Again, we need to accept the reality that Iraq's neighbors have the ability to meddle in Iraqi affairs and to make the course of reconstruction more difficult—very difficult, in the case of Iran. We have to give them an incentive to use that influence constructively, and to contribute far more than they already have. That means treating them as valued partners in the course of reconstruction, although it should not mean giving them veto power over any decision agreed to by the Iraqi government and the United States.

III. Assisting Iraq's Economic Development

It is difficult to make many detailed recommendations regarding the economic aspects of reconstruction because Iraq's economy remains largely held hostage to developments in the security and political arenas. The greatest economic problems in Iraq today derive from the persistent insecurity, widespread corruption, and unsettled political situation that define its landscape. It is hard to envision meaningful progress in reviving or improving Iraq's economy without commensurate—and in many cases, preceding—improvements in Iraq's security and political fortunes. To some extent, any progress in the political and security arenas will have an immediate positive impact on the economy, as has been the case with the semblance of improvement in security resulting from the consolidation of militia control over central and southern Iraq coupled with the successful referendum and elections in Iraq in the fall and winter of 2005. Moreover, it is almost certainly the case that there are deep, structural problems in the Iraqi economy (many of them extant long before the American liberation of the country in 2003 and even before the Iraqi invasion of Kuwait in 1990) that should be addressed as part of the broad program of reconstruction, but cannot really be treated until the security and political

situations improve enough to allow the economic gears to really begin to turn.

Iraq's problems with security, both in terms of insurgent attacks, militia violence and crime, are the first problem for economic reconstruction. Some Iraqis are afraid to leave home, which is especially true for women and girls, making it hard for them to find work or shop for their families. Traveling long distances is always dangerous for Iraqis, and those who must, do so sparingly and often with heavy security. Goods often do not reach their destinations because they are waylaid by militias, insurgents, or thieves. The need for security, both in the form of physical barriers and armed guards adds somewhere between 20–50 percent to all economic costs in Iraq.[1] Anything not properly guarded at all times can vanish in the blink of an eye. Electricity is not always available, to a considerable extent because of sabotage to the power grid, leaving businesses from small shops to enormous factories at the mercy of the fates. According to a report by the Congressional Research Service, in 2004 saboteurs cut over 100 electrical lines and knocked down 1,200 electrical towers.[2] External investment in Iraq is negligible because few foreign entrepreneurs are willing to run

---

1 See for instance Joseph Farinella, "Iraq: Perceptions, Realities and Cost to Complete," Testimony to the Committee On Government Reform, Subcommittee on National Security, Emerging Threats, and International Relations, U.S. House of Representatives, October 18, 2005, p. 8; Renae Merle and Griff Witte, "Security Costs Slow Iraq Reconstruction," *The Washington Post*, July 29, 2005, p. A1; Curt Tarnoff, "Iraq: Recent Developments in Reconstruction Assistance," Congressional Research Service, CRS Report for Congress RL31833, May 12, 2005, p. 11.

2 Tarnoff, ibid, p. 11.

the enormous risks that putting money into Iraq entails. In fact, anecdotal evidence strongly suggests that even wealthy Iraqis (many of them newly-enriched from graft and organized crime) are not investing their earnings back into the country, but are transferring huge amounts of it out for safekeeping to Jordan, the Arab Gulf States, and Europe. Non-Government Organizations (NGOs), which have repeatedly proven themselves critical to the rebuilding of a nation's economy, have mostly fled Iraq because insurgents have deliberately targeted their personnel and the Coalition has been unable to provide for their safety.

For the most part, security problems have caused greater harm to Iraq's larger industries than to its small businesses. Factories need to have workers, managers, power, and materials all present at the same time for any products to be manufactured, and in current circumstances, it is simply too infrequent that such harmonic convergences occur for most factory owners to make the investment in opening their plants. State-Owned Enterprises continue to "operate," but mostly in the sense that the government pays the salaries of the workers, not that anything actually gets produced. Small businesses can usually make do in the face of such shortfalls, and their owners also frequently need to keep them open to earn money in the way that owners of factories generally do not. For instance, small businesses often can buy electricity from neighbors with private generators—or even buy small generators themselves; far fewer owners of large businesses are willing to buy the big generators they would need to meet their power requirements given the ease with which they can be destroyed or otherwise sabotaged. Moreover, larger businesses also tend to be more heavily reliant on foreign investment than smaller concerns, and so they also suffer from the dearth of external investment capital flowing into the country.

Iraq's political problems also hobble its economy. First, there is the indirect impact that politics has on the economy by contributing to Iraq's prevailing insecurity. This is worth noting because it again underscores the intricate interrelationship among military, political, and economic developments in Iraq. Beyond this, however, there are other problems as well. Corruption is the most obvious of these; as noted in Chapter 2, graft is endemic throughout the Iraqi government and, like security, imposes heavy costs on all business transactions. The incapacity of Iraqi ministries means that vast sums of money are simply wasted, as does the infighting among the different ethnic, sectarian and even tribal groups within the government, which paralyzes budgeting, regulations, and other aspects of economic policy. Many major Iraqi enterprises were state-owned, leaving them prey to all of the problems of the central government. These state industries employ roughly 500,000 people, making them a critical employment sector, but they produce little and their workforce is generally overstaffed by 30–40 percent, making them even less efficient as economic engines.[3] Beyond this, Iraq still has numerous other manifestations of a command economy—which inserts an unhelpful and undermanned central bureaucracy into far too many economic activities—not least of which is a mindset among too many Iraqis that they can and should do nothing for themselves but must wait for Baghdad to do it for them.

Consequently, the most useful things that the United States and the new Iraqi government could do to help Iraq's economy would be to embrace the many recommendations regarding security and politics described above.

Of course, there are also a range of pre-existing problems besetting the Iraqi economy from Saddam's mismanagement of the Iraqi economy, the twelve years of UN-imposed sanctions, Iraq's various wars, and the fall of Saddam. Iraq's banking sector remains moribund, in large measure because so much cash appears to be flowing out of the country from graft. This lack

---

3 Ken Dilanian, "Iraqi Business Begins to Boom," *Knight-Ridder Newspapers*, March 16, 2004; The Economist Intelligence Unit (EIU), "Country Report: Iraq," September 2005, p. 24.

of liquidity, manifested in relatively high interest rates, has hindered the service economy and made construction and infrastructure repair efforts heavily dependent on foreign aid rather than internal or external investment.[4] Similarly, the distorting subsidies on fuel and the government-provided rations are also important problems introducing inefficiency into the economy that date to earlier eras in Iraqi history. Iraqi worker productivity remains low thanks to poor education and the mindset among many fostered under Saddam's totalitarianism that receiving a paycheck is not necessarily tied to a person's skill or output.

Another example of this phenomenon is that health care in Iraq remains poor (even by regional standards) as a result of the impact of sanctions, Iraq's wars, and the distortions of Saddam's totalitarian state. Diarrhea, measles, respiratory infections, malaria, and even tuberculosis and cholera, plague the population, especially Iraq's children. These diseases, coupled with malnutrition affecting nearly one-third of Iraqi children under the age of five, have pushed Iraqi infant and child mortality rates well above regional averages and comparable Iraqi figures from before the 1991 Persian Gulf War. Likewise, inadequate healthcare for pregnant women has contributed to high maternal mortality rates.[5] Even here, corruption, crime, violence, and political paralysis also play a role. For instance, pharmaceuticals take long periods of time to reach Iraqi doctors and come with high price tags attached, while many hospitals and clinics lack the resources to care for all seeking their aid. Typically, they charge unofficial "user fees" which make them largely unaffordable for the average Iraqi.[6] Meanwhile, few health NGOs maintain sizable operations in Iraq because of the security threat to foreign personnel.

SIGNS OF LIFE

While the Iraqi economy is not doing well, it is also important to keep in mind that it is not listless either. In fact, there are important signs of life, although the manifestations of progress are important in their own right because of what they say about the fragility and, in some cases, the superficiality of Iraq's economic activity. To some extent, credit for the relative progress of the Iraqi economy is due to the CPA and their successors at the U.S. Embassy, who have done much better dealing with Iraq's economic problems than they have on security and political matters. The transitional Iraqi government also proved far more astute at handling some of its economic problems than it did its political and security problems, thanks to some able ministers in key places, particularly Minister of Finance 'Ali Allawi.

Foreign aid continues to flow into Iraq. The United States alone has appropriated some $25 billion in nonmilitary assistance and a considerable portion of that money has been allocated and even disbursed.[7] Likewise, by August 2005, Iraq had also received about $2.7 billion in bilateral assistance from other countries and recently secured loans of nearly another $1 billion from the IMF and World Bank.[8] Moreover, Iraq and the US have been able to get Iraqi oil exports up to a respectable level, although they are still not at prewar rates. Because Iraq's economy remains almost entirely dependent on oil revenues, increased oil production coupled with very high oil prices in 2004 boosted growth (in GDP per capita) to an astronomical 50 percent. By the same token, the downturn in oil prices coupled with falling exports (thanks mainly to theft and sabotage) meant an equally dramatic slowdown to a growth rate of less than 5 percent in 2005.[9] Although

4   International Monetary Fund, IMF Country Report No. 05/295, Iraq: Statistical Appendix, August 2005, p. 9.
5   USAID, "Assistance for Iraq: Health," available at <http://www.usaid.gov/iraq/accomplishments/health.html>.
6   Medact, "Iraq Health Update – Summer 2005," available at
    <http://www.medact.org/content/communique/iraqupdate.PDF#search='Iraq%20health%20statistics'>.
7   Steven Kosiak, "The Cost of US Military Operations in Iraq and Afghanistan Through Fiscal Year 2006 and Beyond," Center for Strategic and Budgetary Assessments, January 4, 2006, p. 1.
8   Joseph A. Christoff, "Rebuilding Iraq: Enhancing Security, Measuring Program Results, and Maintaining Infrastructure are Necessary to Make Significant and Sustainable Progress," Testimony before the Committee on Government Reform, Sub-Committee on National Security, House of Representatives, October 18, 2005, p. 6.
9   The Economist Intelligence Unit, "Country Risk Service: Iraq," October 2005, p. 8.

far too much of Iraq's oil money is siphoned out of the country in the form of graft, much still remains—even if that too is often in the form of corruption. Thus, legal or illegal, a fair amount of cash still flows into the country. The problem is that it is a bit like a patient with a terrible wound who is being provided with constant blood transfusions: the transfusions are able to keep the patient alive, but he is still likely to die unless the wound is closed because it is impossible to keep maintaining the transfusion rate. In other words, at some point, foreign aid to Iraq is likely to dry up, and when that happens, if Iraq's economy is not on a more sustainable basis, it could experience major dislocations.

The constant flow of money into the country, coupled with the U.S. decision to temporarily lift all import duties after the fall of Baghdad brought in a flood of foreign consumer goods. Tariffs have been reimposed, but the new Iraqi government has generally kept them very low (5 percent) maintaining the attractiveness of Iraq as a destination for foreign goods. Consequently, there is quite a lot of food, household necessities, electronics, and appliances in Iraqi markets and stores. Unfortunately, the same could have been said (with the exception of major appliances) about Iraqi markets at the end of Saddam's reign. There were never real shortages, just an inability on the part of Iraqis to afford to purchase anything. Although inflation has slowed considerably since the fall of Baghdad, it is still high at roughly 20–30 percent, according to the IMF and the Economist Intelligence Unit, respectively.[10] Indeed, the continuing distortion caused by price controls and subsidies has also allowed Iraq's black market to persist and even to thrive. Thus, goods are often available, but they tend to be expensive—too expensive for most Iraqis.

The influx of foreign aid, especially since so much of it was initially earmarked for infrastructure repair, caused Iraq's construction industry to boom. As expected, this has taken some of the edge off of unemployment and has helped push money down into the hands of Iraq's working classes—all of which was beneficial and also helped the recovery of Iraq's consumer economy. However, too much of what was built did not materially affect the Iraqi economy: far more schools were built than were really needed; too many huge "white elephant" projects were built that cannot be sustained by Iraq's limited labor and management force; other projects turned out to be useless because of faulty planning, like the famous electrical generators that were never connected to the national power grid; and too many of these projects have become targets for the insurgents (or local militias) and so are either destroyed or demand scarce resources to pay for security. Moreover, the United States and other aid providers, recognizing these problems, are shifting aid away from construction. While this is probably necessary, to some extent, based on the need to get a better return on the investment, it could undermine Iraq's construction industry, possibly boosting unemployment once again, and leaving a legacy of huge expenditures with little impact on Iraq's long-term economic viability.

Wherever American and other foreign aid has been able to intervene directly in Iraq's healthcare system it has typically done quite a bit of good, but mostly in alleviating immediate problems rather than building a sustainable healthcare system. For instance, USAID-supported programs have resulted in a huge improvement in child immunization rates all across the country. Similarly, infant mortality has been cut in half since the fall of Baghdad through direct intervention in Iraqi pre-, neo-, and ante-natal care; still, only Yemen has a worse infant mortality rate in the Middle East. In contrast to these (relative) success stories, Iraq still averages over 50 infant deaths per 1,000 live births, while Egypt averages less than 33, Syria under 30, and Jordan and the Gulf states are all below 20.[11]

10 The Economist Intelligence Unit, "Country Report: Iraq," September 200 5, p. 12; International Monetary Fund, "Country Report No. 05/295, Iraq: Statistical Appendix," August 2005, p. 18.
11 CIA, *The World Factbook*, 2005.

GRAPHIC 3. BASIC SOCIO-ECONOMIC INDICATORS IN IRAQ, 1989–2005

Socio-Economic Indicator	1989	2002	2003	2005
GDP, in billions of constant 2003 dollars	39	26	20	30*
GDP per capita, in current dollars	1,940	802	518	1,051
GDP per capita, in constant 2003 dollars	2,878	815	518	1,000
Inflation (Consumer Price Index)	30-40	19	34-40**	20-30**
Unemployment	3-5	NA	50-60	25-40
Life Expectancy in years	61	63	59	69
Infant Mortality, per 1,000 live births	40	102	102	50
Maternal Mortality, per 1,000 births	117	310	NA	193 (2004)

* Projected for 2005
** In both cases, the first number is from the IMF, the second from the EIU.
  Sources: CIA, *World Factbook*, 1991 and 2005; Economist Intelligence Unit, "Country Report: Iraq," September 2005, p. 12; International Monetary Fund, "Country Report No. 05/294: Iraq: 2005 Article IV Consultation—Staff Report," August 2005, p. 9, 18; Measuring Stability and Security in Iraq October 2005, Report to Congress In Accordance with Conference Report 109-72, Emergency Supplemental Appropriations Act, 2005, page 11; UNDP, *Iraq Living Conditions Survey, Volume II: Analytical Report*, 2004, p. 51; UNFPA, "Iraq: Reproductive Health Assessment," November 2003, pp. 4–5; World Bank, *World Development Indicators Database*, 8/29/05.

Likewise, in late 2004 one-third to half of Iraqi women were giving birth at home, often with only traditional midwives in attendance, because Iraq's hospitals and health clinics were too few, too understaffed, too short on pharmaceuticals, and too expensive for most.[12] Thus, here as well, there has been a short-term improvement thanks to direct provision of foreign aid, but this has not yet been transformed into overall improvements in Iraq's healthcare system that would allow the system to sustain these improvements (let alone address problems in other areas) in the absence of that foreign aid. All of this suggests that Iraq's current economic activity is superficial and highly dependent on large-scale foreign assistance.

MANAGING EXPECTATIONS

American misunderstanding of Iraqi unhappiness derives at least in part from the different measures that each group employs. Graphic 3 above sets out some basic socio-economic indicators for Iraq, starting in 1989 at the end of the Iran-Iraq War, running through 2002 (i.e. just before the liberation of Iraq), then to 2003 (immediately after the liberation), and finally to the latest estimates for 2005. Americans typically like to compare the last column (current economic indicators) with either the second column (the end of Saddam's reign) or the third column (the immediate postwar situation). These comparisons show progress, both over how well Iraq was doing at the end of Saddam's reign and, particularly, since the nadir of Iraqi fortunes in the chaos immediately following Saddam's fall. To Washington, this suggests both significant progress in both a relative and an absolute sense. In American eyes, these numbers tell the story that Iraqis are better off than they were under Saddam and there is steady upward progress.

Iraqis, however, are often more concerned with the comparison between the first column, when Iraq was doing reasonably well before Saddam's invasion of Kuwait, and the last column. By this standard, Iraq has not improved much at all and in many ways is still very badly off. Moreover, few Iraqis believe 1989 was the golden age of Iraq, an honor that is reserved for the late 1970s, before Saddam's invasion of Iran. Indeed, for Iraqis, 1989 was much like the current moment because it was a time of rebuilding after the hardships of the miserable eight-year war with Iran. Thus, Iraqis see the United States as having done little

---

12 UNDP, *Iraq Living Conditions Survey, Volume II: Analytical Report*, 2004, p. 69.

to improve their lives economically and much to worsen them.

What makes it all the more damaging still is that many Iraqis believed that one of the benefits of the U.S. invasion—to be balanced against its many costs—would be real economic development that would put them in the same league as many of the East Asian countries, or at least the South American states. While most Iraqis always had exaggerated expectations of what the U.S. invasion might accomplish in this area, what they have gained to date has fallen so far short of their expectations that many of them question whether the Americans really know what they are doing or, worse still, whether the Americans are purposely denying Iraq the economic prosperity that they believe the Bush Administration promised. In particular, when adjusted for inflation, Iraqi wealth measured by constant GDP per capita remains less than half of what it had been 15 years ago and unemployment is 8–12 times higher than what it once was. As is well understood at this point, unemployment may be the worst of the economic problems besetting the Iraqi people. Moreover, unemployment may actually be worse than the numbers above convey because these indices do not capture widespread *under*employment. Thus, for the Iraqis, not only is their economy not the dream they had imagined, but it does not even compare well to previous moments in their recent history.

This "expectations gap" is an important element of the problem. But there are two critical "buts" to that statement. The first is that the expectations gap is only part of the problem. There are real structural problems in the Iraqi economy that are regularly exacerbated by the unstable security and political conditions. *The second is that referring to an "expectations gap" inevitably trivializes an extremely dangerous phenomenon.* A dramatic divergence between expectations and reality inevitably breeds anger and frustration. Indeed, this is exactly what has fueled the growth of Salafi Jihadist terrorist groups like al-Qa'ida throughout the Islamic world, where many are deeply unhappy over their lot given where they believe it

ought to be. What's more, in Iraq, many popular expectations were actually quite reasonable. For instance, it was entirely reasonable for the Iraqis to assume that if the United States were going to invade their country, that Washington would employ adequate forces to secure the country after we toppled their government. The fact that we did not do so, and still have not properly filled the security vacuum we consequently created, is causing a great deal of anger and frustration, and is part of the expectations gap. In part, *it is this expectations gap that could drive Iraq to civil war if reconstruction is seen as continuing to fail.*

SHORT TERM VS. LONG TERM ECONOMIC REFORMS

The United States and the new government of Iraq really have two economic challenges ahead of them. The first is the pressing need to begin to provide tangible benefits to the Iraqi people quickly—within the next 6–12 months as the Iraqis assess whether this new government will be any different from its predecessors. As noted repeatedly above, the great danger is that the Iraqi people will see no change from the past and conclude that this government will be no different from its predecessors, and that they therefore need to make other arrangements to get what they need for themselves and their families. The problem is that this will likely mean casting their lot with Sunni insurgents, Shi'i militias, and other extremist groups. The only way to combat this threat is to begin to show the Iraqi people that their lives are getting better. If the new Iraqi government can do so (and this will inevitably require considerable help from Iraq's American benefactors), there is every reason to believe that most Iraqis will continue to support reconstruction if only because the vast majority are so desirous of a better future and so afraid of civil war.

The second, however, is the at-times contradictory need to help Iraq begin to deal with the various structural problems with its economy. At some point, the Iraqi economy will have to move solely under its own power and provide for the Iraqi people without prodigious external assistance, and this will require major changes—physical, organizational, and psychological. The last vestiges of Saddam's command economy need to be dismantled. Iraq's oil wealth needs to be harnessed as an engine to help increase the productivity of the Iraqi worker and diversify the economy so that it is not so wholly reliant on oil revenues. Market forces need to be allowed to operate, and the Iraqi work force is going to have to become integrated into the global economy, which is likely to be a rude awakening for them. In addition to the far-reaching changes this will require, such efforts often run at cross purposes with the need to produce results quickly. For example, the need to create jobs immediately inevitably works against efforts to eliminate distortions and inefficiency in both the labor and investment markets. However, Iraq's economy cannot run on the adrenaline of massive foreign aid contributions forever, and in the coming year the United States must continue to help Iraq reform its economy so that it can survive when the foreign aid runs out.

Unfortunately, there is no easy or obvious way to square this circle. It would be a mistake to simply argue that every effort and every resource needs to be devoted to one course or another. *Iraq must have both immediate economic relief and long-term economic reform.* If it emphasizes the short-term over the long, at best it will require constant infusions of foreign assistance to sustain even its current level of economic growth, and at worst, could mean just postponing an economic crash. However, if it emphasizes long-term reforms without doing enough in the short-term, either the economy or popular support for reconstruction might crash—which would preclude getting to the long-term. This is part of the conundrum facing Iraq in the economic realm: it must simultaneously begin to show immediate progress to people who have been miserable for too long while simultaneously laying the foundation for a more vibrant (and stable) economy to emerge a few years into the future.

Given these conflicting requirements, it is critical that the United States and the new government of Iraq set *clear priorities for economic policy for the next year. We need to identify the sectors of the Iraqi economy that are most important to the short-term well-being of average Iraqis and make focused efforts to produce immediate progress in those sectors. In all other areas of the Iraqi economy, the emphasis should be on long-term structural reform.* In this way, the United States and Iraq ought to be able to strike an adequate balance between providing enough immediate relief to the Iraqi people to keep them committed to reconstruction, while also building a stable, competitive Iraqi economy.

SHORT-TERM EFFORTS

Those sectors of the Iraqi economy that U.S. and Iraqi (and preferably international) officials should target for short-term improvement must be those that the Iraqis have identified as being of greatest concern to them, as well as several other sectors which are indirectly just as vital because they underpin those sectors the Iraqi people are most concerned about. After all, the goal of this effort is to address Iraqi unhappiness to keep Iraqi public opinion from collapsing and causing a mass desertion to the militias and insurgents. *Specifically, the areas in which the U.S. and Iraq should make a determined effort to produce more tangible results are unemployment, electricity, oil production and export, corruption, agriculture, decentralization, banking and investment, and foreign aid.*

While critically important, this overarching recommendation is hardly novel. Although they have not necessarily articulated this approach explicitly, this is effectively what U.S. and international officials have been promoting all along. What's more, they have had some degree of success. Unfortunately, they have not had enough success. Thus this section should be seen principally as a series of recommendations regarding how to improve on efforts that the U.S. government already recognizes as important and has committed a fair degree of resources toward, albeit with varying degrees of impact.

Unemployment. Unemployment is consistently one of the greatest complaints of Iraqis. It is clear that far too many Iraqis are not gainfully employed, although the exact dimensions of the problem are elusive. Various estimates put the range of unemployment as low as about 10 percent to as high as about 70 percent. The Iraqi Ministry of Planning believes that the true unemployment rate is about 28 percent, and most experts concur that somewhere between 25 and 40 percent is probably about right.[13] While this is bad enough, it does not include problems either with underemployment or Iraqis being forced to supplement their incomes with multiple jobs. Thus, there are Iraqis who have jobs, but jobs that do not pay them enough to survive. Either they starve or become homeless, or they take on additional jobs to try to make ends meet. Thus, employment problems extend beyond the large number of people who simply do not have jobs. Moreover, it is important to note that one of the worst problems with unemployment is its concentration among young men—37 percent of educated youth are unemployed, and for uneducated young people, the rates are even higher.[14] This is problematic because young, unemployed men are the principal recruits of the insurgents and militia groups.

The U.S. government is well aware of the problem of unemployment and has made a number of efforts to fight it. In part because of these efforts, and in part because of the resurgence of Iraq's consumer economy, unemployment is not as pervasive as it was even 12 months ago. However, a great deal remains to be done and many of these early efforts must be preserved just to prevent a resurgence of even worse employment problems. This is one of the principal areas in which short and long-term needs run at cross purposes. Economists and reconstruction experts point out that nearly three years into the reconstruction effort, Iraq should be moving away from Works Progress Administration-style aid programs that fund what are often nothing more than make-work projects concentrated in construction and infrastructure repair to take unemployed men off the streets. They correctly argue that Iraq needs to be shifting its emphasis to more economically viable and productive methods of employing its work force. They also note that these kinds of aid programs—particularly those focused on construction—are notorious magnets for corruption, the eradication of which is another short-term priority for Iraq.

However, because progress in Iraq's economy has largely been limited to just a few sectors, it is not yet ready for a radical shift. The jobs do not yet exist in the economy to absorb large numbers of Iraqis if these make-work programs are ended. What's more Iraq's infrastructure is still far from being repaired, let alone modernized, thus construction remains an important demand and it would be deleterious to end these programs too abruptly.

- *Maintain adequate levels of funding for current Iraqi construction projects and other programs that generate large numbers of jobs.* Iraqis and foreign experts complain about the inefficiency of these programs, and they are correct. As a result, USAID and other foreign donors have announced plans to move away from these kinds of grants and instead to focus on longer-term economic development. While the latter is equally necessary, it would be a mistake to do so in the name of ending these projects. Because those working on these projects have not been properly retrained, and because the Iraqi economy does not have other jobs available, the effect could be to quickly swell the ranks of the unemployed (which likely would mean swelling the ranks of the insurgents and militias just as quickly). What's more, while inefficient and susceptible to corruption, these programs have been an important element in the revival of Iraq's consumer economy. There are construction sites all over Iraq and these employ lots of people, pumping lots of U.S. dollars and Iraqi dinars into local economies. Thus a rapid cut in these projects could have severe repercussions for the Iraqi economy in general.

13 The Economist Intelligence Unit, "Country Report: Iraq," September 2005, p. 24.
14 Ibid.

- *Emphasize high-employment projects that will contribute to Iraq's long-term economic health.* A frequent criticism of some of the early American-sponsored construction projects designed to employ large numbers of Iraqis is that they produced "white elephants"—massive facilities that were expensive and difficult to operate in the violent and unpredictable circumstances of Iraq, and that contributed little to Iraq's economy when they were finished. While these programs need to be sustained to some extent to prevent a collapse of the labor market in the short term, it would be useful to learn this lesson. This cuts in two directions. *First, the United States should be willing to provide greater funding to smaller, local projects which are more likely to be sustainable and to have an immediate impact, even if that impact is localized.* USAID does have such programs, but they would need to be greatly expanded. *Second, future U.S. funding for any large projects needs to be based on Iraq's needs and have a reasonable expectation that they can be protected.* To some extent, this builds on the "oil stain" approach to security described in Chapter 1: large infrastructure projects should only be undertaken in those areas secured by Coalition forces. *One possibility would be to build a national light rail system.* Iraq's rail infrastructure is ridiculously inadequate to its needs. A modern, light-rail system that began in the secured areas of the "oil stain" and then slowly expanded outwards as new areas of Iraq were brought into the secured areas. Nothing would do more to make clear the inexorable march of Coalition forces, while simultaneously helping to bind the country together physically and economically.

- *Encourage the creation of job training and retraining programs.* This has been a considerable failing on the part of the United States. Since the fall of Baghdad, too little effort has been put into establishing programs that can teach Iraqis skills that would make them desirable employees, including by multina-

tional firms. As a result, Iraqi worker productivity is low and many firms have preferred to hire foreign workers (even paying to bring them to Iraq) rather than employing Iraqis. Indeed, the mistake that the United States made in disbanding the Iraqi Army and security services was not the decision to disband them *per se*, but the failure to provide for their employment afterwards. Moreover, at this point, after a decade-and-a-half of war and sanctions, many Iraqis lack even basic education: in 2001, the UN Human Development Report observed that 55 percent of Iraqis age 15–24 were illiterate.[15] *The United States should provide grants to Iraqis and to international NGOs to establish vocational schools and job training programs, while the government of Iraq should provide financial incentives for the same.* In particular, the oil redistribution program discussed in Chapter 2 and below specifically would distribute money to individual Iraqis that could be used to pay for various educational programs, including vocational education. *Education and vocational training programs are important not only to ensure that Iraqis have the skills to be productive members of society in future years, but are excellent ways to get large numbers of people off the streets in the short-term.*

- *Increase both aid and other inducements to agriculture, which generates jobs very quickly.* Rebuilding Iraq's agricultural sector is vital for a wide variety of reasons. However, with regard to employment it is important because agricultural work is labor intensive and much of the labor does not need to be skilled. On the specifics of this effort, see "Rebuilding Iraq's Agricultural Sector," below.

Corruption This report has referenced the problems of corruption in Iraq many times, and so a full account is certainly not warranted here. It is worth pointing out that corruption does impose an enormous burden on the Iraqi economy, and so there are economic

---

15 Cited in Christopher Foote, William Block, Keith Crane, and Simon Gry, "Economic Policy and Prospects in Iraq," Public Policy Discussion Papers No. 04-1, Federal Reserve Bank of Boston, p. 7.

incentives to fight it, in addition to the political and other motivations. For instance, a December 2005 Senate Foreign Relations Committee staff report found that Iraqis estimated that corruption generally added about 40 percent to the cost of all business transactions.[16] (To which should also be added the 20–50 percent surcharge imposed by security needs on Iraqi economic transactions to understand why prices in Iraq are often prohibitively high). In addition to the many recommendations for addressing corruption proposed in Chapter 2, above, there is one additional recommendation specifically related to economic matters that can be offered:

• *Remove Ahmed Chalabi as the head of the Contracts Review Committee.* The Contracts Review Committee was established as a corruption-control mechanism. All contracts in excess of $3 million granted by the government of Iraq must be approved by this Committee. Charges of corruption have dogged Chalabi for decades (including a 1992 conviction for embezzlement and fraud *in absentia* in Jordan), and there is a widespread belief in Iraq that he is using his control of the Contracts Review Committee to skim funds, take contracts away from his rivals, and make sure that they go to his friends. Obviously, the government of Iraq should investigate these claims thoroughly. However, under any circumstances, Chalabi should be removed. His reputation for corruption, deserved or not, is seen by many Iraqis as proof that their government is failing them. Like Caesar's wife, the head of the Contracts Review Committee must be above suspicion for Iraqis to have confidence in it.

The oil sector. The Iraqi economy is addicted to oil production, with all of the negative connotations that metaphor implies. However, it would be a mistake to force Iraq to quickly "kick" this habit, and there is the potential for Iraq's oil wealth to be a far more positive factor in Iraq's economic and political health than it has otherwise been, either before or since Saddam's fall. At this point, 95 percent of Iraqi government revenue is coming from oil sales.[17] In the words of the Economist Intelligence Unit, "When the oil doesn't flow, unemployment and poverty increase, creating new recruits for the insurgency."[18]

Unfortunately, too little of Iraq's oil revenues are actually going to meet its vital economic needs. Oil production, distribution, and export are the most lucrative venues for theft and graft, and so are at the heart of Iraq's problems with both crime and corruption. Moreover, the insurgents are well aware of the government's dependence on oil and various groups have mounted a vicious campaign against Iraqi oil production and export capabilities. Consequently, the Iraqi oil ministry claimed that it had lost $11.35 billion worth of oil production to sabotage of pipelines and facilities between April 2003 and July 2005.[19] How much of what the ministry officials claim was lost to sabotage was actually lost to graft, we may never know. But the bottom line remains the same: thanks to crime, sabotage and corruption, far too much of Iraq's oil wealth is not going to fund reconstruction. The problems with corruption, crime, and sabotage are limiting private investment in the Iraqi oil sector, with repercussions for both short- and long-term production.

To make matters worse, sabotage coupled with extensive damage to Iraq's oil fields and production infrastructure over the past 30 years have also combined to keep oil production lower than was hoped (so far) and this, along with increased demand from liberated Iraqis has kept exports down. Exports of oil averaged 1.39 million barrels per day (m b/d) in 2005, down

16 "Iraq: Assessment of Progress in Economic Reconstruction Governmental Capacity," Staff Trip Report to the Committee on Foreign Relations, United States Senate, December 2005, p. 9.

17 Ibid, p. 5.

18 The Economist Intelligence Unit, "Iraq Economy: Iraq's Weak Heart," January 4, 2006.

19 The Economist Intelligence Unit, "Country Report: Iraq," September 2005, p. 28.

from 1.5m b/d in 2004, and about 2.5m b/d in 2002, at the end of Saddam's reign.[20] Finally, Iraq has a major problem with refinery capacity, to the extent that its refineries are able to supply only 55 percent of domestic demand, which forces the country to import gasoline and other refined petroleum products at market rate—which they then sell to the public at the subsidized rate.[21] The results have been disastrous: Iraq is pumping less oil, exporting less of what it is pumping, losing huge amounts of the revenue from what it does export, and then having to use too much of the revenues from what it does export to pay for refined oil products on which it then loses money by reselling these refined products to its own citizens at far less than what it bought them for.

Nor are there easy answers to any of these problems. Recognizing the importance of oil to Iraq's economic future, the United States has invested $2.4 billion to try to get Iraqi oil production up to 3m b/d by 2006, but found that much of that money is instead going to simply maintain the existing infrastructure and repair damage from attacks—which again speaks to the need for greater security efforts on behalf of Iraqi infrastructure.[22] The Iraqis have begun to diminish the extent of the fuel subsidy, raising the price of premium gasoline at the end of 2005 five times from $0.13 per gallon to $0.64 per gallon, but will have to continue to move slowly on this because of the fear of causing widespread political unhappiness and throwing the economy into recession.[23] Privatization of Iraq's downstream oil sector, which is desperately needed to improve efficiency and fight corruption, will also have to proceed slowly to avoid simply turning over Iraq's crown jewels to organized crime as has happened elsewhere in the world.

Neither is decentralization of the management of the Iraqi oil system (in the sense of allowing Iraqi local governments to manage whatever piece of the oil industry lay in their jurisdiction) a good solution. Iraq's oil production system is part of a seamless whole. In addition, in oil production, economies of scale are vitally important to keeping costs down and revenues up. Thus, attempting to divide up the Iraqi oil system among the country's 18 provinces would greatly reduce its efficiency and profitability. As oil analyst Fareed Mohamedi notes, "Without a national [oil] system, fragmentation and increased inequality will impair long term growth and prevent recovery in the short term."[24]

Instead, the longer-term process of structural reform of the Iraqi economy should seek to "unbundle" such enterprises. Iraq does not need vertically integrated, state-owned companies—which have typically proven to be highly inefficient themselves. By unbundling, Iraq would expose the structural weaknesses in these enterprises and give managers a greater sense of responsibility for their part of the firm, rather than allowing them to hide in the enormity of the enterprise. This would then make it possible to privatize discrete pieces of the organization that the state does not need to control. However, eventually unbundling and privatizing Iraq's oil industry is not the same thing as decentralizing it.

All of this means that improving Iraq's oil production and export is vitally important, but fixing it will not be easy. Nevertheless, a number of things can be done:

- *Establish the centralized oil-revenue distribution system described in Chapter 2.* As noted in the previous chapter, such a system is desperately needed for both political and economic reasons.

---

20 The Economist Intelligence Unit, "Iraq Economy: Iraq's Weak Heart," January 4, 2006.

21 "Iraq: Assessment of Progress in Economic Reconstruction Governmental Capacity," Staff Trip Report to the Committee on Foreign Relations, United States Senate, December 2005, p. 5.

22 Ibid.

23 The price of regular gasoline also went up five times, from $0.014 per gallon ($0.034 per gallon in Baghdad) to $0.07 per gallon. However, the price of regular gasoline sold by black marketers to those wishing to avoid lines at state-owned gas stations is $1 per gallon, see Richard A. Oppel Jr., "In Iraq, Rich in Oil, Higher Gasoline Prices Anger Many", *The New York Times*, December 31, 2005 and International Monetary Fund, *Iraq: Letter of Intent, Memorandum of Economic and Financial Policies and Technical Memorandum of Understanding*, December 6, 2005, p. 1. Available at <http://www.imf.org/external/np/loi/2005/irq/120605.pdf>.

24 Fareed Mohamedi, "Accelerating Economic Progress in Iraq," Testimony before the Committee on Foreign Relations, U.S. Senate, July 19, 2005.

- *Keep cutting the fuel subsidies.* The U.S. and Iraqi governments so far recognize the importance of this, but need to stick to this course to eliminate the market distortions that are breeding corruption and draining public coffers. Doing it gradually is fine, as long as the process keeps moving.

- *Press the Iraqi government to invest in natural gas, both for domestic consumption and potentially for export.* Iraq is currently flaring 1,000 million cubic feet per day of natural gas, which could cover 100 percent of Iraqi domestic power requirements.[25] Unfortunately, the Iraqis have always relied on oil for their energy and inertia, the cost of replacing Iraq's oil-based energy infrastructure, plus security and political problems, are preventing them from changing over. This ought to be a priority, and an area where foreign aid might be able to make a considerable difference especially because it can defray many of the costs involved in changing over from oil to natural gas.

- As the Staff Report of the Senate Foreign Relations Committee recommended, *a greater emphasis must be placed on developing a capability for more rapid pipeline repair (along with enhanced security for the pipelines), coupled with the construction of properly guarded storage facilities at Iraq's ports and border crossings to minimize export disruption coming from attacks on the pipelines or production facilities.* This will increase Iraq's revenue streams by making its deliveries more predictable. Iraq also requires more refining capacity, which would mean some very helpful construction projects that would not only mitigate unemployment but also help the economy over the long term—precisely the kind of project recommended above.

- *Make cleaning up the Iraqi Oil Ministry the first priority for the various anti-corruption measures.* A part of this problem is that Ahmed Chalabi is also the chairman of the new Energy Council, which oversees the production, distribution, and export of oil, electricity, and all other sources of energy in Iraq. Again, there are widespread accusations of corruption against him in his handling of this position. Regardless of whether the charges are valid (and they should be investigated thoroughly as part of this effort), he should be removed from this job simply because of the impression that keeping him there, given his long-standing reputation, creates among the employees of the ministry from top to bottom.

Rebuilding Iraq's agricultural sector. As already noted, the revival of Iraq's agricultural sector is critical for a variety of short- and long-term reasons. Iraq has some of the most fertile land in the Middle East and at times in its past was a net exporter of agricultural products. Enhanced agricultural production could be the start of real diversification in Iraq's economy—in terms of labor, production, and exports—away from its current dependence on oil. Moreover, agriculture is far more labor-intensive than oil, making it an excellent way of curbing unemployment.

Unfortunately, Iraq's agricultural sector has not been properly handled, either by the United States or the Iraqis. There are three basic problems that must be solved. First, not enough money, either in the form of grants or loans, has gone to Iraqi agricultural projects. USAID has provided roughly $100 million, which has been enormously beneficial, but has certainly not been adequate to meet Iraq's needs. Second, the Iraqi government continues to purchase food for its food rations (the government-provided "food basket" that is the foundation of most Iraqis' diets) almost entirely from abroad. This is stunningly foolish. It sends Iraq's badly-needed dollars out of the country, does not stimulate Iraq's agricultural sector, and actually undermines it by destroying the ability of farmers to allow the market to set prices and so provide them with

---

25 "Iraq: Assessment of Progress in Economic Reconstruction Governmental Capacity," Staff Trip Report to the Committee on Foreign Relations, United States Senate, December 2005, p. 5.

reasonable incomes. Third, both U.S. officials and Iraqi government bureaucrats have badly hampered the revival of Iraqi agriculture by micromanaging and insisting on procedures and timeframes divorced from the realities of agricultural production. The weather waits for no man, no matter how imposing his office in the Republican Palace or the Ministry of Agriculture. However, too many American and Iraqi officials have insisted on doing things "by the book" and without regard for the timing issues that lie at the heart of all agricultural production. The result has been catastrophic for many farmers unable to take the necessary action, buy needed supplies or equipment, or build necessary facilities in time to meet the needs of their crops and livestock.

To address these three problems, the United States and the government of Iraq should:

• *Increase aid to Iraq's agricultural sector.* Ideally, this should include programs which enable local government (and not the ministry in Baghdad) to provide micro-loans directly to Iraqi farmers. However, the continuation of the original USAID agriculture-assistance programs—which helped establish veterinary clinics, dredged irrigation canals, and provided grants for other communal projects valuable to agriculture across communities—should also be extended and expanded. Andrew Apostolou has suggested that the creation of an agricultural or cooperative bank to take the place of the former state-owned Agricultural Bank would allow farmers to purchase land, machinery, and other needs, that would greatly speed the pace of agricultural expansion. Moreover, making it possible for farmers to hold title over what they till creates collateral, allowing them to borrow against it for further improvements and expansion.

• *Demand that the Iraqi government cease purchasing food for the ration basket internationally.* As described below, it would be best to end the rationing system altogether and instead provide either cash payments or a type of food stamps.

However, recognizing that this will be politically unpopular and therefore slow to unfold, the Iraqi government should be required to purchase as much food as possible domestically before making any purchases abroad until such time as the food basket is entirely phased out.

• *Insist that both Iraqi and U.S. personnel working on agricultural issues have a strong background in agricultural management and have incentives to make the process work for the farmers.* This is part of a broader need to make bureaucratic handling of Iraq issues performance-based; to the extent possible, U.S. and Iraqi officials should benefit when the process works well and should suffer—in their careers and possibly even in their paychecks—when it does poorly.

• *Decentralize control over contracting and administration of agricultural programs to local government to the greatest extent possible.* Many of the problems with the administration of agriculture stem from Baghdad's being overly involved, both because the central government bureaucracy is stultifying and because it is difficult even for well-meaning bureaucrats to properly address problems that frequently vary widely from one locale to another. Consequently, it is far more efficient and effective if the governmental administration of agriculture projects is done at the most local level possible. *The Ministry of Agriculture in Baghdad needs to give up contracting and implementation authority, and should instead concentrate on standards and practices, regulations, and overall governmental policy.*

Electricity. A constant complaint of Iraqis is the ubiquitous, unpredictable blackouts that undermine economic activity and aggravate daily life. To a certain extent, the problem stemmed from the absence of a plan on the part of the United States to quickly increase Iraqi electricity generation capacity and rebuild and improve Iraq's generation and distribution networks immediately after the fall of Baghdad. We have been playing catch-up ever since. However, a problem of equal magnitude is the skyrocketing Iraqi demand for electricity. Immediately after Saddam's fall, Iraqis ran out to buy every type of household appliance imaginable, including refrigerators, televisions, microwaves, and—especially—air conditioners. As a result, demand for electricity to run these items soared from about 4,500–5,000 megawatts per day to nearly 9,000 megawatts per day. Meanwhile, Iraqi and Coalition efforts to repair the Iraqi electrical grid have resulted in current peak capacity of about 4,750 megawatts per day. The United States and the new government of Iraq are presently working to increase Iraq's capacity to import electricity from Iran, Turkey, and Syria, while increasing Iraq's own domestic production to about 6,000 megawatts per day.[26] The Staff Report of the Senate Foreign Relations Committee authored by Patrick Garvey proposed two key recommendations for dealing with Iraq's electricity problems that this report strongly endorses:[27]

• *Limit the demand for Iraqi electricity usage.* This is a three-part process. First, meters need to be installed throughout the country. Second, limits need to be placed on the kilowattage that any home or business can use. Third, the subsidy on electricity which makes it virtually costless to the consumer needs to be slowly eliminated. It should be obvious that this is a process that is easily said, but very hard and painful to do. However, neither is it hopeless. The installation of meters would be an excellent project for foreign aid— a donor nation could purchase the meters and the hardware and software to monitor them, hire local Iraqi contractors to install them, provide advisors to train the government personnel to staff the system, and then hand it over to the Iraqi government. Limits on usage and the gradual elimination of the subsidy will be politically painful, but especially if coupled with ongoing efforts to improve capacity and a new effort to increase the security of the grid, it ought to be a trade-off that Iraqis will recognize as

beneficial by increasing both the number of hours of electricity they enjoy per day and their ability to control when they have power.

• *Demand that Iraqis stop running their electrical grid underfrequency.* For decades, the Iraqis have steadfastly insisted that running the grid underfrequency somehow saved power—like the Middle Eastern habit of not running the headlights in a car (even at night) in the belief that having the headlights on drained the battery (even when the motor was running). This practice does not save power, it simply damages the grid, thereby reducing its efficiency and making it more susceptible to other problems. Given that Iraq needs every kilowatt that it can get, this is a ridiculous and costly practice. Indeed, the United States should make its provision of further aid to the power grid conditional on the Iraqis ceasing it.

Decentralization. Chapter 2 dealt with the need for political decentralization at some length, but it is equally the case that Iraq requires greater economic decentralization in a variety of sectors—other than oil. As noted above, the central government in Baghdad remains a sinkhole of corruption, a bureaucratic bottleneck, and whether through understaffing, inability, or malign intent its overall efficiency has improved little over the days of Saddam. The net effect is that many resources go into Baghdad, and far fewer come out—and when they do, they are often inadequate and late.

Many American bureaucratic and contracting procedures reinforce these problems. Because U.S. personnel tend to congregate in the Green Zone in Baghdad, they also tend to do their business through their Iraqi counterparts nearby—meaning the ministries in central Baghdad. Likewise, U.S. contract regulations often make it hard for small Iraqi contractors: they lack the English-language, accounting, auditing, legal, other skills to successfully apply for, let alone be awarded,

---

26 Ibid, p. 6.
27 Ibid, pp. 6–7.

U.S. government contracts given the tight constraints of U.S. anti-corruption measures. Iraq's is a cash society, and too often the U.S. bureaucracy insists on credit (and electronic banking) capacities that Iraq generally lacks. The U.S. government has done far too little to cut through this red tape in the name of getting more money into the hands of local contractors.

Consequently, one of the challenges of reconstruction will be to push resources directly to the Iraqi people, bypassing Baghdad, and cutting out much of the U.S. bureaucracy. At present, far too much U.S. aid and Iraqi wealth is blocked by this set of reinforcing bottlenecks.

A related matter has been Washington's over-reliance on massive American firms to handle much of the contracting in Iraq. This makes sense from a bureaucratic perspective, but has been bad for reconstruction. Again, it means that resources are not going directly to Iraqis. Indeed, far too much of the funds in each contract stay here in the United States or are directed to subsidiaries of the multinationals in other countries than actually get into Iraq. Whatever graft there might be in Halliburton's dealings in Iraq would actually be secondary compared to the damage done because so little of the money awarded to Halliburton for a contract actually gets spent in Iraq.

In addition to the steps noted in Chapter 2 regarding decentralization, which would apply equally well to both Iraq's political and economic sectors, two further recommendations are worth making:

• *U.S. and other foreign aid programs must be re-focused to provide grants directly to local councils, for infrastructure development and micro-loans to small businesses.* At present, U.S. aid programs have focused too heavily on the development of national-level capacity.

• *Foreign donors and the Iraqi government itself need to focus more on micro-loans.* So far, micro-loans have

had an enormous positive impact in Iraq, but far too little has been disbursed in that form. Micro-loans to small businesses foster less graft, provide more money directly to the people who need it most, stimulate market forces, and are much easier (and more appropriate) for local government leaders to disburse. Moreover, hiring by small business is a far more efficient and practical solution to Iraq's unemployment problems than the creation of massive new economic enterprises.

More donor funding. As noted above, the resurgence of Iraq's economy, such as it is, depends heavily on grant money. Since a key consideration of American-Iraqi policy must be to boost Iraqi popular support for reconstruction over the next 6–12 months by demonstrating tangible signs of progress and the Iraqi economy is not structurally sound enough to do so on its own—now is *not* the time to try to wean Iraq off of its dependence on foreign aid. Moreover, U.S. assistance may have been prodigious so far, but its impact on the Iraqi economy has been less than the raw numbers would suggest. For instance, of $2.2 billion in aid earmarked for civilian reconstruction in 2004, only two-thirds of that was spent on rebuilding the domestic economy and of that money, half was devoted to security, which meant that in practice only about one-third reached the domestic economy.[28] Meanwhile, many countries that pledged money to Iraq have not yet made good on their promises. According to the Government Accounting Office, foreign governments have pledged $13.6 billion to Iraq in the form of various grants and loans. However, only $2.7 billion has actually been provided. In some cases, this is because Iraq has not accessed the loans that it has been offered; however, in other cases it is because grants have not been forthcoming. *Iraq needs to continue to receive large amounts of external funding at least for the next 12–36 months, and the United States must both provide it and encourage others to do so.*

On a related matter, at this point in time 5 percent of

28   The Economist Intelligence Unit, "Country Report: Iraq," September 2005, p. 20.

all Iraqi oil revenues still go to the United Nations Compensation Commission to pay for damages incurred by other countries as a result of Iraq's 1990 invasion of Kuwait and the ensuing Persian Gulf War. Most of this money—about two-thirds of the monies being paid at this point—goes to Kuwait, which is wealthier than its northern neighbor to the tune of a GDP per capita almost twenty times that of Iraq. Kuwait did suffer terribly during the invasion and six months of Iraqi occupation. However, at this point, Iraq has paid over $20 billion to the foreign victims of Saddam's invasion, and Kuwait has received a large percentage of that figure, although exact numbers appear unavailable. There is an argument to be made that the Iraqi people were also victims of Saddam and they are being forced to bear yet another burden by paying for the damages he inflicted on others as well as those he inflicted on them. Indeed, given the risks to Kuwait if Iraq were to fall into civil war, *it would be best for Kuwait if it were willing to defer or assume payment for many of the private claims still uncompensated from the 1990–91 war. At the very least, the United States should press Kuwait to declare a compensation holiday for 1–3 years while the Iraqi economy recovers.*

ECONOMIC DEVELOPMENT: OVER THE LONGER TERM

Unfortunately, providing immediate relief from pressing economic problems is only part of the challenge. The United States also will have to ensure that Iraqi economic growth is sustainable over the long-term. This is an enormously complicated matter, deserving of a paper of its own. Consequently, this report can only highlight several issues that should be part of such an effort.

Debt relief. If Iraq's short-term need is for continued foreign aid and a halt (even if temporary) in payments

to the UN Compensation Commission, its long-term need is for debt relief. On this issue, the Bush Administration has made considerable progress. They took this issue very seriously and, thanks to the labors of special envoy James Baker, have already succeeded in getting huge amounts of Iraq's outstanding foreign debt forgiven. They have, and must continue, to make this a high priority.

In November 2004, the Paris Club of creditor nations struck a deal with Iraq to write off 30 percent of Iraq's international debt immediately, another 30 percent after a restructuring deal with the IMF was agreed to (which it has been) and another 20 percent to be written off when the IMF agreement was completed. While this means that 80 percent of Iraq's non-commercial debt has effectively been forgiven this still leaves Iraq owing foreign nations over $15 billion, according to IMF projections.[29] *This is still a huge amount of money given Iraq's revenue problems and it would be desirable to have more of it forgiven.* In addition, the entire forgiveness package is contingent upon Iraq's deal with the IMF. So far, the IMF has been moderate in its demands upon Iraq, but in the past it has insisted on the kind of rapid privatization of industry that would probably cripple the Iraqi economy for the long-term by delivering up most of Iraq's state-owned enterprises to organized crime and militia leaders of various stripes. The United States must help ensure that the IMF does not begin down this same road with Iraq.

Eliminating subsidies. Iraq's economy remains hobbled by costly subsidies dating to Saddam's era and before. The principal subsidies on food, gasoline and electricity constitute 21 percent of the Iraqi government's budget—over $7 billion of a $33 billion budget for 2006.[30] Imports of gasoline and other refined petroleum products—which are then sold at subsidized prices—cost the government another $3 billion.[31] As numerous economists have pointed out, these subsidies

---

29 Ibid, p. 3. The issue of the disputed debt to Kuwait and Saudi Arabia has yet to be resolved.

30 "Iraq: Assessment of Progress in Economic Reconstruction Governmental Capacity," Staff Trip Report to the Committee on Foreign Relations, United States Senate, December 2005, pp. 7–8.

31 The Economist Intelligence Unit, "Country Report: Iraq," September 2005, p. 21.

are horrifyingly costly to the Iraqi economy, not just in terms of public spending, but in the negation and distortion of market forces, which skews every other aspect of the Iraqi economy. Of course, all are political "sacred cows" and so quickly eliminating them is probably impossible. *All of these subsidies need to be phased out over the next several years.* Washington has already been pushing Baghdad to do so, and has had some success, with the first increases to gasoline prices coming at the end of 2005.

- As argued above, *electricity subsidies should be gradually phased out along with the introduction of meters and the limiting of kilowatt consumption across the country.*

- *Start removing items from the "food basket" and replacing them with food stamps.* It will be impossible to do away with the food basket overnight and there are concerns about the monetization of the food basket because of the problems with corruption and violent crime. Consequently, it might benefit Iraq to employ a system of food stamps that would be redeemable by underprivileged Iraqis for food only. This too could happen gradually. For instance, in late 2005 Iraqi newspapers carried stories reporting that some of the wheat being distributed in the food basket was contaminated, so most Iraqis refused to eat it. That would have provided the perfect opportunity to eliminate wheat from the food basket altogether and instead replace it with food stamps.

- *Make provision of the food basket need-based.* This is another simple remedy. Right now, rations are available to all, including those with plenty of money to buy food. This makes no sense given Iraq's other priorities.

- *Insist that the Iraqi government buy food locally to the greatest extent possible.* As noted above, it is absurd

to have a situation where the government is undermining the country's agricultural sector.

Education. There is nothing more important to Iraq's long-term economic prosperity than improving the state of its educational system. Here as well, the United States and the international community recognized the need early on and have already provided considerable assistance, largely in terms of building schools, raising the pay of teachers, providing revised textbooks, furnishing school supplies, and eliminating Saddam's worst flunkies from university positions. While these were all positive steps, there is still a great deal more to be done. To a certain extent, assistance to the Iraqi educational program will help alleviate the nation's most pressing problems in terms of the decline in literacy and other basic education among Iraq's younger generations, largely as a result of the 12 years of sanctions and Saddam's response to them.

However, in many ways, this is merely the tip of the iceberg. Iraq suffers from all of the same problems in education as the other Arab states: there is little emphasis on interactive learning, instead rote memorization is employed in every subject (including the sciences); creativity tends to be stifled; there is an overemphasis on the humanities (including religion) at the expense of science and math; teachers are provided with few incentives to stimulate or engage with their pupils; and the entire process is rigidly prescribed by the central government which cares only that students can spit back formulaic answers to standardized tests whose questions generally are never changed for decades. The result is that, like elsewhere in the Arab world, students graduate from the educational systems with little facility for critical thinking, initiative, or creativity, and few of the kinds of job skills needed to compete in the globalized economy.[32]

Moreover, Iraq's educational system has problems unique to itself. For instance, there is a pervasive

---

32 The most forthright treatment of this subject by a group of Arab public intellectuals remains the United Nations Development Program's *Arab Human Development Reports*, particularly the 2002 edition.

"culture of violence" in Iraqi schools; teachers employ physical abuse to force unhappy students to obey, creative students to conform, and inquisitive students to stay mute. When the Kurds took over the running of the schools in northern Iraq after 1991, they identified erasing this culture of violence as both one of their highest priorities and biggest problems. It took them a decade to rid their schools of it, but today Kurdish schools tend to be much better in terms of teacher-pupil behavior than those elsewhere in the country.

Ultimately, it will be up to the Iraqis to recognize the failings of their traditional educational methods and move to modernize their schools. However, there are still ways that the United States can help, and in so doing, improve the likelihood that Iraq's economy will remain stable and productive over the long-term.

- *The United States should offer to fund a high-level and comprehensive study of Iraqi education by leading American educators and education specialists.* As always, their ability to conduct their mission will be limited by security considerations. However, American higher education remains the envy of the world and American educational methods remain outstanding—even if not always fully implemented in our private schools. In 1932, a team of American educators made an important study of Iraqi educational practices on behalf of the newly-independent Iraqi government, and 74 years later it might be beneficial to do so again on behalf of the latest, newly-independent Iraqi government.[33] At the very least, this would provide an honest, objective account of what needs to change in Iraqi schools to make their graduates competitive in the global economy. This could then serve as ammunition for those Iraqi politicians who wanted to press the case of reform and as a blueprint if they are able to prevail against the forces of traditionalism.

- *The government of Iraq should commission a compre-*

hensive education survey to assess a current baseline and needs for rebuilding Iraq's educational system. To a great extent, the Ministry of Education does not have the basic information that it needs to plan and implement a rebuilding and reform program. It would be important, especially when combined with the new census recommended in Chapters 1 and 2, to conduct such a survey to establish how many school-age children lived in a particular area, what their literacy rates were, the status of schools and teachers, and other basic information regarding education. This was one of the first things that the Kurds did when they took over the educational system in northern Iraq in 1991 and they found it immensely helpful.

- *Use the centralized oil-distribution plan described in Chapter 2, to fund both vocational and higher education through individual education accounts.*

- *Fund programs to teach English throughout Iraq.* English is the language of the global economy, at least for now, but likely well into the future. The internet is largely English-based, as is the aviation industry, and a variety of new high-tech industries. It would be a tremendous gift to the Iraqi people to help their children to learn English. Here as well, the Kurds kept lowering the age at which students in schools in northern Iraq began to learn English until now it is taught in primary school, and has displaced Arabic as the second language in Kurdish schools. Moreover, it seems particularly appropriate that since the United States has been the primary occupying power since the fall of Baghdad, we would make a major effort to teach Iraqi children English. *The United States could establish programs to send young Americans to Iraq to teach English (obviously, only in the secured areas of the "oil stain"). It could fund English instruction, purchase English-language textbooks and other teaching materials, and provide language fellowships that would allow Iraqi*

---

33 Reeva S. Simon, *Iraq Between the Two World Wars: The Creation and Implementation of a Nationalist Ideology,* (NY: Columbia University Press, 1986, pp. 90–95.

students to travel to the United States, Great Britain, Australia, or other English-speaking nations to improve their language skills.

• *Create scholarships for Iraqi students to study in America.* In a similar vein, the U.S. government could fund a variety of scholarships to bring Iraqis over to study in the United States for varying lengths of time for secondary school, college or graduate school. Doing so would likely improve the ties between the American and Iraqi peoples, breed a generation of Iraqis sympathetic to America, and provide them with educational opportunities they could only dream about in Iraq.

Stemming Iraq's nascent brain drain. An issue closely related to the need to overhaul Iraq's educational system is the corresponding need to staunch the flight of Iraq's best and brightest from the country. The problem is not calamitous yet, because immediately after the fall of Saddam many highly-educated and successful members of the Iraqi diaspora returned to Iraq to participate in the revival of their homeland. Likewise, many of those who had never left saw Saddam's fall as an opportunity to create the kind of Iraq of which they had always dreamed. Only in the last 12–18 months have professional Iraqis—doctors, professors, lawyers, and others—begun to make arrangements to leave. A fair number of Iraq's middle class have begun moving to Jordan, although new Jordanian laws are making that more difficult. They are leaving out of fear that Iraq's pervasive violence will finally catch up with them and their families, and despair that Iraq's political and economic problems will prevent them from living the kind of normal, prosperous life they desire. In many cases, they also express fear that the Shi'i parties that increasingly dominate the Iraqi Council of Representatives intend to impose religious codes of conduct under which they do not wish to live.

In the short term, this problem pales in comparison with Iraq's other challenges, but for its long-term prosperity, this is an important issue and should be nipped in the bud as quickly and completely as possible.

Solving the problem obviously requires a number of transformative changes to Iraq's security, political, and economic situations—like securing the population centers where these urban professionals tend to live through a traditional COIN strategy, ensuring personal freedoms, and creating a vibrant economy where people with these skills can fulfill their own ambitions. *However, it would also be helpful for the Iraqi government to think in terms of providing tax and financial incentives to high-tech firms, limiting corporate taxes generally, and providing other benefits for people working in the sciences, engineering, computers, and medicine to make it more desirable for them to remain in Iraq.*

THE IMPORTANCE OF AN INTEGRATED APPROACH

One of the principal themes of this report has been the criticality of better integrating military, political and economic programs to foster reconstruction across the board. There are always bound to be successes and failures in an effort as grand as the reconstruction of Iraq. If these different fields of action are properly integrated, there should be more successes than failures in each field, and the successes in each will be more likely to spark corresponding successes in the others, creating a self-reinforcing process. Unfortunately the opposite is also true. If activities in these fields are not properly integrated, there are likely to be more failures than successes in each, and failures in one field are more likely to cause failures in the others.

Unfortunately, the United States has made a great many mistakes in handling the reconstruction of Iraq and one of the worst, has been the ongoing failure to create a single, integrated military/political/economic strategy and implement it as such. To some extent, this is understandable because it reflects a badly disintegrated policy approach within the U.S. government, where the interagency process has been functioning very poorly. But this is not the only problem. Another part of the problem has been the unwillingness of agencies other than the armed forces to see the reconstruction of Iraq as their highest priority and every other policy as a distant second. For too much of Washington, the war in Iraq is nothing but a distraction from what they think they really should be doing.

The needs of rebuilding the Iraqi economy illustrate the dangers of this failing most dramatically. According to the Iraqis themselves, economic problems (along with security) are the most important problems they face. Thus, getting the economic piece right will be crucial to the success of reconstruction. Indeed, to some extent, economic progress may be the clearest measure of the success or failure of reconstruction. However, economic progress is wholly reliant on improvements in the security and political situations. Without a safe environment in which goods and people can move around the country, without the rule of law, effective regulatory agencies and practices, and limits on theft and corruption, it is impossible to imagine that Iraq will enjoy any degree of prosperity.

THE SABAN CENTER FOR MIDDLE EAST POLICY

The Saban Center for Middle East Policy was established on May 13, 2002 with an inaugural address by His Majesty King Abdullah II of Jordan. The creation of the Saban Center reflects the Brookings Institution's commitment to expand dramatically its research and analysis of Middle East policy issues at a time when the region has come to dominate the U.S. foreign policy agenda.

The Saban Center provides Washington policymakers with balanced, objective, in-depth and timely research and policy analysis from experienced and knowledgeable scholars who can bring fresh perspectives to bear on the critical problems of the Middle East. The center upholds the Brookings tradition of being open to a broad range of views. The Saban Center's central objective is to advance understanding of developments in the Middle East through policy-relevant scholarship and debate.

The center's foundation was made possible by a generous grant from Haim and Cheryl Saban of Los Angeles. Ambassador Martin S. Indyk, Senior Fellow in Foreign Policy Studies, is the director of the Saban Center. Kenneth M. Pollack is the center's director of research. Joining them is a core group of Middle East experts who conduct original research and develop innovative programs to promote a better understanding of the policy choices facing American decision makers in the Middle East. They include Tamara Cofman Wittes, who is a specialist on political reform in the Arab world; Shibley Telhami, who holds the Sadat Chair at the University of Maryland; Shaul Bakhash, an expert

on Iranian politics from George Mason University; Daniel Byman, a Middle East terrorism expert from Georgetown University, and Flynt Leverett, a former senior CIA analyst and senior director at the National Security Council, who is a specialist on Syria and Lebanon. The center is located in the Foreign Policy Studies Program at Brookings, led by Carlos Pascual, its director and a Brookings vice president.

The Saban Center is undertaking path breaking research in five areas: the implications of regime change in Iraq, including post-war nation-building and Persian Gulf security; the dynamics of Iranian domestic politics and the threat of nuclear proliferation; mechanisms and requirements for a two-state solution to the Israeli-Palestinian conflict; policy for the war against terrorism, including the continuing challenge of state-sponsorship of terrorism; and political and economic change in the Arab world, in particular in Syria and Lebanon, and the methods required to promote democratization.

The center also houses the ongoing Brookings Project on U.S. Policy Towards the Islamic World which is directed by Peter W. Singer, Senior Fellow in Foreign Policy Studies. The project focuses on analyzing the problems in the relationship between the United States and the Islamic world with the objective of developing effective policy responses. The Islamic World Project includes a task force of experts, an annual dialogue between American and Muslim intellectuals, a visiting fellows program for specialists from the Islamic world, and a monograph series.

www.ingramcontent.com/pod-product-compliance
Lightning Source LLC
Chambersburg PA
CBHW080647270326
41928CB00017B/3221